Corporations and Partnerships in Turkey

Corporations and Partnerships in Turkey

Ünal Tekinalp
Melis Aritman Alp

This book was originally published as a monograph in the International Encyclopaedia of Laws/Corporations and Partnerships.

Founding Editor: Roger Blanpain
General Editor: Frank Hendrickx
Volume Editors: Koen Geens

Wolters Kluwer

Published by:
Kluwer Law International B.V.
PO Box 316
2400 AH Alphen aan den Rijn
The Netherlands
E-mail: lrs-sales@wolterskluwer.com
Website: www.wolterskluwer.com/en/solutions/kluwerlawinternational

Sold and distributed by:
Wolters Kluwer Legal & Regulatory U.S.
7201 McKinney Circle
Frederick, MD 21704
United States of America
E-mail: customer.service@wolterskluwer.com

ISBN 978-94-035-0696-8

e-Book: ISBN 978-94-035-0816-0
web-PDF: ISBN 978-94-035-0826-9

The Authors

Professor Dr. Ünal Tekinalp (born October 4, 1935) graduated with a Bachelor of Laws at the University of İstanbul, Turkey, in 1958 and became a research assistant and lecturer at the same university in 1959. He obtained his doctorate in 1961 from the University of İstanbul and spent two years at the Freie Universität, Berlin, as a guest academic in the academic years 1962–1964. He has served as a research associate with the Institute of Commercial Law. Dr. Tekinalp became a member of the İstanbul Bar Association in 1963. In 1966, he was appointed as an Associate professor at the University of İstanbul, Faculty of Law following the acceptance of his thesis and became a professor in 1973 at the same university.

Between 1997 and May 2002, Professor Tekinalp served as the Head of Commercial Law Department at Istanbul University, Faculty of Law. He lectured on Banking Law, Intellectual Property Law, Competition Law, EU Law, as well as on Commercial Law for undergraduate, postgraduate and Ph.D. programs for twenty-nine years. In 2002, having reached the age of retirement, he retired from his post at Istanbul University, Faculty of Law.

In addition to his role as the Head of Commercial Law Department of Istanbul University, until his retirement, Professor Tekinalp also served as the Director of the Center for Research and Practice in European Law and the Chairman of the Department of European Union's Legal Structure which is an academic department responsible for postgraduate and Ph.D. programs available under Social Sciences Institute of Istanbul University.

In 1999, Professor Tekinalp was elected as the chairman of the commission responsible for preparing the draft of the Turkish Commercial Code (NTCC or TCC) (by a unanimous vote of the members of the commission appointed by the Ministry of Justice. The first draft of the code was opened to public opinion in 2005, the second draft was delivered to the government in 2006, and finally, the new Turkish Commercial Code was approved by the Turkish Parliament on January 13, 2011.

Since 2008, he has been a member of ALLEA's (All European Academies) Permanent Working Group on Intellectual Property Rights. Professor Tekinalp has then become a fellow member of the Science Academy and continued his membership with ALLEA Permanent Working Group until his resignation due to health reasons on November 20, 2018.

Dr. Tekinalp publishes extensively in the areas of commercial law, banking law and regulations, corporate/securities law and accounting law, as well as intellectual property law. Among his publications are the section on Turkey in *The European Accounting Guide* [edited by D. Alexander & S. Archer], Academic Press, London (1992); *Banka Hukukunun Esasları* (Principles of Banking Law), İstanbul, (1988) [a comprehensive introduction]; *Sermaye Piyasası Hukukunun Esasları* (Principles of Capital Market Law), İstanbul, (1982). *Anonim Ortaklığın Bilançosu ve Yedek Akçeleri* (The Balance Sheet and Reserves of Companies Limited by Shares), 2nd Ed., İstanbul (1979); *Halka Açık Ortaklıklarda Yönetime Katılma Sorunları* (Problems of Participation in the Management of Publicly Held Companies Limited by Shares), İstanbul (1979); *Kooperatiflerde Ortaklıkların Kişisel Niteliklerinin Önemi, Ortak Sıfatının Kazanılması ve Yitirilmesi* (The Importance of Personal Qualities of Partners in Cooperatives, Acquisition and Losing of Partner Capacity), İstanbul (1972), *Anonim Ortaklıkta Yeni Bağlam Sisteminin Esasları* (Principles of New System of Transfer Restrictions on Registered Shares in Joint-Stock Companies), İstanbul (2012); *Fikri Mülkiyet Hukuku* (Intellectual Property Law), 5th Edition, İstanbul (2012); *Sermaye Ortaklıklarının Yeni Hukuku* (Principles of New Law of Capital Partnerships), 5th Edition, İstanbul (2020). He is the co-author of the following books; Hirsch/Tekinalp, *Das türkische Aktien-und GmbH-Recht*, 2. Aufl., Nomos Verlagsgesellschaft, Baden-Baden (1993); Poroy/Tekinalp/Çamoğlu, *Ortaklıklar Hukuku* (Law on Partnerships), Vol. I and II, 2nd Ed., İstanbul (1976/77) [a comprehensive introduction]; Poroy/Tekinalp/Çamoğlu, *Ortaklıklar ve Kooperatif Hukuku* (Law on Partnerships and Cooperatives), 11th Edition, İstanbul (2009) [a comprehensive and widely used student's book]; Poroy/Tekinalp/Çamoğlu, *Ortaklıklar Hukuku I* [Rewritten] 15th Edition, İstanbul (2021); Poroy/Tekinalp/Çamoğlu, *Ortaklıklar Hukuku II* [Rewritten] 14th Edition, İstanbul (2019); Tekinalp/Çamoğlu, *Türk Ticaret Kanunu* (Turkish Commercial Code (TCC)), 15th Edition, İstanbul (2014) [a short and widely used commentary]; Tekinlap/Çamoğu, *Sınai Mülkiyet Kanunu* (Code on Industrial Property), İstanbul (2017); Poroy/Tekinalp, *Kıymetli Evrak Hukuku Esasları* (Principles of the Law on Negotiable Instruments), 24th Edition, İstanbul (2021); Tekinalp Gülören/Tekinalp Ünal, *Avrupa Birliği Hukuku* (European Union Law), İstanbul (1997). He has also written the section on Turkey for the *International Encyclopaedia of Laws on Commercial and Economic Law in Turkey* (2016).

Melis Aritman Alp is one of the founding partners of AYALAW Firm which is a boutique law firm in Istanbul established in April 2011 and specializes in M&A transactions and arbitrations arising out of M&A disputes. Ms. Aritman Alp has been working as an M&A lawyer for almost 20 years. Before establishing AYALAW Firm, Ms. Aritman Alp was an M&A partner in Esin Hukuk Burosu (Baker & McKenzie).

Ms. Aritman Alp started her law career in the law offices of Noyan Turunc (which was, at the time, named Turunc & Savascin) in Izmir as a legal intern. After completing her legal internship in 1999, she joined Van Bael & Bellis, a law firm based in Brussels, Belgium, as a foreign intern. She then started working in Somay Hukuk Burosu in Istanbul in 2000 and continued working there until 2009 and left her partnership position to join Esin Hukuk Burosu.

Melis Aritman Alp has worked in numerous M&A transactions in Turkey in almost all sectors ranging from banking to retail, cement and logistics. She is also experienced in private equity investments in Turkey.

Ms. Aritman Alp has been nominated for the M&A advisor of the year award for 2012–2013 by Who's Who Intercontinental; recognized as a leading M&A Lawyer in 2012 by Who's Who Legal Turkey; recognized as a leading lawyer by Best Lawyers International in 2012, recognized as a leading lawyer in IFLR for 2013, 2012 and 2020.

Ms. Aritman Alp received her LL.B. from Dokuz Eylul Law Faculty, Turkey and is a member of the Istanbul Bar Association.

Table of Contents

List of Abbreviations

Art	Article
AdŞ	(*Adi Şirket*) Ordinary Partnership
A.Ş.	*(Anonim Şirket)* Company Limited by Shares
AKP	Justice and Development Party
BA	Banking Act(*Bankalar Kanunu*)
BCLR	Banking and Commercial Law Review (Banka ve Ticaret Hukuku Dergisi (Batider))
CMB	Capital Market Board (*Sermaye Piyasası Kurulu*)
CML	Capital Market Law (*Sermaye Piyasası Kanunu*) No. 6362
CRS	Central Registration System
CPL	Civil Procedural Law
Comp.	Comparison
C.Cham.	Civil Chamber of the Supreme Court of Appeal (*Yargıtay Hukuk Dairesi*)
CTL	Corporation Tax Law (Kurumlar Vergisi Kanunu)
CTP	Code of Tax Procedure (Vergi Usul Kanunu)
DCBL	Law on Debt Collection and Bankruptcy (İcra ve İflas Kanunu)
EGA	Extraordinary General Assembly
IAS	Independent Audit Standards
ICPI	Institutions Concerning Public Interest
IFRS	International Financial Reporting Standards
IPL	International Private Procedural Law dated 27 November 2007 No. 5718
ITL	Income Tax Law No. 193
Jud.	Judgment
KŞ/K.Ş	(Kollektif Şirket) The Collective Partnership
L.Ş.	(*Limited Şirket*) Limited Liability Companies
MHP	Nationalist Movement Party
O.G	Official Gazette (*Resmi Gazete*)

List of Abbreviations

OGA	Ordinary General Assembly
Par/para	Paragraph
PL	Law No. 4046 on Implementations of Privatization
PUS	Participation Usufruct Shares
SPBKŞ	*(Sermayesi Paylara Bölünmüş Komandit Şirket)* A commandite partnership limited by shares
Sup. Court	Supreme Court
SCO	Swiss Company Law
SDIF/Fund	Savings Deposit Insurance Fund
TBMM	Grand National Assembly of Turkey (Türkiye Büyük Millet Meclisi)
TurkStat	Turkish Statistical Institute
TCC/NTCC	The New Turkish Commercial Code No. 6102
TCC 1956	Previous Turkish Commercial Code
TCivC	Turkish Civil Code
TCO	Turkish Code of Obligations
TOG	Turkish Official Gazette
VAT	Value Added Tax

Preface and Acknowledgments

This new monograph includes major and fundamental changes that were introduced by the new TCC. Perhaps, "change" is not the right word sufficient enough to describe the reforms that were introduced by the Turkish Commercial Code No. 6102 enacted in 2011 with the intention to primarily comply with European Law and also respond to the developments in modern commercial life. The new TCC entered into force in July 2012 replacing the previous TCC in its entirety. Accordingly, our monograph is revised in its entirety to capture and explain the developments and reforms introduced by the new TCC.

In this new edition, Ms. Melis Aritman Alp, an esteemed lawyer who specialized in Mergers and Acquisitions, undertook the editing of the entire monograph and provided major contributions. Also, two other young lawyers, Ms. Mehtap Mertol Digili and Ms. Melike Demirci, provided some assistance to reflect the reforms of the new TCC. I would like to thank each one of them for all their hard work and valuable efforts. I hope that this team or some of them continue this monograph after me keeping the same level of professionalism and academic depth.

Fenerbahçe
İstanbul
February 2022

General Introduction

§1. General Description of the Country

I. Geography

1. Turkey is a country with a total land area of 776.980 km^2 and is surrounded by water on three sides. It is located at the crossroads not only of Europe and Asia but also of various land and marine transit routes. A small part of its territory (Thrace) is in Europe. The major part, constituting 95% of the territory, extends from the westernmost tip of Asia eastwards to the border with Iran. Turkey is, therefore, a bridge linking Europe and Asia. In fact, the Marmara Sea, an inland sea, lies between these two continents, and there is access to the Black Sea through the Bosporus (the İstanbul Strait) and the Aegean Sea through the Dardanelles (the Çanakkale Strait). The Bosporus Bridge (15 Temmuz Şehitler Köprüsü), Fatih Sultan Mehmet Bridge, Yavuz Sultan Selim Bridge, an underwater railway tunnel called Marmaray and another underwater railway tunnel called Avrasya Tunnel link Europe and Asia in physical, as well as a cultural, sense.

2. With a coastline of 7,126 km, Turkey is bordered by the Black Sea in the north, the Aegean in the west and the Mediterranean in the south. The country is divided into seven geographical regions: the Black Sea Region, the Marmara Region, the Aegean Region, the Mediterranean Region, the Central Anatolian Region, the East Anatolian Region, and the South East Anatolian Region. Turkey's neighbors are Greece and Bulgaria to the west, Iraq and Syria to the south, and Iran, Azerbaijan, Nahjevan and Armenia to the east.

II. Cultural Composition

3. Turkey has a unique culture, which has been enhanced by values from many religions, including polytheist beliefs. It is a culture where various civilizations and cultures have clashed, intermingled, and interacted in succession as a consequence of her diverse and complex geography. This culture is not a mere synthesis of eastern and western cultures, but an indigenous development resulting from her rich history. One cannot point to the dominant influence of any particular culture (and this includes Islam) regarding the culture of Turkey. This is because Turkey, although a Muslim country with historical ties to Islamic culture and values, is secular both constitutionally and with respect to the outlook of her people. It has a long past with an interpretation of Islam different from that of the rest of the Muslim world. This has influenced literature, art, architecture and music and has kept Turkish culture independent of Arab and Islamic cultures.[1]

III. Political System

A. A Brief History of the Turkish Constitution

4. The first written constitution of Turkey was promulgated in 1876 and was the product of a movement of intellectuals.[2] This Constitution, which was based on a system of constitutional monarchy, was repealed two years later and was not put into effect again until 1908.[3] A further constitutional change in 1909 introduced a parliamentary system. This time, the movement had a wider leadership, with the army and a small circle of traders joining forces with the intellectuals.[4]

5. The Constitution of 1921 illustrated the radical change in the concept of sovereignty which had taken place after the fall of the Ottoman Empire and indicated the principles of constitutional order in the new Turkish state, which was shortly to be founded. It declared that sovereignty resides unconditionally with the nation and represented a deviation from the principle of sharing power with the head of state (the Sultan)—which had been the dominant concept in constitutional movements at the time of the Ottoman Empire—in that all powers were concentrated in the hands of Parliament and the executive power was subjugated to the legislative power.[5]

6. The Constitution of 1924, which superseded the Constitution of 1921 with all its amendments, was the first Constitution of the Republican era. Retaining the basic tenet of the 1921 Constitution, the Constitution of 1924 unconditionally empowered Parliament to exercise sovereignty, though it differed from the 1921 Constitution in that basic rights and freedoms were included. Nevertheless, mechanisms for the defense and preservation of such rights and freedoms were not envisaged.[6] The 1924 Constitution was amended from time to time and was later superseded by the

---

1. This is discussed in more detail below; *see* No. 9 paras. 32–37, *infra*.
2. E. Teziç, *Anayasa Hukuku*, 2. Bası [*Constitutional Law*] 139 (İstanbul 2d ed. 1991); T.Z. Tunaya, *Siyasal Kurumlar ve Anayasa Hukuku*, 4. Bası [Political Institutions and Constitutional Law] 129 (İstanbul 4rd ed. 1980); for further discussion *see* O. Aldıkaçtı, *Anayasa Hukukumuzun Gelişmesi ve 1961 Anayasası*, 3. Bası [Development of our Constitutional Law and the Constitution of 1961] 55–64 (İstanbul 3rd ed.). For the text of the Constitution of 1876 *see*, A.Ş. Gözübüyük/Ş. Kili, *Türk Anayasa Metinleri*, 2. Bası [Texts of the Turkish Constitutions] 27–42 (İstanbul 2d ed. 1982).
3. For an in-depth look at this matter, *see* Aldıkaçtı, *ibid.*, 65, 66 and 67–75.
4. Teziç [note 1], 139; for the text of the Constitution of 1908, *see* Gözübüyük/Kili *supra*, 63–67 and accompanying amendments dated 1909–1918, 75.
5. For a more detailed discussion and critique, *see* Aldıkaçtı, *supra*, 77–86; and for the text of the Constitution of 1921, *see* Gözübüyük/Kili, *supra*, 93 et seq.
6. *Ibid.*, 87–93; for the text of the Constitution of 1924 *see* Gözübüyük/Kili, *supra* 11 et seq.

Constitution of 1961.[7] The evident character of the 1961 Constitution was that Parliament was no longer the sole body empowered to exercise sovereignty, and limits were placed on the powers of Parliament. The 1961 Constitution tried to strike a balance between opposing influences through autonomous institutions like independent courts and universities, and indirectly tried to limit political power, i.e., the rule of the executive. The reason for this was that the exclusive exercise of sovereignty by Parliament under the 1924 Constitution had led in practice to the domination of a single party and the prevalence of a system based on the supremacy of the executive power.

7. However, the new order based on an equilibrium of powers did not produce the expected results. The powers not only of the executive but also of the legislative body were disputed and even *de facto* shared by the courts and autonomous institutions.[8] In 1980, when the extra-parliamentary opposition also tried to share power and the country plunged into terror and anarchy, Turkey suspended democracy. The democratic order was restored under the Constitution of 1982.[9]

B. *The Constitution of 1982*[10]

1. General

8. The structure of public authority in Turkey was founded upon the principle of the separation of legislative (Const. 7), executive (Const. 8) and judicial powers (Const. 9) until the change of the government system through a fundamental amendment of the Constitution of 1982 that was accepted in the Referendum that took place on April 16, 2017. The Constitutions of 1924 and 1961 were based on this principle and the Constitution of 1982 maintained the same principle until the 2017 Referendum.

9. The most important change that was introduced by the Constitution of 1982 as opposed to the Constitutions of 1924 and 1961 concerned the fortification of the status and powers of the President of the Republic which were strengthened even more as a result of the 2017 Referendum. Status of the President has been a question that has given rise to much controversy. As indicated by some commentators,

---

7. For the German translation of the Constitution of 1961, *see* E. E. Hirsch, "Die Verfassung der Türkischen Republic", Die *Staatsverfassungen der Welt, Band 7*, Frankfurt am Main-Berlin, 1966; for an outline *see* B. Davran/H. N. Kubalı, Turkey, *International Encyclopedia of Comparative Law*, Vol. I, T-45/4 1974; E. Özbudun *Türk Anayasa Hukuku*, 2. Bası [Turkish Constitutional Law] (Ankara 2d ed. 1992) *See* generally, O. Aldıkaçtı,supra.
8. For a more detailed critique and discussion, *see* E. Özbudun, supra 28.
9. For a survey of legislative history, *see ibid.*, 31–35.
10. For the German translation of the Constitution of 1982, *see* E. E. Hirsch, "Die Verfassung der Türkischen Republik vom 9. November 1982", *Jahrbuch des öffentlichen Rechts der Gegenwart*, Neue Folge/Band 32, Tübingen 1983, text and accompanying introduction, 508–551; *see* generally Özbudun, supra Teziç, supra B. Tanör, *İki Anayasa, 1961–1982* [Two Constitutions, 1961–1982], İstanbul 1986.

to ensure that the executive functions efficiently and with clear goals, the Constitution of 1982 relies heavily on the powers of the President. In accordance with Article 104 of the Constitution, he "shall ensure the implementation of the Constitution, and the regular and harmonious functioning of the organs of the State." This may mean the President *can be everywhere and can do everything.*[11]

10. Others came to the conclusion that although the 1982 Constitution transformed the presidency from a largely symbolic and ceremonial office, (as it was under the 1961 Constitution), into an active and powerful one, with important political and appointive functions, it had not gone, however, to the extreme of adopting an executive presidency, such as in the United States of America until the latest amendments of 2017.

11. Before the amendments of 2017, the system of government in Turkey was essentially parliamentary, in the sense that the executive maintained a dual structure and the Council of Ministers was politically responsible to the legislature. Thus, it may be concluded that the 1982 Constitution had created a "mixed" or "hybrid" system of government, somewhat along the lines of the French Constitution of 1958.

2. 2017 Amendments

12. On January 21, 2017, the Turkish Parliament approved the amendment of 18 Articles of the Constitution of 1982. These amendments introduced major changes to the current parliamentary system and designated the President as the head of the executive powers. A constitutional referendum was held throughout Turkey on April 16, 2017 on whether to approve the 18 proposed amendments to the Turkish Constitution that were brought forward by the governing Justice and Development Party (AKP) and the Nationalist Movement Party (MHP). Results indicated a 51%–49% lead for the "Yes" vote.

13. As a result of the 2017 amendments, the term "Prime Minister" was removed from the Constitution and the then-existing parliamentary system was replaced with the executive presidency and presidential system. Additionally, the number of seats in the Turkish Parliament was raised from 550 to 600 while the president was given more control over appointments to the Constitution Court and Supreme Council of Judges and Prosecutors whose name was then changed to "Council of Judges and Prosecutors" by dropping the word "Supreme."

14. The system introduced by the 2017 amendments, differs from the standard presidential system. In the classical sense, the presidential system requires the election of the president and parliament members in different elections and does not empower the president or the parliament to dissolve each other before the expiry of their respective terms. However, contrary to these established standards, as per the system introduced by the 2017 amendments, the President and parliament members

11. *Ibid.*, 104; *cf.* Teziç, supra 140.

are elected in the same elections and both the president and the parliament have the authority to renew the elections. This governance system is referred to as the "Presidential Governance System" in Turkish practice and doctrine. As per Article 8 of the law amending the Turkish Constitution, executive duty and authority belongs to the President and is performed in compliance with laws and regulations. The President is the head of government and holds the exclusive executive authority. The President also has the authority to issue Presidential/Executive Orders in the force of law on matters that fall within his/her executive powers. As indicated above, the new system removes the "Prime Minister" and also "Council of Ministers" from the Constitution granting the authority to the President to appoint any number of assistants and Ministers from among individuals that are eligible to be elected as a Parliament member.

15. Another important aspect of the amendments is that it changes the election system of the Council of Judges and Prosecutors granting the President and the Parliament to appoint 11 out of 13 members while the remaining two are appointed by the Minister of Justice (who is also appointed by the President) and Undersecretary of Ministry of Justice (appointed by the Minister of Justice).

16. It is also important to note that certain amended provisions of the Constitution had different dates for entry into force. While the provisions changing the election system of the Council of Judges and Prosecutors, abolishing the military courts and permitting the President to be a member of a political party entered into force immediately, the remaining amendments were to enter into force upon the next elections which had been scheduled to take place on November 3, 2019, for the election of the President and the Parliament members. However, the amendments also made it possible for the Parliament to decide for early elections. Indeed, the Parliament decided for early elections and all amended provisions of the Constitution entered into force on June 24, 2018, upon the election of the President and the members of the Parliament.

C. Political Parties

17. During the Republican era, a "*one-party*" regime dominated Turkey from 1923 to 1945, and the country was ruled by the Republican People's Party. The foundations of the Republican People's Party had been established during the War of Independence (1919–1922), and the party was active after the declaration of the Republic in the promulgation and consolidation of Atatürk's reforms. Turkey adopted a "multi-party" political system in 1945. In 1950, the Democratic Party—then in opposition—defeated the Republican People's Party, despite its historical importance, and came to power. Statism was dominant in the economy during the period from 1923 to 1950. In fact, statism was a fundamental principle conscientiously followed by the Republican People's Party, together with the principles of nationalism, populism, revolutionism and secularism. The Democrat Party advocated a liberal economic system in its bid for power and took the first significant practical steps towards this.

18. Many parties were founded in Turkey between 1960 and 1982, and these formed coalition governments with the two major parties, the Justice Party (the successor of the Democratic Party founded after the military intervention of 1960) and the Republican People's Party.

19. Similarly, after the military intervention of 1982, various new parties were founded, such as the Social Democratic Populist Party, the Nationalist Labor Party and the Democratic Left Party, on the left and the Motherland Party, the True Path Party and the Welfare Party, on the right. It was the Motherland Party, which came to power after the general elections in 1983.

20. In addition, in 1992, all the previous parties which were closed down in 1981 were revived by a special Act of Parliament.

21. Many parties considered the possibility of unification, but it was only the Social Democratic Populist Party who agreed to merge into the Republican People's Party in 1994.

22. In 1994, the Republican People's Party and the Social Democratic Populist Party merged retaining the former's name and the country was ruled by a coalition government formed by the Welfare Party. Between 1982 and 2002, Turkey was mostly governed by coalition governments. Founded in 2001 by members of a number of existing conservative parties, the Justice and Development Party (AKP) won over two-thirds of parliamentary seats in the 2002 elections. Since then, the country has gained a stable government. Following the 2002 elections, the influence of armed forces gradually decreased. The general political view in Turkey became more conservative after 2009.

IV. Population and Employment Statistics

23. Turkey's population has been growing steadily over the past years. The first census in Turkey was conducted in 1923; the census was conducted every year ending with zero and five digits during the period falling between 1930–1990. According to the results of the last 2016 Address Based Census, the population of Turkey is 82,003,882.[12]

24. Turkish Statistical Institute ("*TurkStat*") is the Turkish government agency commissioned with producing official statistics on Turkey, its population, resources, economy, society and culture. According to TurkStat data, population density is expressed as "A number of people per square kilometer," Turkey in general has increased by 2 to 107 people in comparison to 2017. Istanbul is the province with the highest population density with 2,900 people per square kilometer. This is

12. https://eacea.ec.europa.eu/national-policies/eurydice/content/population-demographic-situation-languages-and-religions-103_en.

respectively followed by Kocaeli with 528 people and İzmir with 360 people. The province with the lowest population density is Tunceli with 12 people per square kilometer as in the previous year. The population density of Konya, which ranks first in terms of surface area, is 57 and the population density of Yalova with its smallest area is 310 people. In 2017, the proportion of those residing in provincial and district centers was 92.5%, which was 92.3% in 2018. The rate of residents living in towns and villages was 7.7%.

25. As per the labor force statistics issued by TurkStat on December 10, 2020, the unemployment rate realized as of September 2020 is 12.7% and employment rate is realized as 44%. The number of persons in the labor force realized 31 million 724 thousand persons with 1 million 282 thousand persons decrease in the period of September 2020 compared with the same period of the previous year. Labor force participation rate was 50.5% with 3.0 percentage point decrease.

V. Enterprise, Corporations and Partnership Statistics

26. Number of companies and partnerships in Turkey as of January 31, 2021 as per the statistics held by the Central Registration System (CRS) of the Ministry of Trade is provided below:

Type	*Number*
Joint-Stock Company	152,230
Limited Liability Company	918,614
Collective Partnership	10,872
Commandite Partnership	1,926
Co-operative Societies	31,833
Commercial Enterprise	678,895
Branch	214,351
Total	2,008,721

27. As per the information obtained from the Capital Markets Board of Turkey, the total number of public companies in Turkey as of January 31, 2021 is 508 and the number of public companies actively traded on the Istanbul Stock Exchange (Borsa Istanbul) is 395.

VI. Social and Cultural Values

28. As has been stated previously, although Turkey is a predominantly Muslim country, it is also a secular country, with a perception of Islam filtered through its rich history rather than a perception based on rigid Islamic doctrines. Despite the fact that the conservative political view has gained dominance since the 2002 elections, the great majority of the Turkish people identify themselves with this secularism. Secularism today is not just a constitutional principle but a way of looking at the world, a way of life, and a national, social and cultural value conscientiously defended by all classes. This sets Turkey apart from many other Islamic countries and places it in a different position in the world of Islam.

29. The second feature of Turkey's system of social and cultural values is that Turkey possesses reformist dynamics orientating it towards the west. The movement of modernization, started by Mustafa Reşit Paşa in 1839 with the Royal Decree of Gülhane, led to the permeation of society with western institutions. The restructuring of the state also initiated changes in the social and cultural infrastructure. This transformation was hastened by Atatürk. Through the legal revolution and the adaption of the Latin alphabet, as well as other comprehensive social reforms, the country reached a point of no return in the process of westernization, and a wide social consensus for progress was created. This consensus, which was adopted by ever wider and more diverse classes, is also a social value, and this transformation has in turn been significantly reflected in Turkey's culture.

30. The great majority of Turkish men and women today have adopted a western lifestyle and global outlook. Exponents of the western lifestyle and global outlook have greatly increased in numbers during the last thirty years because of accelerated immigration to the cities and industrialization. Turkey is unique in the experience of having successfully passed through a process of westernization and of having neared the completion of that process. It, therefore, has been the subject of many scientific studies in sociology, culture, and law.

31. Westernization has, however, neither ruptured nor weakened Turkey's ties with tradition. This has created a unique synthesis between Turkey's culture and the social and cultural values which are independent of Islamic and Arab culture, in spite of being Muslim and despite her geographical proximity to the Arab world. Contractual freedom, which is significant from the viewpoint of partnership and company law in Turkey—though it does not have the cultural quality and weight of a social value—is a generally accepted fundamental principle of civil law. In fact, the Constitution provides that everyone—whether a natural or a legal person—has freedom of contract in whichever area that person may desire.

32. A liberal system prevails in Turkey, which allows capital to select its type of business, location and operations freely within the country. The five-year development plans and the annual programs are not mandatory for private enterprises and provide only encouragement by means of incentives and government subsidies. The freedom to choose the subject matter of business is now unrestricted. The Constitution provides that everyone—whether a natural or a legal person—is free to work in any desired field and free to establish private enterprises. The State does not have a monopoly in any field. State monopolies dating from the early years of the Republic, and surviving into the 1980s, were limited to tobacco, salt, spirits except for wine and matches. These monopolies were gradually abolished prior to and during the 1980s.

33. Thus, there is a wide consensus today on the matter of a free market and a free enterprise economy.

VII. Privatization Efforts and Golden Shares

34. Law no. 2983, dated February 29, 1984 is the first privatization law of Turkey which set forth the methods of privatization as transfer of shares, operation rights and income participation certificates. The Privatization Administration of Turkey was founded on November 27, 1994, as per Law No. 4046 on Implementations of Privatization (PL) as the governmental agency responsible for public sector companies, public assets and services. PL has been subject to various amendments over the past years but maintained its position as the general framework of privatization in Turkey.

35. Turkey has pursued a vigorous privatization program since 1990s and certain important services such as telecommunications, certain highways, sea ports, electricity production and distribution companies and the state's right to organize lottery games have been privatized over the years leading to a total revenue of USD 70,421,355,979[13]

36. Implementation of golden (privileged) shares in privatizations started in the privatization of TELETAŞ which had foreseen the golden share to automatically convert to a standard share (unprivileged share) once the shareholding of the state in the company falls below 3%.

37. As per Article 13 of the PL, Privatization Administration is entitled to determine the strategically important fields and entities under the privatization program, amount of the privileged shares to be issued to the state in case its shareholding in the company falls below 50% granting the state veto right on important decisions to be obtained by the corporate bodies, the scope of the privileges to be granted to such shares, the number and amount of privileged shares and amend the granted privileges.

38. The aforesaid article also stipulates that the formation of golden shares to be granted to the state is required for the following entities in case 49% or more of their shares are privatized:

- Turkish Airlines
- Turkish Republic Agriculture Bank (*Türkiye Ziraat Bankası*)

---

13. https://ms.hmb.gov.tr/uploads/sites/6/2021/05/yillar-itibariyle-uygulama-.pdf.

– Turkish Petroleum Company (TPAO)
– Alkaloid Institution of Turkish Agricultural Products Office.

§2. The Historical Background of Corporations and Partnerships

I. The Mediaeval Period

39. One of the earliest business associations in Islamic Law was the "*Kirad*" which was an early form of *commenda*, in which a financier, as a sleeping partner, lent capital to his active partner, whose liability was limited to the amount of such capital. The *Kirad* was regarded as a purely temporary arrangement for trading purposes.[14]

40. Another form of business association was the "*Şirket-i-inan,*" which had always been associated with the idea of a personal relationship founded on mutual confidence and trust. In contrast to partnership, the partner of the *Şirket-i-inan* acted for himself and accordingly bound himself, but not his co-partners. At the end of a business venture, the profit or loss was shared among the partners proportionately to the shares held by each of them.[15]

II. The *Tanzimat*[16] Period (1839–1876)

41. Although the concept of incorporation has been of the greatest importance in the development of trade and industry, it remained unknown in Turkey until 1850. In 1850, however, the Commercial Code (Kanunname-i-Ticaret) was enacted and Commercial Courts were established. Consequently, company law entered a phase of development.

---

14. *See* H. Arslanlı, *Kollektif ve Komandit Şirketler*, 2. Bası [General and Limited Partnerships] (İstanbul 2d ed. 1960) [*see SB*] 6, 9; (Poroy/Tekinalp/Çamoğlu) *Ortaklıklar ve Kooperatif Hukuku*, Ders Kitabı, 5. Bası [Law on Partnerships, Companies and Co-operatives Textbook] (İstanbul 5rd ed. 1993) [Partnerships] [*see* SB].
15. *Ibid.*, [*see* SB], 12.
16. The literature on the "*Tanzimat*" is immense; among the contributions in English and French *see* E. Z. Koral, *Osmanlı Tarihi*, C. IV [Ottoman History Vol. IV], Ankara 1954; T. Z. Tunaya, *Türkiye'nin Siyasi Hayatında Batılılaşma Hareketleri*; [Westernization activities in Turkey's political life] İstanbul, 1960; H. V. Velidedeoğlu, "*Kanunlaştırma Hareketleri ve Tanzimat*" [Legal codification activities and the Tanzimat], *in: Tanzimat* I, İstanbul 1941; F. Ahmad, *The Young Turks*, The Committee of Union and Progress in Turkish Politics 1908–1914, Oxford University Press 1969 [Turkish version: İttihat ve Terakki, 1908–1914, N. Ülken, (trans.), Sander Yayınları: İstanbul 1971], ed. Engelhardt, *La Turquie et la Tanzimat* une *histoire des reforms dans l'Empire Ottoman depuis 1826 jusqu'a nos jours*, Paris 1882–1884 [Turkish version: *Tanzimat*, A. Düz (trans.) İstanbul 1976, Milliyet Yayınları]; B. Lewis, *The Emergence of modern Turkey*, 2ed., Oxford University Press, 1968 [Turkish version: *Modern Türkiye'nin Doğuşu* M. Kıratlı (trans.), Ankara 1970]; H.W.V Temperley, "British Policy towards Parliamentary Rule and Constitutionalism in Turkey (1830–1914)", in: *Cambridge Historical Journal*, IV (1923–24), 156–191; F.D. Bailey, *British Policy and the Turkish Reform Movement*, Cambridge, Mass., 1942.

42. The situation was radically changed in the Ottoman Empire as a result of the *Tanzimat* legislation. The *Tanzimat*, or "programme of reforms," was prepared by Mustafa Reşid Paşa, who was one of the statesmen and westernizers of the reform period. This vast plan of reforms was issued under the name of *Gülhane-hatt-ı hümayunu* (Royal Decree of Gülhane). From this royal decree dates the fundamental change of the Ottoman Empire from an archaic system, based on *shari'a* and theocratic principles, to that of a modern state.[17]

A. *The* Mecelle[18]

43. The *Mecelle* (literally "*book*" or "*volume*"), the largest legislative act of the Tanzimat period, was a civil code still under the influence of the shari'a. It consisted of several books on such subjects as sale, rent and hire, order pledge, loan for use, gifts and mandat. One of the books of the *Mecelle* was allocated to companies and partnerships.

44. These were divided into two major categories. The first category consisted of two commercial enterprises: *Şirket-i-mülk and Şirket-i-ibaha.*[19] Neither was an association in the literal sense of company law, since neither was an association of two or more persons for the purpose of gaining, managing and sharing profits (or losses) in a business enterprise, nor an association that had *affectio societatis*. Some features of *Şirket-i mülk* were similar to joint tenancy and others were like co-ownership. *Şirket-i ibaha*, however, meant the right of collective use by every one of the places open to the public, such as rivers and lakes and it is not possible to describe it as a company in the modern sense.

45. The second category consisted of several types of commercial enterprises: if the shares of the partners in capital and profit were equal, the company was called *Şirket-i mufaveze*; if the shares were not equal, the company was called *Şirket-i inan*. Moreover, the *Mecelle* named companies differently according to the types of capital and purposes of the company. If the capital was cash and/or in kind and the type of business was the sale and purchase of goods, then the company was called *Şirket-i emval*; if personal work was performed as capital and the type of business was the provision of services, then the company was called *Şirket-i âmâl*; if personal credit was contributed as capital and the type of business was a sale and purchase on credit, the company was called *Şirket-i vücüh.*[20]

---

17. *Shari'a*, literally "road to a watering place" *see Encyclopaedia Britannica*, Vol. 12, 1972, 679.
18. *See* generally A. Haydar, *Mecelle Şerhi*, [Commentary on the Mecelle] İstanbul 1914. E. Mardin, *Medeni Hukuk Cephesinden Ahmet Cevdet Paşa* [Ahmet Cevdet Paşa from the point of view of Civil Law], İstanbul 1946; S.S. Onar, "The Macalla", *in*: Majid Khadduri and Herbert J. Liebensny (eds.), *Law in the Middle East*, I, 1955, pp. 292–308.
19. *See* Arslanlı, [Partnerships] [*see* SB], 11.
20. *Ibid.*, 11–13.

*B. The Commercial Code (*The Kanunname-i-Ticaret) of 1850[21]

46. Legislation, in the modern sense, concerning partnerships and companies was enacted for the first time in the Ottoman Empire in 1850 with the *Kanunname-i-Ticaret* (literally "*Commercial Code*"). It was based on the French Code de Commerce of 1807. After the promulgation of the Kanunname-i-Ticaret, secular courts, including commercial courts, were set up to apply these modern codes under modern forms of procedure.

47. The Commercial Code of 1850, in its third chapter, contained certain provisions regulating the structures of the various types of partnerships and companies and, to a lesser extent, the rights of their members and shareholders.

48. Partnerships and companies formed under the *Commercial Code of 1850* had certain common principal features. One of the distinguishing features was legal personality. Both partnerships and companies were legal entities, e.g., both could own property, enter into contracts, and sue and be sued. Under the terms of the *Commercial Code of 1850*, the characteristics which distinguished a company from a partnership were a limited liability and the establishment of the company by Seniyye-i Şahene (royal charter).

49. The types of partnerships and companies created by the *Commercial Code of 1850* were collective companies (general partnerships), commandite partnerships (limited partnerships) and capital companies, i.e., joint-stock companies and limited liability companies. It was possible, however, to establish a partnership limited by shares (Article 29) or an "association commerciale en participation" (Article 47). Co-operative societies were regulated in 1924 through the amendment of Article 10.

50. A general partnership (Articles 11–13) was an association of two or more individuals, with unlimited liability to the creditors of the partnership, formed under a firm name for the purpose of operating a trading enterprise. The relationship between the partners was determined primarily by a partnership agreement in written form, which was not a *conditio sine qua non* for the creation of the partnership but was necessary to prove and demonstrate the relationship. The limited partnership differed legally from the general partnership in that at least one partner was fully liable for the debts and obligations of the firm, while the liability of the other partner or partners was limited to a fixed contribution.

51. A company was defined as a company with a firm name of its own whose capital was divided into shares and whose liabilities were met exclusively by its assets. It did not follow its model, the French Code of Commerce, very closely as the minimum amount of share capital and minimum value of each share were not fixed. Equally, there was no provision relating to the organization and bodies of the

21. *Selected Special Bibliography:* Ahmet Reşit, *Hukuku Ticaret* [Commercial Law], İstanbul, 1890. Further *see* Arslanlı, *ibid.*

company. The partnership limited by shares was incorporated through the *İrade-i-Seniyye-i-Şahane* (royal charter) and its Articles of Association had to be announced by a notice on the wall of the premises rather than in the Trade Registry and Official Journal.

III. The Period of the Republic of Turkey (1923 to Date)

A. *The Turkish Commercial Code (TCC) of 1926*[22]

52. The mid-1920s was a time of innovation when the social, political and cultural landscape of Turkey began to undergo fundamental changes. A series of legal reforms took place in 1926. By these reforms, Ottoman Law was replaced by a system based on various European precedents, such as the Civil Code and the Code of Obligations (Switzerland), the Penal Code (Italy), the Code of Penal Procedure (Germany) and the Code of Procedure (Neuchâtel, Switzerland). This was the climate in which the Commercial Code of 1926 was born. It was described as a "home-made" act, in spite of its being taken from a wide variety of sources.

B. *The TCC of 1956*[23]

53. The Commercial Code was completely replaced by the TCC of 1956, which was drafted by Professor Ernts Eduard Hirsch of the Free University of Berlin and, for many years, Professor of Law at the Universities of İstanbul and Ankara. Its various provisions regarding partnerships and companies were adapted from Swiss precedents. In 1983, 1989, 1992 and 1994, the TCC was amended.[24] Finally, in 1995, the TCC was amended by Decree having the force of Law No. 95/559.[25] The Ministry of Industry and Trade was given powers to issue communiqués in order to regulate the application of the Code provisions concerning companies. Commercial registries were now administered by Chambers of Commerce instead of Courts. Under TCC Article 299, a joint-stock company could not be established without court approval. This provision was then repealed, which obviated the need for court approval, but which also had the consequence that, contrary to the earlier law, a company could now be declared null and void after its establishment. Under the old system, a company could be deemed not to have been established if illegalities in

---

22. *See* generally K. Arar, *Şirketler Hukuku* [Law of Partnerships and Companies], Ankara 1952; E. E. Hirş (Hirsch), *Ticaret Hukuku Dersleri*, 3. Bası [Lectures on Commercial Law] (İstanbul 3rd ed. 1948); K. Ş. Onsun, *Ticaret Şirketleri* [Commercial Companies], Ankara 1949; M. A. Bilgişin, *Şirketler Hukuku*, C. 2 [Law of Partnerships and Companies, Vol. 2], İstanbul 1950.
23. *See* SB.
24. Law No. 2915 [O.G. No. 18192, Sep. 15, 1983], Law No. 3585 [O.G. No. 20215, Jul. 4, 1989], Law No. 3809 [O.G. No. 21273, Jul. 3, 1992], Decree having the force of Law No. 94/537 [O.G. No. 21991, Jul. 15, 1994].
25. Decree having the force of Law No. 95/559 [O.G. No. 22326, Jun. 27, 1995], Law No. 4128 [O.G. No. 22426, Nov. 7, 1995].

its establishment jeopardized or infringed in a major way the interests of shareholders and creditors. Legal action seeking such a declaration could only be initiated within one month of the establishment of the company. The repeal of Article 299 has removed this time limit so that a challenge to the legal existence of a company is possible at any time. The new Turkish Commercial Code No. 6102 (NTCC or TCC) regulated this concept under Article 353. As per Article 353 of the current code, it is not possible to declare a joint-stock company as null and void, however, the board of directors, shareholders or creditors of a joint-stock company or the Ministry of Trade may initiate a lawsuit for the cancellation of a joint-stock company in case the interests of shareholders, creditors or the public have been significantly risked or violated due to violation of the TCC at the time of incorporation of the company. This lawsuit may be initiated within three months following the incorporation of the company.

C. *The TCC No. 6102*[26]

1. Passage of the Act and Entry into Force

54. The Commercial Code of 1956 was replaced in 2011 by the new TCC of 2011, which was drafted by an academic commission of experts formed in 1999 by the Ministry of Justice, chaired by Professor Ünal Tekinalp of the University of Istanbul. The new TCC was passed by the Grand National Assembly of Turkey (Türkiye Büyük Millet Meclisi, TBMM) on January 13, 2011. After being signed by the President, it was published in the Turkish Official Gazette (TOG) on February 14, 2011. Its various provisions regarding partnerships and companies are adapted from Swiss models. Except in the case of Book 3, which is about negotiable instruments, the approach was to write a completely new code rather than revising the existing text of the then-current law. With the exception of certain number of its provisions, TCC came into force on July 1, 2012. The other provisions consisting of two groups came into force on July 1, 2013. The first group deals with the requirements applicable to capital companies, such as the obligation to have an internet website. The other group of provisions that came into effect on July 1, 2013 includes requirements concerning (1) Turkish Accounting Standards, which are identical to International Financial Reporting Standards (IFRS) and with which all business undertakings (including legal entities and private persons that qualify as merchants under the TCC) will be required to comply and (2) Turkish Auditing Standards, which are identical to International Auditing and Assurance Standards and which apply to auditing of capital companies. Law No. 6103, which contains

26. Turkish Commercial Code (Law No. 6102), OG 27846, Feb. 14, 2011. For the "General Explanatory Note" (which sets out TCC's aims, objectives, principles, and philosophies) and for the "Explanatory Notes" (which reveal the thought behind each clause so as to assist in its interpretation), *see Türk Ticaret Kanunu Tasarısı ve Adalet Komisyonu Raporu (1/324)* [*The Draft of the Turkish Commercial Code and Report of the Justice Commission (1/324)*] TBMM, S 96.

provisions governing the transition to the new rules and the adaptation to them, was also signed by the President and published in the TOG along with NTCC and came into effect on July 1, 2012.

2. Considerable Short-Term Amendments

55. However, the TCC and Application Law No. 6103 were amended by Law No. 6335[27] dated June 26, 2012, just a few days before the said laws entered into force. The TCC 2011 system regarding commercial offenses and penalties, which was already more relaxed than the systems applicable in EU countries, especially those in France and Germany, has become even less strict. Various TCC articles regarding commercial offenses, such as Articles 33, 38, 51(1), 52(2) and 562(1)-(14) were amended and penalties were lightened. Some prison sentences were converted into fines, while fines imposable by courts were converted to fines imposable by governmental agencies due to the fact that in case of nonpayment of fines ordered by a court, such a fine may be converted to imprisonment.

56. One of the reforms made by TCC 2011 was in regard to the auditing system. The new law would have compelled 95,000 corporations, 600 of which were publicly held companies, and 78,000 limited liability companies to build a new auditing system consisting of only independent auditors. The reason for this reform was that for ninety-five years since TCC 1926 entered into force, i.e., also during the application of TCC 1956, commercial companies had been audited by non-professional "controllers" whose auditing reports typically consisted of two or three sentences at most and almost always reached a positive conclusion. In other words, auditing was deemed to be a procedural requirement having no significant effect or importance. It was an established view that the previous TCC provisions related to the auditing of corporations were archaic. For this reason, the new TCC attempted to introduce an audit system whereby the audit would be carried out by qualified independent auditors.

57. However, the lobby activities of business circles, declaring that it would be costly for the companies to build the new auditing system, provoked an amendment to the auditing requirements introduced by the new TCC. As a result of these lobbying efforts, TCC Article 397 was amended by Law No. 6335 and the audit requirement applicable for all capital companies was abolished granting the right to the Council of Ministers to determine the criteria which would require a capital company to be subject to a mandatory independent audit requirement.

58. In accordance with TCC 2011 all joint-stock and limited-liability companies would have been under the obligation to build a company website. These companies were obliged to publish on their websites information that may be needed by the public, including investors and creditors as well as outside advisors and even

27. TOJ 28339, Jun. 26, 2012.

the media focusing on financial news which makes use of companys' financial statements in their broadest sense. The information and documents (which the law referred to generally as "content") included (but was not limited to) public announcements which a company must make; documents that shareholders, partners and stakeholders generally need to see and be aware of in order to protect their own interests and exercise their rights; board and general assembly resolutions pertaining to the exercise of preemptive rights, rights of first refusal, options and similar rights; annual reports as well as reports pertaining to audits, valuations and public offerings; general assembly related meeting announcements, invitations, agendas, etc.; amounts of money paid by the company to directors and senior managers as salaries, representation and travel expenses, pensions, bonuses, premiums, compensation and other forms of remuneration. As the result of the strong campaign against this new transparency system and misinformation extended to the public in this regard, the related articles were significantly amended although not entirely abolished. The items to be disclosed on the website have been restricted; particularly, the requirements to disclose the remuneration of senior managers, financial statements and auditing reports have been canceled.

59. Articles 358 and 395 concerning shareholder's and director's loans (i.e., loans extended by the company to its shareholders and/or directors), which were thoroughly discussed in public, have been relaxed. With the changes introduced by Law No. 6335, shareholder's loans are permitted, provided that the shareholder has paid all outstanding capital contribution and the company's profit and expendable reserves are sufficient to cover previous year's losses. Directors loans, however, are still prohibited.

60. Article 39(2) which was adopted from AktG §. 80 and GmbH §. 35a has been changed. Accordingly, the requirement to include the company's trade registry number, tradename, registered address and, if the company is obliged to set up a website, the address of the website in the company's letterhead was replaced with the requirement to announce the company's capital and the name of its directors only on the company's website.

61. One of the significant reforms of TCC 2011, which has also been abolished by Law No. 6335, was that the important transactions of a company, such as merger, division, conversion and an increase and decrease of capital, were to be subject to a special auditing. The auditor would have been elected only in respect of such transactions and his duty would have been limited to the examination of such transactions. This new system has also been canceled in its entirety because of high-cost concerns.

3. TCC as a Unified Code

62. While upholding a number of traditions inherited from previous Turkish commercial codes (notably those of 1926 and 1956), TCC is a unified code consisting of six books, each of which deals with a specific subject, but all of which are concerned with various aspects of commercial law. Like previous manifestations of the TCC, TCC's attitudes towards "commercial law" very much resemble those of the *Handelsgesetzbuch* (HGB) of the previous 1897 version which was in force before its revision dated January 30, 1937. Other examples of this type which may be mentioned are the Swiss *Obligationenrecht* (OR), the 1942 *Codice Civile Italiano*, and the French *Code de Commerce*. In that respect, TCC is a "zentrales Handelsgesetzbuch."[28] Book 1 is concerned with "commercial enterprises," Book 2 with "commercial companies," Book 3 with "negotiable instruments," Book 4 with "carriage of goods," Book 5 with "maritime law," and Book 6 with "insurance law." The "unified code" approach also embodies the uniformity of Turkish private law. As was the case with the previous TCC (TCC 1956), Article 1 of TCC states, "The Turkish Commercial Code is an inseparable part of the Turkish Civil Code," thus making a reference to the integrality of Turkish private law. Article 646 of the Turkish Code of Obligations underscores the same integrality because it states that the Turkish Code of Obligations is the fifth book of the Turkish Civil Code and complements it. The principle of uniformity does not detract from the independency of TCC with respect to either the Turkish Civil Code or the Turkish Code of Obligations. The previous TCC 1956 consisted of five books. It did not address transport law as a separate book and "negotiable instruments" were dealt with under the rubric of "Freight bills." TCC's approach to dealing with transport law as a whole and recognizing its independence from negotiable instruments are two of its innovations.

4. The Objectives of TCC

63. The first objective of TCC is to ensure that the "language" that Turkish businesses speak is compatible with what is used in international markets. This is done in order to gain recognition for Turkish businesses as potentially trustworthy actors and to increase their competitive strength in such markets.[29]

64. The second objective to which TCC gives importance—and this runs through all six books though it applies in particular to "commercial companies"—is to achieve transparency at the most effective and comprehensive levels possible.

65. For a country such as Turkey that is currently engaged in negotiations to become a full member of the EU, compliance with the *acquis communautaire* is the third objective of TCC, to which it attaches as much importance as it does to the first two.[30] For this reason, not only were all European Community (EC), and European Union (EU) regulations, directives, and recommendations touching upon the

---

28. For the term "das zentrale Handelsgesetzbuch" and debate on this issue *see* Hopt, "Reformprobleme im Handels-, Gesellschafts- und Abschlussprüferrecht: Bemerkungen zur türkischen Handelsrechtsreform 2008" in Kompatabilität des türkischen und europäischen Wirtschaftsrechts: der neue türkische HGB-Entwurf und benachbarte Rechtsgebiete (ed Atamer and Hopt), Tübingen 2009, pp. 21 and 22.
29. General Explanatory Note 5.
30. General Explanatory Note 3.

issues dealt with by all six books reflected in TCC, but even high-level expert reports, communications, and action plans were also taken into account.

66. The fourth objective was to ensure that the impact of developments in technology (especially in internet technology) on commercial enterprises would be reflected not only just in company law but also in maritime and insurance law.[31]

67. Finally, as a further objective, a number of safeguards and mechanisms designed to deal with the challenges of globalization were integrated into TCC. The effects of globalization have not always been beneficial, especially in the case of countries that were unprepared for all of its ramifications. While globalization-driven transparency and developments like Basel I, II, and III are good, such things as "hot money" (short-term deposit movements), ill-conceived—or even malicious—"securitization," and contagious financial market volatilities are not.

5. Innovative Initiatives Concerning Limited Liability and Joint-Stock Companies

68. In addition to the adoption of IFRS, the following initiatives concerning limited liability and joint-stock companies are of an innovative nature.

a. Websites, Information Society Services, and Free Access Rights

69. Transparency is an issue of particular importance and a fundamental pillar of TCC, particularly where limited liability and joint-stock companies are concerned. Under TCC, all capital companies which are subject to mandatory independent audit must have at least one internet website and devote an appropriate part of that website to "information society services." This is a mandatory requirement, non-compliance with which is subject to civil and even criminal penalties.

70. The law sets forth a number of specific features that are applicable to the websites of capital companies:

(i) All persons have the right to enter any company's website. In this respect, TCC defines an internet website "free access right" that is not contingent upon the possession of any qualifications or other conditions of interest or benefit.[32]

(ii) All persons have the right to initiate a lawsuit in case of violation of this right of access.

(iii) This right of access entails a number of specific shareholder and stakeholder rights. Therefore, failure to publish statutorily prescribed information and documents on a company's website could lead to suits to challenge any company decisions on which they are based; such non-compliance also gives rise

31. General Explanatory Note 4.
32. Ünal Tekinalp, "Erişim Hakkı" ["Access Right"], Batider 2006, B. XXVIII:4, pp. 5–12.

to the complete gamut of legal consequences, for which managers in positions of authority can be held responsible and liable for the penalties provided for under TCC Article 562(12).

(iv) Information and documents published on company websites must remain there for at least six months unless a longer period of time is called for in TCC or by other laws, regulations, or administrative provisions. In the case of financial statements, for example, the mandated publication period is five years (this last rule is to allow financial statement users to make comparisons between different years).

b. Adoption of the Corporate Governance Philosophy

71. TCC does not regard the fundamental principles of corporate governance (such as equitable treatment of shareholders, interests of other stakeholders, accountability, justice, the role and responsibilities of the board, integrity and ethical behavior, and disclosure and transparency) as being limited exclusively to listed joint-stock companies. It takes the view that these principles are an essential part of the theoretical and dogmatic legal structure of every joint-stock company whether publicly traded or not. This approach is evident in everything from the formulation of legal structures to the scope and effectiveness of shareholders and stakeholders rights and from public disclosure to provisions on financial reporting and auditing.[33]

72. TCC gives Capital Market Board (CMB) the exclusive right to lay down the corporate governance rules that are applicable to public companies. Every publicly traded company's board is required by law to prepare a report on an annual basis assessing the company's compliance with corporate governance principles and have these compliance reports publicly disclosed (TCC 375 (1/f), 1524 (1/i), 1529).

c. Company Board and General Assembly Meetings in an Electronic Environment

73. Provided that it is so specified in the partnership agreement or Articles of Association, partners and managers meetings (in partnerships) and board meetings

33. Selected literature assessing TCC from the standpoint of corporate governance: Kemal Erol, "Yeni Türk Ticaret Kanunu Tasarısının Kurumsal Yönetim İlkeleri Açısından Getirdikleri" ["The Implications of the Draft of the New Turkish Commercial Code from the Standpoint of Corporate Governance Principles], *Kurumsal Yönetim Dergisi* 2008:14, pp. 18 et seq.; Gül Okutan Nilssonn, "The Draft Turkish Commercial Code and Corporate Governance", *Unternehmen, Markt und Verantwortung Festschrift Hopt* 2 (ed S. Grundmann, B Hear, H Merket), Berlin-New York: 2010, pp. 3177 et seq.; Ünal Tekinalp, "Türk Ticaret Kanunu Tasarısının Kurumsal Yönetim Felsefesine Yaklaşımı" ["The Approach of the Turkish Draft Commercial Code to the Philosophy of Corporate Governance"], *Uğur Alacakaptan Armağanı* [*Festschrift for Uğur Alacakaptan*] II, İstanbul: 2008, pp. 637–652; Veliye Yanlı, *Kurumsal Yönetim İlkeleri Açısından Türk Ticaret Kanununun Değerlendirilmesi: Türkiye ve Avrupa Birliğinde Sermaye Şirketleri Reformu,* (*"Evaluation of Turkish Commercial Code in respect of Corporate Governance Principles: Capital oriented Companies Reform in Turkey and European Union"*) İstanbul: İstanbul Ticaret Odası (2007), pp. 45 et seq.

(in companies) may be conducted by the participation of all members online. Furthermore, members who are not physically present at actual meetings may take part in them online, in which case they are also allowed to advance motions and cast votes (TCC 1527.1, 2). There are three specific requirements for votes to be cast in this way. The first is that the partnership or company should have a website that is specifically designed to facilitate such voting. The second is that it must be established (by means of a "technical report") that the partnerships' or companies' equipment enabling voting in an electronic environment is fit for enabling effective participation in meetings and the technical report evidencing such fact must be duly registered and announced. The third is that the identities of those who voted in the general assembly must be kept confidential (TCC 1527.3).

74. As per TCC 1527.5, it has become mandatory for public joint-stock companies to use systems enabling participation and voting to general assemblies electronically upon the enactment of the Regulation on Electronic General Assemblies of Public Companies issued by the Ministry of Trade and Customs on August 28, 2012.

d. Independent Auditing[34]

75. Under TCC 1956, capital-oriented companies in Turkey were subject to an auditing system that was widely criticized as being archaic, futile, and "a mere formality." Joint-stock companies under TCC 1956 were supposedly "audited" by statutory auditors for whom no expertise whatsoever was required and who—apart from a duty of auditing—had fiduciary duties that consisted of little more than summoning a general assembly of shareholders when necessary, checking budget compliance, and determining, in collaboration with the board of directors, how an annual balance sheet was to be drawn up. Statutory auditor's "reports" were rarely longer than a few sentences in length. Limited liability companies with more than twenty partners were subject to the same auditing rules as joint-stock companies.

76. Although, according to the TCC of 2011, all capital companies[35] were to be subject to independent auditing such requirement was then changed by Law No. 6335 limiting such requirement only to those companies that fall under the determinations made by the Council of Ministers. The Council of Ministers adopted a decision on May 26, 2018 and determined certain thresholds in terms of total assets, turnover, number of employees which would qualify a capital company to be subject to independent auditing.

34. Korkut Özkorkut, *Türk Ticaret Kanunu Tasarısına Göre Anonim Şirketlerin Denetiminde Yeni Bir Dönem* ["A Sea Change in the Auditing of Joint-Stock Companies according to the Draft of the Turkish Commercial Code"], Batider 2005, XXII, pp. 29–70. Ünal Tekinalp, "Türk Ticaret Kanunu Tasarısının Merkez Kurumu Bağımsız Denetimin, Denetçi, Denetimin Konusu ve Yöntemi Bakımından Analizi" ["Analysis of Audit, The Central Notion of the Draft Turkish Commercial Code from the Standpoints of Independent Auditing, Auditors, Auditing scope, and Auditing methods"], *Türkiye Muhasebe Standartları Sempozyumu* X, 2006, pp. 24 et seq.

35. *See* footnote 2.

77. Companies which fall under the scope of the aforementioned decision of the Council of Ministers must be audited by an independent, impartial, and qualified auditing firm or auditor[36] in accordance with Turkish Auditing Standards (which are essentially International Auditing and Assurance Standards).

78. Auditors are not only required to scrutinize companies' annual financial statements and their boards' annual reports but also to determine whether or not companies have to set up a risk management committee and whether or not the committee is functioning effectively (NTCC Article 378).

e. Single-Shareholder Joint-Stock Company and Limited Liability Company

79. TCC recognizes single-shareholder joint-stock companies and limited liability companies parallel to the *Directive 89/667/EC on Single-Member Private Limited-Liability Companies.*[37] Accordingly, as per the new TCC, it is now possible for joint-stock and limited liability companies to be established by only one person or legal entity. It is also possible for a limited liability company or joint-stock company established by multiple shareholders to drop down to one shareholder and maintain its legal existence. If a company is incorporated with one shareholder, the name and identity of such shareholder and its tradename and address are required to be registered with the Trade Registry and announced. Similarly, if the number of shareholders in a company established with multiple shareholders drops down to one, such change has to be registered with the Trade Registry Gazette and announced together with the information pertaining to the single shareholder. The requirements regarding registration are intended to achieve transparency and ensure the separation of the assets of the company and its shareholder thereby laying the foundations for the implementation of the "piercing the corporate veil" doctrine in Turkey. This is a fundamental change compared to the previous TCC of 1956 which did not allow limited liability or joint-stock companies with one shareholder and was deemed such as a cause for dissolution.

36. Auditors must be chartered accountants (YMM) or certified public accountants (SMMM).
37. Selected literature: Feyzan H. Ş. Çelik, Hukukun Ekonomik Gerçekliğe Yanıtı: Tek Kişilik Şirketler (A Response of Law to the Economic Reality: Single Member Companies), Batider 2007, C: XXIV Türk Hukukunda Tek Ortaklı Şirketler (Single Member Companies in Turkish Law), Hukuk Dergisi 2008, p. 1253; Gül Okutan, Tek Kişi Ortaklığı (Single Member Company), Türk Hukukunun Avrupa Hukukuna Uyumu (Harmonization of Turkish Law with European Law) (Ed. Ünal Tekinalp), The Project Included in the "Administered Projects" of Research Fund of İstanbul University and Prepared Under Supervision of İstanbul University European Law Research and Practice Center, İstanbul 2001, p. 587 et seq.; Ünal Tekinalp, Tek Kişilik Ortaklık I: Tek Paysahipli Anonim Ortaklık (Single Member Company I: Single-Shareholder Joint-Stock Company); Ünal Tekinalp, Yeni Anonim ve Limited Şirketler Hukuku ile Tek Kişi Ortaklığının Esasları (Principles of New Law of Joint-Stock Companies and Limited liability Companies), 2. Bası (2d Edition), İstanbul, 2011; Veliye Yanlı, Zulässigkeit der Einpersonen—Aktiengesellschaft im Hinblick auf Ihre Existenz und Gründung, Annales de la Faculté de Droit d'Istanbul 1998, XXXII No.48, pp. 200 et seq.

f. Corporate Groups

80. A group of companies ("Corporate Groups") has been regulated for the first time in Turkish Law under the new TCC. As a result, an important loophole has been closed by the detailed provisions of the new TCC concerning Corporate Groups.

81. The new TCC introduces the concepts of parent (controlling) company and subsidiary (dependent company) while also bringing certain brand-new reporting requirements applicable to the Corporate Groups. The Board of Directors of the controlling and dependent companies are required to report on inter-group transactions and relations on an annual basis.

82. Also, a new requirement is introduced in terms of registration and announcement of certain share transfers that take place in companies which are a part of a Corporate Group. As per Article 198 of the TCC, in the event that an undertaking acquires, directly or indirectly, the shares constituting 5%, 10%, 20%, 25% 33%, 50%, 67% or 100% of the share capital of a capital company or its shareholding falls below such percentages, such undertaking is required to notify the capital company and other relevant authorities as per applicable law within ten days following the completion of the relevant share transfer transaction. The notifications shall be made in writing and registered with the relevant Trade Registry and announced in the Trade Registry Gazette. Voting and other shareholding rights pertaining to the transferred shares shall freeze until the registration and announcement requirements are duly fulfilled.

83. This is a significant provision promoting transparency since, in the case of joint-stock companies (other than public companies and companies active in certain regulated markets), share transfers were not subject to any registration or announcement requirement before the enactment of the new TCC and could be freely conducted without becoming public.

84. The new provisions of TCC on Corporation Groups also regulate the consequences of abuse of controlling power of the parent company on the subsidiary and introduce certain protection mechanisms. Among these mechanisms is the sell-out right provided to the shareholders of the subsidiary (dependent company) which has incurred losses due to the abuse of power of the parent (controlling) company.

85. Also, a squeeze-out mechanism is introduced in the new TCC allowing the controlling company holding, directly or indirectly, at least 90% of the share capital of another company to force the minority shareholders to sell their shares in the company if the minority acts in bad faith, hinders operations of the parent company, creates a significant discomfort in the company or acts irresponsibly.

D. The Capital Market Law of 2012

86. Capital Market Law of 1982[38] was replaced in its entirety by new Capital Market Law No. 6362 (*CML*) which entered into force on December 30, 2012.

87. The new CML consists of eight chapters: (1) General Provisions, (2) Principles Regarding Issuance of Capital Market Instruments, Public Disclosure and Issuers, (3) Capital Market Institutions and Activities, (4) Exchanges in Capital Markets Association of Capital Markets of Turkey and Other Institutions, (5) Supervision and Measures in Capital Markets, (6) Actions Requiring Administrative Fine and Capital Market Crimes, (7) Principles Regarding the Capital Markets Board, (8) Final and Transitional Provisions.

88. The new CML did not change the system of the former CML. The main objective of the new law is to achieve harmonization with EC law and the new TCC. Its second aim is to introduce rules that reflect the lessons learned from the mistakes that led to the 2008 global economic crisis. However, the new law focuses on regulating and supervising the relevant institutions rather than improving the capital market.

89. The CML's main objectives have been to establish the control of the CMB over new issues of securities offered to the public and the requirements for the registration of corporations; to obtain permission for the issue of securities by companies; and to enlarge the scope of application of the disclosure principle and to enhance its effectiveness. Under CML, the CMB is empowered to issue regulations which are necessary to supervise the following:

- companies offering their securities to the public or which have more than 500 shareholders (CML 16/1);
- capital market instruments;
- stock exchanges and other secondary markets;
- mutual funds and investment trusts;
- auditing firms which offer their services to institutions operating in the capital market; and
- other similar entities which operate in the capital markets.

90. Some of the subjects regulated under the new CML for the first time are listing on the stock exchange (CML 68), suspension of trading and delisting (CML 69), supervision of financial and information systems of stock exchanges and market operators. The new law has also introduced a number of new institutions such as investment partnerships with variable capital, investor compensation center, trade repositories, and some new associations such as the Turkish Capital Markets Association and the Turkish Appraisal Experts Association.

38. *See generally* Ü. Tekinalp, *Sermaye Piyasası Hukukunun Esasları* [Fundamentals of the Capital Market Law], İstanbul 1982.

91. The authority of the CMB also extends to financial reporting requirements. According to the Communiqué No. II-14.1 Regarding Financial Reporting in Capital Markets, as a rule, Turkish Accounting Standards/Turkish Financial Reporting Standards is applicable to the issuers and other capital market institutions.

§3. Definitions and Structure of Corporations and Partnerships

92. It is more difficult in Turkish jurisprudence—compared to some continental jurisprudences such as French, German and Swiss—to adopt the distinction between a partnership and a corporation which is prevalent in English and American jurisprudence. This is due to the fact that in the Turkish legal system, contrary to those others mentioned above, all Commercial Enterprises—including general partnerships and limited partnerships—are regarded as corporations. A further difficulty arises from the fact that the agreement for setting up any Commercial Enterprise must be in writing and the signatures of the promoters must be certified by a notary public or the Trade Registry officer. Furthermore, the same formality must be observed for any amendments to be made to the incorporation agreement. In fact, all types of Commercial Enterprise—including ordinary partnerships—are covered by the designation "company" in Turkish jurisprudence, as in many continental jurisprudences. Different words designating "partnership" and "company" are used neither in law nor in academic texts. Instead of the distinction between partnership and company, Turkish doctrine prefers the classification between the personal or non-corporate company—to include partnership as well—and the capital or corporate company. It can be said that this is more suitable for Turkish company law and can explain better some sub-models created in practice. However, a classification that would be more useful for this purpose would be possible by the addition of a third category (mixed types) to those mentioned above since some legal models, such as cooperatives, are of a mixed character, i.e., they possess the features of both personal companies and capital companies.

I. Different Forms of Corporations and Partnerships

93. In Turkish Civil Law, partnerships and companies cannot be distinguished from each other, but a distinction exists between ordinary partnerships and Commercial Enterprises.

A. Ordinary Partnership

94. The Ordinary Partnership is regulated in the Turkish Code of Obligations (Articles 620–645) and has no legal personality.

B. Commercial Enterprises

95. Commercial Enterprises are commandite partnerships (*komandit şirket*), collective partnerships (*kollektif şirket*), limited liability companies (*limited şirket*), joint-stock companies (*anonim şirket*) and co-operative societies (*kooperatifler*). The first five types of Commercial Enterprises are provided by the TCC. Co-operative societies used to be regulated by the commercial code, but, since 1965, they have been the subject of a special legislation and are now regulated by the Law Concerning Co-operative Societies. Since this, there has been disagreement as to whether it is a Commercial Enterprise or an association of persons who have joined together to safeguard their own economic interests.

C. Joint Ventures[39]

96. A joint venture means an association of persons or legal entities in the domain of civil law which is established under a contract to accomplish a specific and common objective.

97. In most forms of joint ventures, both natural and legal persons may be partners, however, in certain forms only natural persons may become partners.

98. Joint ventures are established under a contract. If a cooperation or an association is created by law, such collaboration cannot be considered a joint venture. Article 776 of the Turkish Civil Code ("TCivC") provides a classic example of *ex lege* (by law) co-ownership, which may not be considered a joint venture. In accordance with Article 776 of the TCivC, where assets belonging to different owners have been intermixed or merged in such a way that they cannot be separated without causing material damage or excessive labor and expense, the interested parties become co-owners of the new merged asset (*communio incidends*). Their shares in it are proportionate to the value of the different assets they own in the merged asset. In this sense, another common example is the "community of creditors." According to Article 221 and of the Debt Collection and Bankruptcy Law, the creditors constitute by law a community called "the General Meeting of Creditor's," which is a legally created "partnership" among creditors with limited power to decide on matters that relate to the debtor and assets subject to the bankruptcy. Since this partnership is not established under a contract, it cannot be considered an association or an ordinary partnership.

99. A third typical example of an *ex lege-created* community which may not be considered a joint venture is a "partnership among heirs." According to Article 640 of the TCivC, where there are several heirs, all the rights and obligations included in the inheritance constitute a "community/partnership" among the heirs until final

39. *See generally*, G. Tekinalp/Ü. Tekinalp, "Joint-Venture", *Prof. Dr. Yaşar Karayalçın a 65 Yaş Armağanı* ["Joint-Venture", in: Festschrift to Professor Yaşar Karayalçın on the occasion of his 65th birthday] Ankara 1986, pp. 143–176; K. Dayinlar.

distribution. The heirs are joint owners of the property forming the inheritance estate and they act jointly in relation thereto. Since this "*community/partnership*" has been created by law, not by contract, it is not a joint venture.

100. In certain cases, the creation of a joint venture might be legally flawed so that it would be legally invalid. Such collaboration, which is called a *de facto association*, survives in the business world until the flaw is noticed, and is considered to have been legally valid until that time so as to protect the interests of third parties.

101. The important criterion for a joint venture having as its purpose the accomplishment of a specific and common objective is *affectio societatis*. Each partner has to contribute to the accomplishment of the common objective through joint endeavors and means. The interests of partners are parallel in a joint venture, in contrast with *synallagmatic* contracts.

II. Distinction Between Structure and Consequences

102. The following are certain characteristic features of Commercial Enterprises which distinguishes it from similar enterprises:

- legal personality;
- leaving the "*Numerus Clausus*" Doctrine;
- the requirement for a written form of partnership agreement/Articles of Association; and
- "merchant" status.

A. *Legal Personality*

103.

(a) *General*: As per Article 125 of the TCC, all commercial companies have legal personalities and are distinguished as legal entities. Unlike most civil law and common law systems, not only limited liability companies but also collective and commandite partnerships are recognized as separate legal entities under the TCC. They own their assets, may own property, enter into contracts, sue and be sued. Each Commercial Enterprise must register its formation agreement or Articles of Association with the Trade Registry within the area of its main office. With this registration, the Commercial Enterprise acquires the status of a legal entity.

(b) "*Lifting the Corporate Veil*":[40] Under Turkish Law, shareholders of only certain types of companies may be held personally liable for the liabilities of the company. Such companies are identified as collective companies, commandite partnerships and the general partner of the commandite partnerships limited by

40. *See* Poroy/Tekinalp/Çamoğlu [Textbook] [*see* SB], 121–124, 61–63.

shares in the TCC. Although, in principle, the shareholders of a capital company (e.g., a limited liability company or a joint-stock company) may not be held liable for its liabilities, the concept of lifting of the corporate veil has developed in recent years in Turkish Law, especially after 2010.

104. Under Turkish law, the concept of the corporate veil was first introduced by an article by Professor Tekinalp in 1995 whereby, for the first time, the legal basis of and the reasons for lifting the corporate veil were introduced. In the Turkish doctrine, the legal basis of piercing of the corporate veil finds its roots in the principle of good faith defined under the Turkish Civil Code. In other words, in cases where the corporate veil is used as a shield in violation of the principle of good faith, the veil may be pierced. In practice and as per the precedents of the Supreme Court of Appeals, the existence of a deliberate deceitful act may be required for such purposes. Under Turkish law, there is not any lawsuit type identified specifically for the lifting of the corporate veil. Usually, lawsuits initiated for such purpose are indemnification lawsuits requesting the person hiding behind the corporate veil to be held liable. In such lawsuits disguising the actual debtor through creating corporate structures is considered as both an abuse of right and a violation of the prohibition of contradictory behavior (*venire contra factum proprium*) which are special cases of violation of the good faith principle.

105. The following decisions of the Supreme Court of Appeals may give guidance on the approach to the lifting of the corporate veil under Turkish Law:

(a) In the decision numbered 2013-15772/4589 and dated March 10, 2014 of 11th Chamber of the Court of Appeals concerning a corporation group, the request for lifting of the corporate veil was rejected, indicating that the organic tie between the parties was not itself sufficient for the lifting of the corporate veil and requesting the payment of the company's receivables from the shareholders (defendant companies). The court decision further stated that, for granting such a request, it must be ascertained with tangible data that these companies have made transactions in bad faith and with the intention to damage the creditors through hiding of assets. Although it is usually considered that the existence of a corporate group is sufficient for the lifting of the corporate veil due to the controlling power of the shareholder company dictating the policies of its subsidiary, this decision of the Court of Appeals closed the door for such interpretations in Turkish Law.
(b) In the decision numbered 2016-5148/7084 and dated December 11, 2017 of 11th Chamber of the Court of Appeals, it is indicated that the corporate veil may be lifted and the shareholders may be held liable for the liabilities of the company against its creditors in cases where the identity and assets of the shareholder are intertwined with the legal entity and with the purpose to avoid liability through hiding behind the corporate shield in a manner that may be considered as abuse of right. This decision correctly underlies the following five aspects in relation to the lifting of the corporate veil concept: (1) principle of prohibition of contradictory behavior is violated as clearly underlined in the decision through the use of a powerful terminology as "intertwining of the

shareholder with the legal entity," (2) the debtor hides behind the corporate shield of the legal entity with the purpose to evade assets from the creditors, (3) hiding behind the corporate shield constitutes an abuse of right shields behind the veil of incorporation in order not to pay to its creditors (by way of abusing the legal personality), (4) shareholder is calculated and acts with ill intentions, and (5) the shareholder's power to act this way stems from its controlling position.

106. Under the terms of the TCC, the bankruptcy of a collective partnership does not entail the bankruptcy of the partners. However, if, as part of the bankruptcy proceedings, the court decides to pay and deposit a certain amount by the collective partnership to the court and the collective partnership fails to deposit such amount, the creditors may request the court to notify the partners of the company of its payment decision and declare the partners bankrupt together with the collective partnership should they fail to make the requisite payment (TCC 240). This provision also applies to the fully liable partners of a commandite partnership (TCC 317).

107. A similar liability is imposed by the Banking Act ("BA"). According to Article 108 of the BA, the controlling shareholders and managers of banks whose operating permission has been revoked or which have been transferred to the Savings Deposit Insurance Fund (SDIF/"Fund") are required to pay and return to the bank all misused resources and compensate bank's losses suffered due to such unlawful use.

108. If the resources misused and the losses incurred are not returned to the bank or compensated within the period given by the Fund, or are not guaranteed in a form acceptable to the Fund or if such controlling shareholders fail to transfer their shares in the bank to third persons within the period given by the Fund, irrespective of the amount of the resources misused and/or losses incurred, the shares of the controlling shareholders shall be directly transferred to the Fund without being subject to any legal procedure.

B. *Leaving the Ultra Vires Doctrine*[41]

109. One of the unique features of the TCC 1956 was that all Commercial Enterprises, partnerships and corporations were subject to the ultra vires rule (TCC 1956 136). The power to bind the association was limited to the scope of the stated purpose in the partnership agreement or the Articles of Association. Transactions outside the defined scope of business activities were not valid and could not be ratified by the partners afterward; any such contract was ultra vires and void.

110. This basic principle, which applied to all commercial enterprises (commercial partnerships and companies) governed by TCC 1956 and which was inherited

41. *Ibid.*, paras. 125, 126.

from the ultra vires doctrine of British company law was not included in the new TCC. This is in line with the requirements of the First Company Law Directive (68/151/EEC).

111. As a result of leaving the Ultra Vires Doctrine, the new TCC introduced the necessary provisions under Article 371. As per the aforesaid article, the authorized representatives of the company are entitled to enter into transactions on behalf and in the name of the company for matters that fall within the scope of activity of the company. However, the company has the right of recourse against the representatives that act in violation of its Articles of Association by entering into transactions that are outside its scope of activities.

112. Article 371 also explicitly indicates that the transactions executed by the authorized signatories of the company with third parties shall be binding upon the company even if such transactions are outside its scope of activity unless the company proves that the relevant third party knew or was in a position to know the fact that such transaction was indeed its scope of activities. The said article specifically sets forth that registration and announcement of the Articles of Association of the company shall not constitute sufficient evidence to prove such fact. In other words, registration and announcement of the scope of activities of the Company shall not release the Company from liability against such third party.

113. This has created certain difficulties in terms of proving the knowledge of a third party entering into a transaction outside the scope of the company. The concept of "explicit knowledge" should be utilized for this purpose and knowledge of the third party may be proved by the signature of such third party. For instance, if a document involving the relevant fact was signed by the third party, the company may use such document to prove that the third party had the knowledge that the transaction in question was outside the scope of its activities. The documentation used between parties while conducting negotiations may be useful to serve as evidence to prove explicit knowledge.

C. Numerus Clausus[42]

114. The number of commercial enterprises (or commercial associations or companies) which are provided by law is exhaustive, i.e., there is a *numerus clausus*, or limited number of possible legal forms of Commercial Enterprise. Article 124 of the TCC indicates that commercial enterprises consist of collective companies, commandite partnerships, joint-stock companies, limited liability companies and cooperatives. In other words, ones that wish to incorporate a commercial enterprise shall be required to choose from these types determined by the aforesaid article.

115. However, despite the provisions of Article 124 of the TCC, Article 50 of the Capital Markets Law (CML) No. 6362 has introduced a new type of company

42. *Ibid.*, para. 165.

called "*investment partnership with variable capital.*" In this partnership, the capital of the company is always equal to its net asset value. Net asset value means the amount remaining after the deduction of the total payables of the company from its total assets. The shares of this partnership are divided into two categories. The first category consists of the investor shares and the second category is the founder shares. On the one hand, transfer and cancellation of founder shares are subject to the approval of the Capital Markets Board. Investor shares, on the other hand, do not have a nominal value and new investor shares may always be issued. The "Investment partnership with variable capital" which has a legal personality under Turkish Law resembles the open-ended funds under Anglo-Saxon Law.

116. All types of commercial enterprises indicated under Article 124 of the TCC are legal entities and fundamental elements and principles pertaining to each type of commercial enterprise are provided by law. However, provided that the minimum requirements provided for a certain type of company are complied with, the shareholders are free to adopt rules and mechanisms specific to their requirements. Article 124 of the TCC defines collective and commandite partnerships as "*personal (non-capital)*" companies and joint stock, limited liability and commandite partnerships limited by shares as "*capital*" companies.

117. TCC recognizes single-shareholder limited liability companies in compliance with *Directive 89/667/EC on Single-Member Private Limited-Liability Companies,*[43] and it also allows joint-stock companies that have but one shareholder. The law makes it possible for a single private person or legal entity to own one or more single-shareholder companies and for a single-shareholder company to set up other single-member companies. No restrictions are imposed on the status (private person versus legal entity) of a company's single shareholder. TCC provides various registration requirements for a single-shareholder company that are intended to ensure that the assets of the owner of a single-shareholder company and of the company (or companies) are kept strictly separate and to achieve transparency in such matters, thereby laying the foundations for the implementation of the "piercing the corporate veil" doctrine in Turkey as discussed above.

43. Selected literature: Feyzan H. Ş. Çelik, Hukukun Ekonomik Gerçekliğe Yanıtı: Tek Kişilik Şirketler (A Response of Law to the Economic Reality: Single Member Companies), Batider 2007, C: XXIV Türk Hukukunda Tek Ortaklı Şirketler (Single Member Companies in Turkish Law), Hukuk Dergisi 2008, p. 1253; Gül Okutan, Tek Kişi Ortaklığı (Single Member Company), Türk Hukukunun Avrupa Hukukuna Uyumu (Harmonization of Turkish Law with European Law) (Ed. Ünal Tekinalp), The Project Included in the "Administered Projects" of Research Fund of İstanbul University and Prepared Under Supervision of İstanbul University European Law Research and Practice Center, İstanbul 2001, pp. 587 et seq.; Ünal Tekinalp, Sermaye Ortaklıklarının Yeni Hukuku (New Law of Capital Partnerships) Istanbul, Vedat Kitapçılık, 2020; Veliye Yanlı, Zulässigkeit der Einpersonen—Aktiengesellschaft im Hinblick auf Ihre Existenz und Gründung, Annales de la Faculté de Droit d'Istanbul 1998, XXXII No. 48, pp. 200 et seq.

D. Written Form of the Agreement

118. The agreement forming the Commercial Enterprise must be made in written form and the signatures of the promoting shareholders must be either certified by a notary public or the founding agreement (i.e., *Articles of Association*) must be executed before the director or assistant director of the relevant Trade Registry (*Article 339 for joint-stock companies, Article 212 for collective companies, Article 556 for commandite partnerships and Article 575 for the Limited Liability Companies*). The Articles of Association of a commercial enterprise must regulate at least those matters which have been set forth in the TCC for the relevant form of legal entity.

E. Merchant Quality

119. Each commercial enterprise is designated as a merchant as per Article 16.1. This means that the association must keep commercial books and be registered with the Commercial Registry. As per Article 18 of the TCC, all merchants, including the commercial enterprises, are subject to bankruptcy, required to have a trade name and registered with the relevant trade registry and keep commercial books as required by the applicable law. Merchants are also required to act diligently and prudently in all their dealings concerning their commercial activities. All notifications among merchants aimed to declare the other party in default or terminate or rescind an agreement have to be sent through a notary public, registered mail, telegram or registered electronic e-mail system through the use of a registered electronic signature.

F. Structural Changes (Conversions, Mergers and Divisions)[44]

120. The provisions of the TCC pertaining to conversions, mergers and divisions may be classified as provisions on "structural changes."

1. Conversion

121. Conversion of a commercial enterprise is regulated both in the former TCC 1956 and the new TCC. While the former TCC did not specify which form of company could be converted into which enterprise making it possible for a personal (non-capital) company to be converted into a capital company, the new TCC introduced various restrictions to such effect. Article 181 of the new TCC introduced that: (1) a capital company could only be converted into (i) another capital company or (ii) a cooperative; (2) a collective partnership may only be converted into

---

44. *See* generally H. S. Türk, *Die Umwandlung der Handelsgesellschaften, Eine vergleichende Untersuchung nach dem deutschen und türkischen Recht*, Diss., Köln 1968; Ü. Tekinalp, "Typenumwandlung von Handelsgesellschaften", *Annales de la Faculté de droit d' İstanbul* 44/981: Poroy/Tekinalp/Çamoğlu [Textbook] [*see* SE], 165–189.

(i) a capital company, (ii) a cooperative or (iii) a commandite partnership; (3) a commandite partnership may only be converted into (i) capital company, (ii) a cooperative or (iii) a collective partnership; and (4) a cooperative may only be converted into a capital company.

122. The above-mentioned restrictions introduced by the new TCC do not have much significance in practice as the transformation of a capital company into a non-capital (personal) company was very exceptional in practice.

123. As per the new TCC, the executive organ of the relevant commercial enterprise prepares a plan for the anticipated conversion and submits such plan to the approval of the general assembly together with the Articles of Association of the new commercial enterprise to be converted into.

124. The new TCC provides different quorum and decision majority requirements for a conversion decision to be adopted by the shareholders of the relevant commercial enterprise. According to Article 189 of TCC, a conversion decision may be adopted: (i) in a joint-stock or commandite partnership limited by shares by two-thirds of the shareholders present at a general assembly convened by shareholders representing at least two-thirds of total share capital of the company; provided however that if the conversion decision involves a conversion into a limited liability company whereby additional payment requirements or personal obligations are imposed on the shareholders the conversion decision has to be obtained by the affirmative votes of all shareholders; (ii) in a limited liability company by the three-fourths of the affirmative votes of the shareholders representing at least three-fourths of the total share capital of the company; (iii) by the affirmative votes of all shareholders if a capital company is converted into a cooperative; (iv) in a cooperative company, by the majority of the members present at a general assembly convened by members representing at least two-thirds of total members of the cooperative; provided however that if the conversion decision imposes additional payment requirements or personal obligations on the members of the cooperative or extends the scope of the existing obligations, the conversion decision has to be obtained by affirmative votes of members constituting two-thirds of total members of the cooperative; (v) in a collective or commandite partnership, by the affirmative votes of all partners unless the Articles of Association of the relevant company foresees that a conversion decision may be obtained by two-thirds of all partners.

125. Once the conversion decision is approved by the general assembly of the commercial enterprise by the above-referred decision majority requirements, such decision of the general assembly is registered with the relevant trade registry together with the Articles of Association of the new entity into which the commercial enterprise is converted. Conversion shall have legal effect once the registration is completed. The conversion decision is announced in the Trade Registry Gazette.

2. Mergers

126. The TCC foresees that mergers may be conducted through acquisition or formation of a new entity. In the former method, one entity acquires one or more entities in their entirety and the acquired entities cease to exist whereas, in the latter method, two or more entities come together and form a new entity.

127. As per Article 137 of the TCC: (i) capital companies may merge with (1) capital companies, (2) cooperatives; and (3) collective and commandite companies, provided that they remain the acquiring entity in the merger transaction; (ii) non-capital (personal) companies may merge with (1) non-capital companies, (2) capital companies and cooperatives, provided that they are the acquired entities in the merger transaction; (iii) cooperatives may merge with (1) cooperatives, (2) capital companies and (3) non-capital (personal) companies, provided that they remain the acquiring entity in the merger transaction.

128. While the new TCC includes detailed provisions regulating mergers of the commercial enterprises, it also introduces a simplified system for certain capital companies. The simplified system is applicable to the merger of capital companies (i) whereby the entity being merged into (*acquiring entity*) holds the entire voting rights of the merging entity; or (ii) if a company or real person or a group of persons that are considered affiliated as per the applicable law or based on an agreement holds the entire voting rights of the merging entities. As per the simplified procedure, the merger agreement includes limited items concerning only the title and specifications of the merging entities, the names and identities of the shareholders with unlimited liability (if any) and exit payment/premium if the merging entities would like to grant the shareholders the right either to acquire shares in the acquiring entity or, instead of becoming a shareholder in the acquiring entity, relinquish such right in exchange of an amount corresponding to the market value of the shares to be acquired in such entity.

129. In the standard system applicable to mergers, the merger agreement has to include those provisions indicated in Article 146 of the TCC which are as follows: (i) the title and specifications of the merging entities, the names and identities of the shareholders with unlimited liability (if any); (ii) conversion ratio of the shares to apply for calculating the shares to be granted to the shareholders of the acquiring entity, (iii) balancing payment amount, if any, to be offered to shareholders of the merging entity (entity being acquired by the merged entity) which shall not exceed one-tenth of the market value of shares to be acquired by such shareholders in the merged (acquiring) entity; (iv) explanations as to the shareholding amount and rights of to be acquired in the merged (acquiring) entity by the shareholders of the merging entity; (v) rights to be granted by the merged entity to the privileged shareholders, holders of shares with no voting rights and holders of usufruct shares; (vi) method foreseen for the conversion of shares; (vii) the date as of when the shares acquired as a result of the merger shall be entitled to dividend rights and other related details; (viii) exit payment, if any; (ix) the date as of when the actions and transactions of the merging entity shall be deemed to be conducted on behalf of the merged entity; (x) special rights and benefits to be granted to the executive bodies and managing shareholders; (xi) names of the shareholders with unlimited liability, if applicable.

130. The managing bodies of the merging companies shall also prepare a merger report whereby the details concerning the merger, such as the objectives and results of the merger, are indicated. The merger agreement and the merger report are discussed and approved in the general assemblies of the merging entities.

131. As per Article 151 of the TCC, the merger agreement has to be approved:

- in joint-stock companies and commandite partnerships limited by shares, by three-fourths of the shareholders present in a general assembly meeting whereby at least the shareholders holding the majority of the capital are represented (in commandite partnerships limited by shares, provided also that the unlimited partner of the commandite partnership approves the merger in writing);
- in capital companies to be acquired by a cooperative, by three-fourths of the shareholders present in a general assembly meeting whereby at least the shareholders holding the majority of the capital are represented;
- in limited liability companies, by three-fourths of the shareholders provided that such shareholders also represent at least three-fourths of the share capital of the company;
- in cooperatives, by two-thirds of the votes casted in a general assembly provided, however, that if additional payment or other obligations are introduced in the Articles of Association of the cooperative or an unlimited liability is accepted or the scope of existing liabilities are extended, the merger should be approved by three-fourths of all registered members;
- in collective and commandite partnerships, by all shareholders unless the Articles of Association of these companies allow for approval by three-fourths of all shareholders; and
- in a joint-stock company or a commandite partnership limited by shares to be acquired by a limited liability company, by all shareholders if additional payment or other obligations are introduced in the Articles of Association or an unlimited liability is accepted, or the scope of existing liabilities are extended.

132. The managing bodies of the merging entities are required to apply to the relevant Trade Registry for registration of the merger immediately upon approval of the merger agreement. The merging entity shall become dissolved upon registration of the merger. Merger shall become valid upon registration with the Trade Registry and all the assets and liabilities of the merging entity are automatically transferred to and assumed by the acquiring entity.

133. In the event that the creditors of the merging entities request from the acquiring entity within three months following the registration of the merger, the acquiring entity is required to provide guarantee for their receivables.

3. Divisions

134. The new TCC regulates spin-offs and split-ups. A split up is a "complete division" in which all the assets of a commercial company are divided into units and transferred to an existing or a new company or companies, where the partners of the company subject to spin-off acquire shares and rights in the transferee companies and where the company subject to division ceases to exist and dissolves without liquidation. A spin-off is a "partial division" in which the assets of a commercial company are divided into units whereby certain unit or units remain with the company subject to division while other units are transferred to an existing or a new company or companies in which the shareholders of the divided company acquire shares.

135. Divisions may be symmetrical or asymmetrical. In symmetrical divisions, the shareholding structure of the divided company remains the same in the transferee company or companies, whereas, in asymmetrical divisions, the shareholding structure may differ. Alternatively, the transferee companies may become the subsidiaries of the divided company.

136. The provisions pertaining to the division are newly introduced in TCC. In line with the provisions of EU regulations, the new TCC contains various provisions protecting the shareholders, creditors and employees of companies participating in a spin-off.

137. The protective provisions concerning division may be briefly listed as follows:

- It is ensured that the shareholders of the divided company acquire shares in the transferee company in proportion to their shares in the divided company.
- If privileged shares are available such privileges are kept in the transferee company.
- In the division agreement, shareholders that do not wish to become a shareholder in the transferee entity may be offered an exit payment/premium.
- A detailed and transparent division agreement and plan must be submitted for the approval of the general assembly.

138. Shareholders are entitled to inspect the division agreement and plan, division plan and the financial statements of the last three years, annual reports and interim financial statements.

139. Creditors of the companies participating in the division are invited to declare their receivables and request guarantees securing such receivables through three announcements published on the websites of the companies and in the Trade Registry Gazette in seven days intervals.

140. Companies participating in the merger are required to provide guarantees to secure the receivables of the creditors which submit such requests to the relevant company within three months following the issuance of the announcements referred to above in the Trade Registry Gazette. In the event that the collectability of the receivables of the other creditors is not going to be adversely affected, the company may pay the debts instead of providing guarantees for the respective creditors. Additionally, if it is proved that the receivables of the creditors shall not be adversely affected by the division, the company shall be released of its obligation to provide guarantees.

III. Commercial and Civil Corporations and Partnerships

141. Turkish Law has eight types of Commercial Enterprises under the terms of the numerus clausus principle. These are:

(1) Ordinary Partnership (*adi ortaklık*)
(2) Collective Partnership (*kollektif şirket*)
(3) Commandite Partnership (*komandit şirket*)
(4) Joint-Stock Company (*anonim şirket*)
(5) Commandite Partnership Limited by Shares (*sermayesi paylara bölünmüş komandit şirket*)
(6) Limited Liability Company (*limited şirket*)
(7) Co-operatives (*kooperatifler*)
(8) Foundations operating commercial entities.

A. Ordinary Partnership

142. An ordinary partnership is an association of two or more persons that have come together to carry on a specific business or project. An ordinary partnership may have a financial purpose or not. For example, manufacturing, transportation, farming, commerce or pleasure are all qualifying purposes for ordinary partnership. For a temporary business, an ordinary partnership is the most convenient form of association, e.g., joint venture, consortia or syndicates of banks for issuing loans or debentures.

143. The ordinary partnership is not a separate legal entity. It is, therefore, not registered with the Trade Registry and does not have a trade name in accordance with TCC and TCO. However, pursuant to the Communiqué dated April 1, 2009 related to "*Registration With The Trade Registry of Commercial Enterprises Which Are Operated By Commercial Companies under a Partnership Structure That Does Not Have A Legal Personality*," partnerships that do not have a legal personality but founded and managed jointly by commercial companies that are legal entities to realize a specific purpose and generate profits may be registered with the Trade Registry upon the request of the parties and provided that the partnership agreement is in writing.

144. The distinctive feature of an ordinary partnership as opposed to an entity with a corporate form is the representation power of its partners. As per Article 637 of the TCO, in case a partner enters into a transaction with a third party in its name and on behalf of the ordinary partnership, the liabilities and rights arising out of such transaction shall inure on that partner vis-à-vis the relevant third party. If a partner enters into a transaction with a third party in the name of the ordinary partnership or all partners thereof, other partners shall be liable against or inure benefits from the relevant third party to the extent that they are duly represented as per the provisions of the TCO pertaining to representation. In case one of the partners is granted the right of management of the ordinary partnership, it is deemed that such partner is authorized to represent the partnership and the remaining partners to third parties. However, the managing partner should have been authorized by the unanimous vote of all partners for representation in important transactions and such power should have been duly indicated in the representation certificate. Unless agreed otherwise, the partners shall be jointly and severally liable against the third party for obligations they have undertaken for the ordinary partnership together or through a representative.

B. Collective Partnership (i.e., General Partnership)

145. A collective partnership (may also be referred to as "*general partnership*") is an association of two or more natural persons to operate a commercial enterprise under a trade name and in which the liability of the partners to the creditors of the partnership is unlimited. Corporate bodies cannot become partners in a collective partnership.

146. The partners are jointly and severally liable with their personal assets for the debts of the partnership, but this is a secondary liability. No partner can be sued personally unless the partnership first becomes bankrupt or is dissolved.

C. Commandite Partnership (i.e., Limited Partnership)

147. The commandite partnership (may also be referred to as "*limited partnership*") differs legally from the collective partnership because at least one partner (who is called the "general partner") should be personally liable against third parties without any limitation for all debts and obligations of the partnership while the liability of other partners ("*limited partners*") may be limited up to a certain capital amount contributed to the partnership.

148. The TCC permits only a natural person to be a general partner, while a legal entity or a natural person may be a limited partner.

149. The capital contributed by either general or limited partners may take the form of cash or other property or labor; in the latter two cases, valuation method of the property or labor must be indicated in the Articles of Association of the company.

150. A commandite partnership, like the collective partnership, is created by drawing up a written contract of partnership, which must be registered at the Trade Registry.

D. Joint-Stock Company (i.e., Company Limited by Shares)

151. A joint-stock company is an entity with a trade name formed for the purpose of business, whose capital is divided into shares and whose liabilities are covered exclusively by its assets. The shareholder's liability is limited to the obligations imposed on them by the Articles of Association; they are not personally liable for the company's debts.

152. Turkish Law provides for two types of capital systems: basic (fixed) capital system and authorized (registered) capital system.

E. Commandite Partnership Limited by Shares

153. The commandite partnership limited by shares combines the characteristics of both the joint-stock company and the commandite partnership. Its capital is divided into shares and one or more partners are jointly and severally liable to the creditors of the partnership without limitation as a general partner.

F. Limited Liability Company (i.e., Partnership Limited by Shares)

154. The limited liability company is another mixed type of commercial entity, merging the characteristics of the joint-stock company, the collective partnership and the ordinary partnership. It operates under a trade name and with a capital fixed in advance. Each shareholder participates in the capital of the partnership with a contribution. The liability of a shareholder is limited to its capital contribution. The amount of capital contribution of each shareholder determines the ratio of its participation in a liability.

G. Co-operatives

155. The co-operative is an association of an indefinite number of natural and legal persons, the main object of which is the furtherance or safeguarding of a defined economic interest of its members by their common effort. It is incorporated by registration at the Commercial Registry. It is considered as a merchant and a legal entity.

156. The capital of the cooperative is not fixed in advance and its liability is limited to its own assets unless the by-laws contain express provisions to the contrary.

157. Before the enactment of the new TCC, it was disputed in the doctrine whether the cooperative was, indeed, a partnership. Article 124 of the new Turkish Commercial Code has ended the discussions on the matter and categorized the cooperative society as a commercial company. However, the second paragraph of the aforesaid article does not make a reference to the cooperative society while differentiating between capital companies and partnerships. This paragraph defines collective and commandite companies as partnerships and limited liability and joint-stock companies as capital companies without any mention of the co-operative societies.

158. There are two main reasons for such omissions. The first reason is that an alternative liability system is adopted for cooperatives. As per Article 28 of the Law on Cooperatives, unless there is a provision to the contrary in its Articles of Association, the liability of the cooperative against its creditors is limited to its assets. In other words, the law determines, in principle, a limited liability mechanism for the cooperatives. However, Article 29 of the said law indicates that the Articles of Association of a cooperative may foresee the partners of the cooperative to be held liable personally and without any limitation in case the assets of the cooperative are not sufficient to pay off its debts. In such cases, the partners of the cooperative shall be jointly liable for the unpaid receivables of the creditors with all their personal assets if the creditors fail to collect their receivables from the cooperative upon its bankruptcy or dissolution.

159. Article 30 of the Law on Cooperatives sets forth that it is possible to indicate in the Articles of Association of cooperative that partners may be held liable in succession to the cooperative with their personal assets in amount more than his/her share in the cooperative but up to a certain limit. The said article also permits the Articles of Association to limit the amount for which the partners may be held liable personally with their shares in the cooperative.

160. Albeit the above-referred provisions, the Law on Cooperatives also includes provisions which emphasize the partnership status of the cooperatives. The definition of the "cooperative society" includes such qualifications. In this respect, a "cooperative society" is a legal entity incorporated by real persons or legal entities which aim to generate benefits for their professional requirements or general living costs by contributing their work power and funds and, as well as providing charity, support and surety.

The second reason for the omission of cooperatives while differentiating between capital companies and partnerships in the new Turkish Commercial Code is that the cooperative society carries the qualifications of both partnerships and capital companies and thus does not directly fall under neither of the categories creating a sui generis status.

IV. Nonprofit Associations and Other Corporate Legal Persons

A. *Foundations*

161. A foundation is an association of persons who have joined together for a non-profit purpose, such as scientific, cultural, political, charitable or social activities. A foundation acquires the status of a legal person as soon as its articles of association are drawn up. Its liability is limited to its assets.

B. *Associations*

162. Associations are generally regulated under Turkish Civil Code and Law No. 5253 on Non-Profit Associations. As per Article 56 of the Turkish Civil Code, an association is a group of persons with a legal entity status which is established by at least seven persons (legal entity or real person) to realize a certain and common purpose other than sharing of revenues by way of joining their knowledge and efforts.

§4. Sources and Hierarchy of the Law on Partnerships and Companies

I. International Sources

163. International sources of the law on companies and partnerships are to be found in certain bilateral and multilateral agreements. Both bilateral and multilateral treaties are mostly concerned with foreign investment and its protection and cover both direct investment by foreign companies and groups in Turkey. Multilateral Investment Guarantee Agreement and the International Centre for the Settlement of Investment Disputes Treaty between the members of the Islamic Conference regarding the Protection of Investments are certain examples of such agreements. There are also provisions in certain bilateral agreements concerning residence, relocation and operations of foreign companies in Turkey.[45] These provisions apply to all companies in certain cases, and sometimes they concern only those companies in specific fields of business, such as transportation or insurance.

164. The following may be identified as certain significant International Treaties that Turkey has ratified or acceded to are:

45. For a list of said agreements, *see* A. Çelikel/C. Şanlı, *Türk MilletlerarasıÖzel Hukuk Mevzuatı*, 8. Bası [Turkish Legislation on Private International Law] (İstanbul 8th ed. 1988) p. 265, note 1.

- the Hague Convention Concerning Civil Procedure of 1954;[46]
- the Hague Convention of October 5, 1961 abolishing the Requirement of Legalisation for Foreign Public Documents;[47]
- the Hague Convention of November 15, 1965 on the Service Abroad of Judicial and Extrajudicial Documents in Civil or Commercial Matters;[48] and
- the UN Convention on the Recognition and Enforcement of Foreign Arbitral Awards of 1958.[49]

165. Turkey is an associate member of the EC and there is an Agreement (the Ankara Agreement)[50] of December 12, 1964, and a Supplementary Protocol[51] dated November 23, 1970 between the EEC and Turkey. The Ankara Agreement and the Supplementary Protocol contain all the freedoms incorporated in the Treaty of Rome concerning the circulation and location of goods and capital. Article 58 of the Supplementary Protocol prohibits discrimination with respect to companies limited by shares. Article 52 of the Supplementary Protocol relates indirectly to companies limited by shares. It states that the Parties will resist imposing restrictive regulations which may harm capital movements and payments, and that the Parties will simplify the control of, and the permission procedures applied to the transfer of capital and will consult with each other regarding this simplification.

166. On March 6, 1995, the EC-Turkey Partnership Council[52] adopted a decision (No. 1/95) to initiate the final phase envisaged in Article 5 of the Ankara Agreement. Accordingly, a customs union between the EC (EU) and Turkey has been in effect since January 1, 1996. The content and scope of the customs union include free flow of goods, harmonization of trade policies and legislation, provisions concerning agricultural commodities and simplification of customs formalities. Turkey has joined the Agreement Establishing the World Trade Organization with all its annexes, thereby becoming a party to the Agreement on Trade-Related Aspects of Intellectual Property Rights including Trade in Counterfeit Goods.[53]

167. Turkey has been in negotiations to be a full member of the EU since October 2005. In order to satisfy the membership conditions and maintain harmonization with the EU, Turkey has passed various new laws and regulations. However, due to various political and other constraints, Turkey seems to be long away from completing the membership negotiations and becoming a full member of the EU.

46. O.G. No. 14119, May 23, 1972.
47. O.G. No. 18517, Sep. 16, 1984.
48. O.G. No. 14218, Jun. 17, 1972, the Communiqué of the Ministry of Justice [O.G. No. 14454, Feb. 20, 1954].
49. O.G. No. 21002, Sep. 25, 1991.
50. O.G. No. 11858, Nov. 17, 1964.
51. O.G. No. 14406, Aug. 29, 1972.
52. The Partnership Council was established pursuant to Art. 6 of the Ankara Agreement.
53. Decree No. 95/6525 [O.G. No. 22213*bis*, Feb. 25 1995].

II. National Sources

A. *Legislation*

168. Turkey is a unitary state, and therefore, it does not have federal laws. The "general" provisions are those provisions which are applicable to all commercial enterprises. Under this title are the provisions pertaining to the types of commercial enterprises, principles of *numerus clausus*, the definition of all commercial associations, the cooperation groups and provisions relating to the merger, division and conversion of commercial associations.

169. Other significant national legal sources concerning partnerships and commercial enterprises are the Turkish Civil Code and the Code of Obligations.[54] Ordinary partnerships are regulated by Articles 620–645 of the Turkish Code of Obligations, and these provisions apply, together with Articles 47, 49, 50 and 51 of the Civil Code, to commercial associations as well, insofar as they are appropriate for the characteristics of each type of commercial association.

170. Another law which requires mention is the Foreign Direct Investments Law No. 4875 and dated June 17, 2003 which regulates principles to encourage foreign direct investments, protect the rights of foreign investors, establish a notification-based system rather than screening and approval for foreign investment and establish that foreign investors shall be subject to equal treatment with domestic investors.

171. Secondary sources are certain presidential execution orders, regulations and other decrees that concern commercial enterprises, such as Trade Registry Regulation, Communiqués Concerning the Principles Regarding the Procedures of Establishment and Amendment of Articles of Association of Joint-Stock Companies.[55]

172. Other legal sources of significance with respect to commercial enterprises are as follows:

- Law No. 5174 concerning the Association of Turkish Chambers and Exchange and Chambers and Exchange.[56]
- Law No. 6361 concerning Financial Leasing, Factoring and Finance Companies and related legislation.[57]
- Law No. 1567 concerning the Protection of the Value of Turkish Currency[58] and related legislation, in particular Decree No. 32.[59]

---

54. *See* SL.
55. O.G. No. 22233, 13 Aug. 1995.
56. O.G. No. 25479, Jun. 1, 2004.
57. O.G. No. 28496, Dec. 13, 2012.
58. O.G. No. 1433, Feb. 25, 1930.
59. O.G. No. 20249, Aug. 11, 1989.

- Law No. 5718 on Private International Law and Procedural Law.[60]
- Law No. 6769 on Industrial Property Law.[61]
- Law No. 5846 concerning Intellectual and Artistic Works.[62]
- Law No. 4054 concerning the Protection of Competition.[63]
- Law No. 6502 concerning Consumer Protection.[64]
- Law No. 5148 concerning the Regulation of Implementations Relevant to Privatization and the Amendment of Certain Laws and Decrees with the force of law[65] and related legislation.

B. By-Laws or Articles

173. Turkish Law does not have or use the term "by-laws." Each commercial enterprise is required to register its Articles of Association with the relevant trade registry having jurisdiction in the area where its headquarters are located. Commercial Enterprises have to comply with law and the provisions of their Articles of Association while conducting their operations.

174. Depending on the type of the company or partnership, the requirements applicable to the Articles of Association vary. Certain types of entities, such as joint-stock companies, have more strict mandatory rules to abide with while drafting their articles whereas partnerships that have a more personal type, such as limited liability companies, have more flexibility while determining the provisions of their Articles of Association.

C. Relationship Between Articles and Legislation

175. Articles of Associations of Commercial Enterprises have to comply with general principles of Turkish Code of Obligations and Turkish Civil Code and the specific provisions of the Turkish Commercial Code applicable to the relevant enterprise type. Also, certain specific laws may apply to the Articles of Association of commercial enterprises that are active in areas that are regulated by special laws. For instance, Articles of Associations of banks have to comply with the Banking Law whereas Articles of Associations of public companies have to comply with the CML.

176. The real problem in Turkish Law arises with respect to the provisions of shareholder's agreements which are contradictory to the articles of the company or the applicable law.

60. O.G. No. 26728, Dec. 12, 2007.
61. O.G. No. 29944, Jan. 10, 2017.
62. O.G. No. 7981, Dec. 13, 1951.
63. O.G. No. 22140, Dec. 13, 1994.
64. O.G. No. 28835, Nov. 28, 2013.
65. O.G. No. 25455, Nov. 27, 2004.

D. Hierarchy of the law on Corporations of Partnerships

177. Norms of a legal system are hierarchically ordered according to the validity relationship between them. This is called the hierarchy of a norm. Any legal act within the definition of "norm" has a place in this hierarchy. Articles of association of a joint-stock company is no exception to this. Hierarchical standing of Articles of Association can be ascertained by examining its hierarchical relationship with statutes, delegated legislation, decisions of Commercial Court of First Instance, board of directors resolutions and resolutions of the general assembly. Legal regime of Articles of Association shows that it is hierarchically inferior to statutes, delegated legislation and decisions of the court while superior to the resolutions of board of directors and general assembly. The hierarchy of norms in a legal system provides general information regarding the system. Therefore, it mostly has theoretical value. However, the fact that the application of the principle *lex superior derogat legi inferiori* demands prior determination of the hierarchy of norms can be seen as a factor which increases the practical importance of the hierarchy of norms.[66]

§5. International Private Law (Conflict of Laws)[67]

I. Jurisdiction[68]of the Court

178. International Private Procedural Law (IPL) dated November 27, 2007 numbered 5718 (IPL) constitutes the principle source of the Turkish Private Interna

---

66. Yahya Berkol Gülgeç, The Place of Joint Stock Companies' Articles of Association in Normative Hierarchy, Ankara Barosu Degisi, 2019/3, 41–93.
67. Aysel Çelikel-Bahadır Erdem Milletlerarası Özel Hukuk 15. Baskı-2018. Vahit Doğan Milletlerarası Özel Hukuk Ankara 2010. Ergin Nomer Devletler Hususi Hukuku XXXXXX Gülören Tekinalp Ayfer Uyanık Çavuşoğlu Milletlerarası Özel Hukuk Bağlama Kuralları XXXXX Gülören Tekinalp Erdin Nomer Ayşe Odman Boztosun Private International Law in Turkey Walters Kluwer Law and Business, the Netherlands 2012 . Gülören TEkinalp 2007 Turkish Code concerning Private International Law and International Civil Procedure, Yearbook of Private International Law Vol.XI "2007-313-343". For the German translation of the Turkish Private International Law and "Law of International Civil Procedure" [O.G. No. 17701, May 22, 1982], *see* Gülören Tekinalp, "Gesetz über Internationales Privatrecht und Zivilverfahrenrecht", *Rabels Zeitschrift für ausländisches und internationales Privatrecht*, 47 [1983], 131–140 and accompanying note; *ibid*., at 74–78 and "*Der Türkische Gesetzentwurf über internationales Privat und Zivilverfahrensrecht, Rabels Zeitschrift für ausländisches und internationales Privatrecht*", 46 [1982], 26–140; *see* H. Krüger, "Das türkische IPR-Gesetz von 1982", *IPRax* [1982], 252–254 and accompanying text at 254–259; for the French translation of the same Statute, *see* N. Uluocak, "Loi sur le droit international privé et la procedure internationale No. 2675, du 20 mai 1982", *Revue Critique de droit international privé*, 141–148 and accompanying note (Quelques reflexions sur loi de 1982), 149–155. *See* generally Gülören Tekinalp, *MilletlerarasıÖzel Hukuk-Bağlama Kuralları*, 6. Bası [Private International Law-Conflicts, 6th Ed.], İstanbul 1999; N. Uluocak, *MilletlerarasıÖzel Hukuk Dersleri* [Lectures on Private International Law], İstanbul 1989;.
68. *Special Selected Bibliography:* S. İ. Ansay, *Hukuk Yargılama Usulleri*, 7. Bası [Civil Procedure Law, 7th Ed.], 1960; N. Bilge/E. Önen [Textbook on Law of Civil Procedure] (Ankara 3rd ed. 1978); B. Kuru, *Hukuk Muhakemeleri Usulü*, C. 1, 5. Bası [Civil Procedure Law, Vol. I] (5th ed. 1990); I. Postacıoğlu, *Medeni Usul Hukuku Dersleri*, 6. Bası [Lectures on Civil Procedure Law] (İstanbul 6th ed. 1975); S. Üstündağ, *Medeni Yargılama Hukuku*, C. 1, 3. Bası (1984), C. 2, 4. Bası (1989) [Civil Procedure Law] (İstanbul Vol. 1 (1984), 3th ed., Vol. 2, 4th ed. (1989)); Gülören Tekinalp, "Über die gerichtliche Zuständigkeit und die Vollstreckung ausländischer gerichtlicher Entscheidungen in Zivil- und Handelssachen in der Türkei", in: *Ein internationales Zivilverfahrensrecht für Gesamteuropa-EuGVÜ, Lugano-Übereinkommen und die Rechtsentwicklungen in Mittel- und Osteuropa*, Heidelberg 1992, 143–154.

tional Law. In accordance with this law, international jurisdiction of the Turkish courts is determined by territorial jurisdiction rules of national law (IPL 40).

179. The general rules concerning the jurisdiction of the courts are determined by Civil Procedural Law (CPL).

A. *Rules of CPL Concerning Jurisdiction*

180. As per Article 6 of the CPL, the court having general jurisdiction is the court located in the domicile of the plaintiff's real person or legal entity. In the event that there are several plaintiffs, the lawsuit may be initiated in the court located in the domicile of any one of the defendants. However, if a special court is designated by law for a specific matter for all plaintiffs, the lawsuit has to be initiated in the territory of such court. If it is determined based on circumstances or other evidence that the lawsuit concerning multiple plaintiffs is brought before a court with the sole purpose to force one of the plaintiffs to come to a court which is not located in the domicile of such plaintiff, the court may decide to separate the lawsuit for the concerned plaintiff by deciding that it does not have jurisdiction over such plaintiff.

181. A legal person may be sued at the place of its head office. In the event of legal persons having their places of business at different *loci*, a suit involving the transactions of a branch office (with the exception of bankruptcy case) may be filed at the court of the place where the branch office is located.

182. As per Article 14/2 of the CPL, the court located in the domicile of the headquarters of the private legal entity shall have absolute and final jurisdiction for lawsuits initiated by the legal entity against its shareholders or members and by shareholders and members against other shareholders or members strictly in relation with matters concerning shareholding or membership.

183. For plaintiffs that do not have a permanent residence in Turkey, the court located in the habitual residence of the plaintiff shall have jurisdiction; provided, however, that lawsuits concerning property rights may also be initiated before the court in the venue where the concerned property is located. As per Article 10 of the CPL, lawsuits concerning contractual disputes may also be initiated before the courts in the venue located where the contract is performed. Lawsuits that concern tort may be initiated before the courts located where the tort is committed, or damage has occurred or may occur or where the person that has incurred damages is resident (CPL 16).

184. As per Article 561 of the TCC, lawsuits concerning the liability of the founders, directors, managers or liquidators of a joint-stock company, limited liability company or cooperative may be initiated before the court where the head offices of the company are situated.

185. The same court has jurisdiction for resolution of disputes arising out of the general assembly decisions of joint-stock companies, limited liability companies, commandite partnerships and cooperatives.

186. For claims relating to real estate, the court where the property is situated has exclusive jurisdiction.

187. It is also possible to choose courts to have jurisdiction by mutual agreement.

B. Agreement for the Submission of Jurisdiction to Foreign Courts

188. The IPL contains a general provision relating to agreements regarding the submission of jurisdiction to foreign courts. As per Article 47 of the IPL, except for matters where jurisdiction is exclusively determined by mandatory provisions, the parties to an agreement may designate foreign courts to have jurisdiction over disputes having a foreign element and pertaining to obligations. Such agreement on jurisdiction is required to be in writing. In case of existence of a jurisdiction agreement to such effect, Turkish Courts may only have jurisdiction over such dispute in case the foreign court designated by the parties declares itself incompetent or parties do not object to the jurisdiction of the Turkish court if the lawsuit is brought before Turkish courts.

II. The Enforcement and Recognition of Foreign Judgments[69]

A. Enforcement of Foreign Judgments

189. In order for a foreign judgment to be enforced in Turkey, the following four conditions have to be met:

(1) existence of a reciprocal agreement between the Republic of Turkey and the state where the court decision is given or a de facto practice or a provision of law enabling the authorization of the execution of final decisions given by a Turkish court in that state;
(2) the foreign judgment must have been given on matters not falling within the exclusive jurisdiction of the Turkish courts or the judgment is not granted by

69. *See* A. Çelikel, *MilletlerarasıÖzel Hukuk*, 4. Bası [Private International Law] (350–364 İstanbul 4th ed. 1995); E. Nomer, *Devletler Hususi Hukuku*, 9. Bası [Private International Law] (384–405 İstanbul 9th ed. 1998).

a foreign state court declaring itself having jurisdiction over a dispute with which such court does not have an actual relation (provided, in such case, one of the parties had objected to the jurisdiction of such court);

(3) the foreign judgment is not granted on a matter that is clearly against Turkish public order; and

(4) the person against whom enforcement of the foreign judgment is requested has not objected before the Turkish courts arguing that he/she/it was not duly summoned to the foreign court or duly represented before such court or that the judgment was not granted in his/her/its absence in violation of the applicable law.

B. Recognition of Foreign Judgments

190. In order for a foreign court decision to be accepted as a final decision or final order in Turkey, a recognition decision must be granted by a Turkish Court provided that the conditions indicated in Article 54 of the IPL for enforcement cases are met whereby the condition pertaining to reciprocity between Turkey and the relevant foreign country is not sought for recognition decisions.

III. Capacity of Partnerships and Companies

191. As per Article 9/4 of the IPL capacity of legal entities or group of persons or assets shall be determined in accordance with the laws applicable in the jurisdiction of domicile indicated in their status documents; provided, however, that Turkish Law may apply to such determination if the legal entity is actively managed through headquarters located in Turkey.

192. This rule is applicable to group of persons or units of assets which are obliged under applicable law to indicate a central office address in their statutes which includes all commercial associations, co-operatives, non-profit associations and foundations. However, the said rule does not apply to persons and units of assets which are not required to have a statute as per the applicable law or for those which are not required to show the address of its central offices.

193. The rules to be applied to the capacity of a corporate body to enter into internal and external transactions are generally described as the "*personal statutes*" of the corporate body (*lex societatis*). However, the criteria to be used in determining the law to be applied have given rise to dispute. In the laws, Supreme Court rulings or academic doctrine of various countries, either the domicile theory or the incorporation control theory has been adopted as the applicable criteria in this respect. Since it has been stated in academic texts that the rule of the IPL which determines the law to be applied to the capacities of corporate bodies, also determines the *lex societatis*, it can be assumed that the domicile theory has been adopted by Turkish jurisprudence. This is because the law has adopted the principle of an irrefutable presumption, subject to a single exception, in the determination of the *lex societatis*.

194. Because Turkish Law categorically demands that legal entities must indicate the location of their central offices in their statutes—i.e., in their partnership agreement or Articles of Association—the *lex societatis* for all commercial enterprises in Turkey is determined according to the provision in their statutes.

195. The point where the legal capacity starts and terminates and the duration of the existence of legal capacity shall be determined by application of the same rule. Therefore, the law applicable to the capacity of legal persons—the law of domicile indicated in the statutes—determines the scope of the capacity as well. Determination of the capacity of legal entities to be a party in lawsuits is also subject to the same law. The same rule is accepted to apply to the organs of the legal entities, their duties and their authority to represent. The law of domicile indicated in the statutes also governs the shareholders or members of the legal entities and their rights and liabilities towards one another and their liabilities as shareholders and/or executives towards third persons.

196. The law has one exception to this general principle, which is as follows: if the address of the central office/headquarters of a legal entity is in a foreign country, but it has offices in Turkey, Turkish Law may still apply if it can be proved that the legal entity is de facto managed and controlled through its offices located in Turkey. In other words, if the offices of the legal entity from where its operations are administered are located in Turkey, the court will be free to decide whether or not to apply Turkish legislation to such entity on matters covered by the *lex societatis.*[70]

IV. Transfer of the Head Office

A. *From a Foreign Country to Turkey*

197. As per Turkish Law, the headquarters of a foreign entity may be transferred to Turkey without being subject to liquidation and establishing a new company in Turkey. In this respect, it has a liberal system.

198. According to Article 115 of the Trade Registry Regulation, in the event that the headquarters of a commercial enterprise is transferred to Turkey certain documents are required to be submitted to the Trade Registry in addition to those that are submitted for incorporation of a new company. These additional documents include a certificate of incorporation and existence issued from the relevant governmental authority where the legal entity is located, a document issued by competent authorities indicating that the transfer of headquarters to Turkey is admissible as per

70. For a more detailed discussion, *see* Gülören Tekinalp [note 1, §5], 69.

the law of incorporation of such entity and the Articles of Association of the commercial enterprise adopted to Turkish Law. Furthermore, although it is not indicated in the Regulations, the prevailing view is that the company transferring its headquarters to Turkey should prove that its capital has been fully paid up in its country of origin.

199. Once its application is duly made, the emigrant company will be registered with the Trade Registry as any Turkish company. As part of this process, the registration officer will investigate whether the conditions required for registration have been fulfilled.

200. The law governing the Turkish equivalent of the type of company in the original country will be applied to the emigrant company.

B. From Turkey to a Foreign Country

201. Articles 116 and 117 of the Trade Registry Regulation set forth the rules applicable to the transfer of headquarters of a Turkish commercial company to a foreign country.

202. As per the aforesaid provisions, a Turkish company which intends to transfer its headquarters is required to apply to the Trade Registry together with (i) documents evidencing that the creditors of the company have been duly informed through announcements in the Trade Registry Gazette and such other media as required in the Articles of Association of the company, (ii) documents evidencing that the consent of all the creditors of the Company are obtained, the receivables of the creditors are paid in full or are secured through guarantees, (iii) certificates obtained from the tax offices indicating that the company does not have any unpaid tax or social premium liabilities or all existing liabilities are secured, and (iv) decision of the competent body of the company pertaining to the transfer of headquarters to a foreign country. Upon filing of the application prepared in compliance with the regulation, the Trade Registry deregisters the company and registers the corporate decision resolving for transfer to a foreign entity, the new title of the company and the trade registry to which it is registered in the foreign country and documents evidencing that all precautions for the protection of the creditors are obtained.

V. Recognition of Foreign Companies[71]

203. The fact that another country has accepted the legal capacity of a company whose head office is located in a foreign country and/or which has been set up under a foreign law means that the second country has recognized the company and its legal status. In other words, the recognition of a foreign legal entity means the acceptance of its capacity by another country. In principle, the recognized legal

71. *See* generally, Gülören Tekinalp [note 1 §5], 74–78.

entity can, in the country which has granted recognition, perform certain permissible operations, incur debts and receivables, sue and be sued.

204. The aforementioned rule of the IPL (in Article 9/4) which foresees that legal entities are to be governed by the legislation of the country of their headquarters as designated in the statutes of the legal entity constitutes the legal basis for the recognition of foreign corporate bodies by Turkish jurisprudence.

205. According to Article 9/4 of the IPL, a foreign legal entity is deemed competent if such a determination may be made as per the laws of the country where the headquarter of the foreign legal entity is located. However, any restrictions imposed by Turkish Law on the capacity of foreign legal entities to conduct certain transactions in Turkey—e.g., those relating to the acquisition of real estate—shall also be taken into consideration. Furthermore, even if the law of the original country has granted extensive rights and powers, any rights or powers more extensive than those recognized in respect of the same (or closely related) type of Turkish company will not be accorded to the foreign corporate body by Turkish courts.

§6. Labor Law Connection: Co-determination and Corporate Structure

206. Turkish legislation does not include any specific regulation pertaining to the concept of employee consultation and participation in company decisions; however, it is possible to include privileged rights to shares held by employees or grant stock options to employees as per the provisions of TCC.

Part I. Companies

Chapter 1. Big Corporation-Public Corporation Share Company (The Joint-Stock Company)

§1. Characteristics

207. A joint-stock company, which is called "*Anonim Şirket (A.Ş.)*" in Turkish, a term derived from the term *Société Anonyme* from French law, is one of the most common type of commercial enterprise in Turkey. Certain distinguishing features of the A.Ş. are the limited liability of the shareholders, freely transferable shares and its institutionalized management.

208. Turkish Commercial Code defines a joint-stock company as a company with a certain determined capital that is divided into shares and which may be held liable for its obligations only with its own assets (TCC 329). In other words, the shareholders of a joint-stock company may not be held liable for the obligations of the joint-stock company. As per Article 480 of the TCC, save for the exceptions provided in law, no obligation other than the obligation to pay its subscribed share capital portion and, if any, the premium exceeding the nominal value of the corresponding shares may be foreseen for the shareholders of a joint-stock company in its Articles of Association. In case a creditor has a claim against the A.Ş., the claim must be satisfied from the assets of the company.

209. The A.Ş. may be formed by one or more real person(s) or legal entities unless otherwise provided for in any special laws (TCC 338) that may be applicable to a joint-stock company depending on its field of activity.

210. As a legal entity, an A.Ş. can sue and be sued.

211. An A.Ş. may be formed for any economic purpose and scope not legally prohibited (TCC 331). It is the mandatory form foreseen in various laws for certain fields of activities. Banks, including investment and development banks, insurance companies[72] and financial leasing[73] and factoring companies,[74] general and private

72. *See* Article 4 of the Law Concerning the Supervision of the Insurance Company No. 7397 [O.G. No. 10394, Dec. 30, 1959].
73. *See* Article 10 of the Law Concerning Financial Leasing (LCFL) [O.G. No. 18795, Jun. 28, 1985]; for a survey of this law, *see* Ünal Tekinalp, "Turkey's New Financial Leasing Law and Industry",

financial establishments (PFE),[75] intermediary institutions and certain other capital market institutions,[76] must be established in the form of an A.Ş. These organizations are established, operated and audited according to the provisions of special legislation applicable to their activities, but additionally, they are also governed by the TCC.

212. As mentioned earlier, the TCC applies to privately held companies and public companies. However, there are certain provisions in the TCC which are specifically applied or not applied to public companies. For instance, the new TCC set forth different provisions for the prohibition of the transfer of the registered shares which are quoted in the stock exchange and the ones which are not.

213. Publicly held A.Ş.s must be registered with the CMB and they may not leave this status unless the conditions set out in Communiqué II/16.1("Communiqué on Principles Pertaining to Removal of Corporations from the Scope of Law and Obligation of Trading of Shares on the Stock Exchange") are met. The said communiqué foresees that a company may be removed from the scope of Capital Markets Law (CML): (i) by a general assembly decision, (ii) due to the shareholder structure of the company, (iii) due to its number of shareholders, (iv) due to its financial status, (v) due to matters concerning the continuance of operations of the company, (vi) ex officio by the decision of the CMB.

214. The CML applies generally to public offering of shares or other securities and capital market instruments by companies, public companies, companies operating in the capital markets, such as intermediary institutions, investment partnerships and real estate investment partnerships. The provisions of the CML pertaining to the public companies concern various requirements that the public companies are subject to, such as public disclosure requirements and corporate governance principles central securities; however, public companies are also subject to the provisions of TCC.

Fordham Law Review, Vol. LX, No. 6 [1992], 117–134. The LCFL is Turkey's principal law regulating financial leasing. It regulates the organization, nature, and structure of Turkish financial leasing companies and Turkish branches of foreign financial leasing companies. The statute contains various provisions relating to finance leases and provides several incentives to promote this type of leasing activity.

74. Because of the common practice of the Undersecretariat of Treasury and Foreign Trade, a factoring company must be established in the form of an A.Ş.

75. Decree of the Council of Ministers No. 88/7506 [O.G. No. 18256, dated Dec. 19, 1985]. PFE are unique financial institutions that purchase products chosen by a customer and resell them to that customer at prices determined by the length of the repayment term, the financing cost and the profit margin. PFEs also make joint investments with clients, operating on a profit-sharing basis. They provide financing, not in cash, but in the form of goods chosen by the client. The PFE sells these goods to the client on a "profit-and-loss" basis, not on an interest-collecting basis. In this respect, PFEs differ from deposit-taker banks and more closely resemble financing leasing companies. *See* further Tekinalp, *supra*, 124.

76. Such as investment companies and venture capital establishments (Communiqué VIII/21; *see* SL).

§2. FORMATION

I. Formal Requirements and Minimum Content of the Articles

A. In General

215. One of the most important innovations introduced by TCC is related to the incorporation of joint-stock companies. The process of incorporation has been simplified and streamlined. It is also made possible to conduct incorporation proceedings in an electronic environment.

216. The "gradual formation" process (which has hardly ever been used) foreseen in the former TCC was removed in the new one whereby "public company incorporation" was introduced as a new formation method.

217. Article 344 of TCC requires that at least 25% of the total cash subscriptions of the founders of a joint-stock company has to be paid in advance before the registration of the incorporation of the company and the remaining amount to be paid within twenty-four months following the incorporation. However, such requirement does not apply to the joint-stock companies incorporated to be offered to public. Cash value of the shares undertaken to be offered to public in the Articles of Association of the company within two months following incorporation and guaranteed by the founder shareholders may be paid through proceeds of the public offering. Through the application of this new concept in a single-shareholder joint-stock companies, the formation of publicly held companies will be greatly simplified and speeded up. The law also allows the shares held by public to be sold at a premium (that is, above their face or nominal value). Entire amount corresponding to the cash value of the shares which are offered to public but not sold within the period prescribed in the Articles of Association (i.e., two months) and 25% of the cash value of the shares which were not offered to public within the period indicated in the Articles of Association are required to be paid by the relevant founding shareholders within three days following the expiry of the two month term.

218. As indicated above, the system of approval requirement for all joint-stock companies was abandoned at the time of former TCC and the new TCC retains this approach. Accordingly, only joint-stock companies which operate in certain specific fields of activity require the pre-approval of the Ministry and certain other governmental institutions as per the legislation applicable thereto.

B. Ordinary and Qualified Formation

219. Incorporations of joint-stock companies may be "ordinary" or "qualified." In case the incorporation of the company involves (i) a capital in-kind contribution, (ii) acquisition of an enterprise or assets in the name of the joint-stock company being incorporated, or (iii) granting founders preferential dividend rights, such incorporation may be deemed as a "qualified" incorporation. This last case is different from the preceding ones since the first two require an expert valuation appointed by court whereby the last one only requires the benefits to be indicated in the Articles of Association. However, the requirement seeking the benefits granted to the founders to be indicated in the Articles of Association indicates the intention of the TCC to deem such incorporations as qualified as well.

220. Article 339/2(e) of the TCC requires the following to be indicated in the Articles of Association of the founding Articles of Association of a joint-stock company: (i) rights and assets contributed to the capital of the company other than cash, their values and the shares issued for such assets and rights; (ii) if an enterprise or asset is acquired at the time of incorporation, the purchase price of such enterprise or asset; (iii) values of assets and rights acquired by the founders, if any, in the name and on behalf of the company for its incorporation; and (iv) fees, premiums and benefits determined to be paid to the ones that provided services for the incorporation of the company.

221. The aforesaid paragraph of the TCC aims for transparency in the incorporation of the company by requiring the incorporation expenses to be indicated in the Articles of Association. Professor Tekinalp is the only commentator in the Turkish doctrine who suggests that incurring high incorporation expenses is another reason that may make the incorporation of a joint-stock company qualified since the trade registry is entitled to reject the incorporation application in case such expenses are significantly higher than the expenses incurred for the incorporation of similar companies.[77]

222. The TCC includes various new provisions compared to the previous one pertaining to capital-in-kind contributions. As an example, the new TCC accepts all kinds of intellectual property rights to be contributed as capital in kind whereas the former one only accepted copyright as the intellectual property right that may be contributed as capital in kind.

223. In addition to the rules foreseen in the former TCC requiring the type and value of the capital in-kind contribution to be determined by a court-appointed expert, the new TCC also requires: (i) the annotation in the title deed registry of the fact that an immovable asset is contributed as capital in kind to a company, (ii) annotation in the special registries that may apply to certain assets such as intellectual property rights pertaining to the contribution of such asset as capital in kind to a company, (iii) delivery of movable assets to a trustee. If these conditions are not met, such assets shall not be deemed as capital in-kind contributions even if they are indicated as such in the Articles of Association of the company. Such annotations are given to the title deed registry, and specific registries remove the good faith of third parties.

---

77. Comp. WINDBICHLER (2013), 26 N. 13.

224. One feature of Turkish company and partnership law should be mentioned at this stage. According to Article 706 of the Turkish Civil Code, a contract for the transfer of ownership of an immovable is null and void unless the official perfection requirements are duly fulfilled. In other words, as per Article 706 of the TCC, ownership of an immovable asset may only be transferred upon execution of a sale contract before the title deed registry. However, according to Article 128 of the TCC, provisions of the Articles of Association foreseeing an obligation to transfer the ownership of an immovable or a *right in rem* that is or will be established on an immovable is valid without being subject to any other perfection requirement.

225. This constitutes an exception to Article 706 of the Civil Code and an example of the objectives of the new TCC introducing various measures and protections to ensure the smooth transfer of assets that are contributed as capital in kind to the company.

C. Articles of Association

226. The most important step in the formation of an A.Ş. is the preparation of the Articles of Association. The Articles of Association must be in writing and executed by all founding shareholders before the notary public or the director or assistant director of the relevant trade registry.

227. In accordance with Article 339 the TCC, the following is indicated in the Articles of Association of a joint-stock company: (i) trade name of the company; (ii) address of the head offices; (iii) scope of activity of the company reflecting and defining the significant aspects thereof; (iv) company's capital and the nominal value of each share and terms and conditions applicable to payment of the capital; (v) whether share certificates are registered or bearer; privileges, if any, provided for certain shares; transfer restrictions, if any; (vi) rights and non-monetary assets contributed as capital in kind and their values; number of shares to be issued for such capital in-kind contributions, in case of an acquisition of an enterprise or a non-monetary asset, the respect value of such asset or enterprise; value of assets and rights acquired on behalf of the company by the founders for the incorporation of the company; fees and premiums to be paid by the company to the ones that have provided services for the incorporation of the company; (vii) benefits, if any, to be provided from the company profits to the founders, members of the board of directors and other persons; (viii) number of members of the board of directors; board members who are authorized signatories on behalf of the company ; (ix) details on calling for a general assembly and exercise of voting rights; (x) if the duration of the company is limited to a period, such period for which the company is incorporated; (xi) details on how the announcements of the company shall be made; (xii) types and amounts of capital shares subscribed by shareholders; (xiii) accounting period of the company; and (xiv) details pertaining to the members of the first board of directors of the company.

228. The Articles of Association of a joint-stock company may deviate from the provisions of the TCC applicable to joint-stock companies only if such deviation is explicitly permitted in law. This is a new principle introduced by the TCC which adopts a more deterministic approach compared to the previous one for the Articles of Association of the joint-stock companies. As per the new TCC, if the law does not explicitly permit the determination of a certain matter contrary to the general rule provided thereunder, it will not be possible to reflect such in the Articles of Association of the joint-stock company. This principle becomes important especially in terms of share transfer restrictions to be reflected in the Articles of Association as will be explained in more detail hereinbelow.

II. Notification, Registration, Incorporation and Publicity

229. The stages of the incorporation (ordinary and/or qualified) are set forth under Article 329 *et seq.* which can be summarized as follows:

- Preparation of Articles of Association (applies to both types of incorporation).
- Expert valuation of capital in-kind contributions (only for qualified incorporation).
- Execution of the Articles of Association by the founder shareholders before the notary public or the relevant trade registry.
- Payment of the capital contributions of the founder shareholders (in case of cash capital contribution undertakings, at least 25% of the total amount has to be paid before the registration of the incorporation before the trade registry).
- If applicable, obtaining the pre-approvals of the relevant governmental authorities as per the Communiqué of the Ministry of Trade published in the Official Gazette dated November 15, 2012 and numbered 28468 and the regulations that may apply to the field of activity that is to be adopted by the company being incorporated.
- Registration with the relevant Trade Registry and acquiring legal personality (applies to both types of incorporation).
- Announcement of incorporation in the Trade Registry Gazette (applies to both types of incorporation).

230. As a final step of incorporation, the Articles of Association of the company is registered with the Trade Registy authorized in the location where the headquarters of the company is located. Upon registration with the relevant Trade Registry, the joint-stock company assumes legal personality as a legal entity (TCC 355).

231. After incorporation, Articles of Association of the company is announced in the Trade Registry Gazette (TCC 354).

III. Contracts Made on Behalf of a Company in Formation

232. As mentioned above, the joint-stock company assumes legal personality upon registration of its incorporation with the relevant trade registry. Before the completion of registration but after the declaration of the founders of their intent to form a joint-stock company under a duly executed Articles of Association prepared in line with the provisions of the TCC whereby the founders unconditionally undertake to pay in full their subscribed portions of the capital, a "*pre-company*" or "*pre-partnership*" is formed among the founders. Formation of this "*pre-company*" is clearly foreseen in Article 335 of the TCC.

233. Provisions of Turkish Code of Obligations pertaining to the Ordinary Partnerships (*Adi Ortaklık*) shall apply for agreements entered into and relations conducted before the formation of "pre-company" among the founders or by the founders with third parties.

IV. Number of Subscribers

234. As per Article 338 of the TCC, a joint-stock company may be established by one or more subscribers.

235. In the event that the number of subscribers falls down to one, such a situation has to be registered with the relevant Trade Registry and announced in the Trade Registry Gazette upon the application of the board of directors. In case of a joint-stock company with one shareholder/founder, the name, address and nationality of such person also need to be registered with the Trade registry.

236. The Articles of Association should be signed by all founders or their duly appointed representatives and their signatures should be approved by the notary public or the director or assistant director of the relevant trade registry.

237. As per Article 348 of the TCC, the founders may not receive payment or gratis shares or such other benefits which may result in decrease of the share capital of the company in consideration of their efforts for the incorporation of the company. The provisions of the Articles of Association in violation of this principle shall be considered null and void. However, usufruct shares may be issued to the founders granting them the right to receive at most 10% of the profits remaining after setting aside reserve funds and a minimum of 5% dividend for the shareholders as permitted by Article 339/2 (f) of the TCC.

V. Initial Share Capital

238. A joint-stock company be established with a minimum share capital of TRY 50,000 (approximately EUR 3,250)

239. At least 25% of the nominal value of the shares subscribed in cash must be paid before registration and the remaining shall be paid within twenty-four months following the registration. If the shares are issued with premium, the entire premium of shares shall be paid before registration. These are the minimum requirements applicable to payment of the share capital. In other words, the Articles of Association may foresee the entire portion of the capital or a portion of it higher than 25% be paid before registration or shorten the period of twenty-four months for the payment of any remaining amount if the capital is not paid in full before registration.

240. Capital contributions in cash are paid by the founders to a special bank account designated for capital payments and opened on behalf of the company to be incorporated. As part of the incorporation application, the founders are required to submit to the relevant Trade Registry a bank letter evidencing the total amount of cash contributions made to such capital account. This bank letter is submitted to the Trade Registry to evidence that the minimum capital contribution amounts required by the TCC and the Articles of Association of the company are duly paid by the founders. The bank may pay the deposited amount only to the company and only upon submission of a letter by the Trade Registry evidencing the duly registration of the company.

241. In the event that the Company fails to complete its formation procedures and acquire the status of a legal entity within three months following the execution of its Articles of Association before the notary public or the relevant trade registry, the Trade Registry issues a certificate evidencing such fact. The bank may, only upon submission of such letter of Trade Registry, pay to the founders the amounts they paid to the capital account of the company to be incorporated

VI. Contributions in Kind

242. Contribution of capital in kind and/or acquisition of an enterprise or non-monetary assets during incorporation and granting benefits to founders in the profits of the company are the two main factors that require the qualified incorporation procedures to be followed.

243. Qualified incorporation requires certain steps, such as a court-appointed expert valuation, to be followed in addition to the steps identified above for ordinary incorporation.

244. In accordance with Article 342 of TCC, assets which (i) are not encumbered by pledge, attachment, injunction or any other liens and (ii) are convertible to cash and transferable may be contributed as capital in kind. Article 342 also foresees that service obligations, personal work, goodwill and unmatured receivables may not be contributed as capital in kind.

245. In other words, all assets, other than cash, listed in Article 127 of the TCC may qualify as capital in-kind contributions to the extent the conditions set forth under Article 342 of the TCC are met. These assets include (i) receivables, negotiable instruments and shares representing the share capital of capital companies, (ii) intellectual property rights, (iii) movable properties and all kinds of immovable properties, (iv) usufruct rights pertaining to movable and immovable properties, (v) commercial enterprises, (vi) transferable electronic environments, domains, names and marks that are used based on a legal right, (vii) mine licenses and other rights having similar economic value and (viii) any kind of asset that may be transferred and valued in cash. Although Article 127 which is a general provision applicable to commercial enterprises qualifies service obligations, personal work and goodwill as capital in-kind contributions such cannot be contributed as capital for joint-stock companies due to the restriction provided under Article 342 of the TCC.

246. The Articles of Association of the joint-stock company should provide details pertaining to the capital in-kind contribution and specify the type and nature thereof. In other words, the Articles of Association should clearly state what is being contributed as capital, its value and the value determination method and number of shares issued in exchange of such capital in-kind contribution.

247. Capital in-kind contributions are required to be valued by experts appointed by the Commercial Court of First Instance in the judicial area where the headquarters of the company is located. The valuation report should clearly indicate with satisfactory evidence and in compliance with the accountability principle (i) that the valuation method used for the particular asset is a fair and appropriate method for all concerned parties taking into consideration the specifics of the matter at hand; (ii) the existence and validity of receivables (if any) being contributed as capital in kind, their compliance with the provisions of Article 342 and confirmation as to the collectible nature thereof; (iii) the number of shares to be issued in exchange of the capital in-kind contribution and TRY equivalent thereof. The evaluation can be made before the preparation of Articles of Association or both can be done simultaneously. In any case, until the evaluation is finalized and reflected in the Articles of Association, the Articles of Association may not be completed and be signed by the founding shareholders.

248. The capital in-kind contribution of immovable properties are required to be annotated with the relevant Title Deed Registry whereas movable properties contributed as capital in kind have to be entrusted to a trustee and intellectual property rights and other economic rights and assets being subject to registration requirements have to be registered with the relevant special registries. In case of capital contribution of immovable property or any other usufruct right on immovable properties, the Company shall have the right of disposal over such assets only upon registration of the ownership of the company with the relevant Title Deed Registry.

249. As indicated above, intellectual property rights have to be registered in order for them to be contributed as capital in kind to a joint-stock company. However, the 11th Chamber of the Court of Appeals have a more tolerant approach to the registration requirement. In its decision dated October 10, 2017 and numbered 2016-1756-5174, it concludes as follows: "Article 128 of the TCC indicates that intellectual property rights and other assets may be accepted as capital in kind so long as such capital in kind contribution is registered with the relevant special registries, if any." Therefore, it may be concluded that intellectual property rights may be contributed as capital in kind.

250. A joint-stock company may require acquiring an enterprise (e.g., a factory) or a non-cash asset (e.g., patent rights or a land) during the process of its incorporation. Such acquisition may be from a third party or a founding shareholder. This process is different than contribution of assets as capital in kind since it requires a sale and transfer agreement to be executed between the parties and the seller receives the purchase price rather than shares of the company. The value of the enterprise and non-cash asset is determined by a court-appointed expert through the same procedure that applies to capital in-kind contributions. Following the completion of the purchase procedure, the company gains possession of the enterprise or the non-cash asset.

VII. Other Material Formation Requirements

251. As mentioned above, the former TCC used to apply a pre-approval system for incorporation and amendments in the Articles of Association of all limited liability and joint-stock companies and cooperatives. This system was abandoned by the amendment of Article 273 of the former TCC by Law No. 4884 in 2003. As per this new system, which may be identified as the "selective normative system," only those companies determined by the Ministry were held subject to the pre-approval requirement. The same system is still applicable under new TCC as indicated in Article 333 thereof.

252. Article 5 of the Communiqué on the Pre-Approval Requirement which was published in the Official Gazette dated November 15, 2012 determines the joint-stock companies incorporation which shall be subject to the pre-approval of the Ministry as follows:

- Banks
- Financial leasing companies
- Factoring companies
- Consumer financing and card services companies
- Asset management companies
- Insurance companies
- Holding companies established in the form of joint-stock companies
- Companies operating foreign exchange offices
- Public Warehousing companies
- Companies engaged in warehousing of agriculture products
- Independent audit companies
- Management companies of technology development areas

- Export-import inspection companies
- Companies subject to the CML
- Founder and management companies of free trade zones.

253. Amendments to the Articles of Associations of the companies mentioned in the paragraph above are also subject to the approval of the Ministry provided, however, that capital increases of public companies in the registered capital system up to the ceiling approved by the Capital Markets Board shall not require the approval of the Ministry.

VIII. Court Case for Termination for Incorporation Violations

254. The new TCC allows for the initiation of a termination lawsuit against the company within three months following its incorporation for violation of the applicable laws at the time of incorporation. This lawsuit may be initiated by the board of directors, shareholders or creditors of the company or the Ministry of Industry and Trade in case the interests of creditors or shareholders of the Company or the public are significantly endangered or harmed as a result of violation of the applicable law at the time of incorporation of the company. This change introduced by the new TCC is in line with the requirements of the First Company Law Directive.[78]

255. According to the Article 353 of the TCC, a joint-stock company cannot be declared null and void. However, in case of the situations indicated above, it is possible to initiate a lawsuit for the termination of the Company. The court can give time to the Company to complete pending matters and correct discrepancies conflicting with the Articles of Association or with the law.

IX. *Fraudem Legis Agere*[79]

256. As stated previously, the qualified formation of an A.Ş. enables the protection of the creditors and shareholders through transparency and court-appointed expert evaluation requirements.

257. In order to prevent the circumvention of this aforesaid rule (*fraudem legis agere*), Article 356 of the TCC introduces an additional protection mechanism. As per this mechanism, agreements executed by the Company for the acquisition or lease of enterprises or assets within two years following its incorporation and for a value in excess of 10% of the capital of the Company shall be considered null and void unless such agreements are approved by the general assembly and registered with the relevant trade registry. Upon the request of board of directors, an expert

78. Directive 68/151/EEC, EU-OJ L. 65/8, Mar. 14, 1968.
79. *See* generally H. Ülgen, *Anonim Ortaklıgın Kuruluştan Sonra Malvarlıgı Degerini Satın Alması* [The Acquisition of Assets after the Establishment of a Company Limited by Shares], Ankara 1969.

assigned by the Commercial Court of First Instance at the location of the company shall evaluate the enterprise and the asset to be acquired or leased by the company prior to the general assembly's resolution.

X. Liability of the Founders[80]

258. The provisions pertaining to the liability of the founders used to be at the end of the section relating to the incorporation of the joint-stock companies in the former TCC. The new law has regulated the liability of founders under section 11 of the provisions governing the joint-stock companies under the heading "Legal Liability."

259. The founders may be held liable if: (1) the documents and statements pertaining to the incorporation are in violation of the applicable law (TCC 549), (2) statements pertaining to the capital of the company are not true or the inability of the subscribers to pay their capital portions was known (TCC 550), (3) there are irregularities or fraud pertaining to valuation (TCC 551), (4) funds are collected from public in violation of the applicable law (TCC 552). The nature of liability and joint liability of founders are regulated under a common provision which applies to founders, board members, managers and liquidation officers (TCC 553).

260. Liability pertaining to the documents and statements being in violation of law may occur not only in case of incorporation but in capital increases and decreases, mergers, acquisitions, spin-offs and issuance of securities. The term "documents" means the documents used for the aforesaid transactions which may include declarations of the founders or shareholders, offering circulars, prospectuses and guarantees and undertakings. The types of documents are not listed exhaustively in TCC 549. In the event that the documents are incorrect, untrue or fraudulent or if the facts are concealed, the persons that have prepared these documents or made such declarations may be held responsible under TCC 549 for the damages that are incurred in relation thereto. Liability of the founders (and also board members, managers and liquidation officers) arise in case of existence of fault. The degree of fault (recklessness, gross negligence and intent) has a role in determining the level of liability and, thus, the determination of the indemnification amount. Also, it has to be noted that all persons that are at fault in preparation of the documents in a way to cause liability under TCC 549 may be held liable even if they may not be classified as founders. For instance, notary publics, court-appointed experts, auditors and accounts may be held liable under TCC 549. Article 567 of the TCC regulates the criminal liability of the persons that prepare the documents indicated in Article 549 of the TCC as explained above. As per Article 567, the persons that have forged the documents indicated in Article 549 and the ones that have intentionally made incorrect entries to the commercial books of the company are punished with imprisonment from 1 to 3 years.

80. *See* generally H. Domaniç, *Anonim Ortaklıkta Kuruluştan Dogan Hukuki Mesuliyet* [Responsibility Resulting from the Formation of a Company Limited by Shares], İstanbul 1964.

261. Article 550 of the TCC regulates the liability of the persons that have made or allowed incorrect declarations pertaining to the capital of the company or the ones that had knowledge of but remained silent in relation to the payment incapability of the subscribers to the share capital of the Company. As per the aforesaid article, (i) the persons that have shown that the capital of the company is undertaken or paid in full despite the fact that it was not as per the applicable law and the Articles of Association of the company and, (ii) in case of existence of their fault in such declarations, the representatives of the company shall be deemed to have undertaken such shares and are jointly liable for the payment of the value of shares together with any damages that may occur due to such incorrect declarations. The differentiated joint liability indicated hereunder is a concept introduced in the new TCC. Failure to pay the undertaken capital should be interpreted in a broad manner. For instance, in case of capital contributions in cash, payment with negotiable instruments is to be interpreted as a failure of payment. Similarly, subscription of unmatured receivables as capital or any other irregularities in capital undertakings shall be considered as an event giving rise to liability under TCC 550. TCC 550 also foresees that the ones that had the knowledge of the fact that the subscribers to the capital of the company did not have adequate payment capabilities and have consented to their subscription may be held liable for damages that may occur due to failure of payment of such capital contributions. This liability, like the one defined under TCC 549, requires the existence of fault.

262. As per Article 551 of the TCC, the ones that have (i) determined the value of the asset to be contributed as capital in kind or of the enterprise and assets to be acquired by the company higher than the value of their comparable equivalents; or (ii) shown the quality, type or condition of the asset or enterprise not consistent with its actual quality, type or condition; or (iii) committed other fraudulent acts valuation are liable for damages that occur in relation thereto.

263. Article 552 prohibits, save for the provisions of the CML, the raising of funds through public offerings for incorporation or capital increase of companies by any means. This provision is far from being a complete or perfect provision since it fails to determine the types of fund-raising methods and introduce the ability to obtain a preliminary injunction to cease any violating activity. As per Article 560, the statute of limitations is two years from the date of acquiring knowledge of the irregularity and five years in any case from the occurrence of the event. In case the act constitutes a crime under the Criminal Law and is subject to a longer statute of limitations, the indemnification lawsuits shall be subject to the same statute of limitations. The liability lawsuit shall be initiated before the Civil Court of First Instance in the judicial area where the headquarters of the company is located. As this lawsuit is classified as an indemnification lawsuit, it will be subject to mandatory mediation as per Article 5/a of the TCC.

§3. Essential Elements of the Joint-Stock Company

264. All commercial enterprises have a legal entity status under the Turkish system. This principle is set forth under Article 125 of the TCC. As commercial enterprises have the status of a legal entity, the owner of the assets of the partnership shall be the commercial enterprise.

265. Mandatory elements of each commercial enterprise are set forth in the TCC and in case an enterprise loses or misses any one of these elements it may also lose its status as a legal entity.

266. Likewise, the joint-stock company is defined under Article 329 of the TCC as a company which has a determined capital that is divided into shares and which is liable for its debts only with its own assets. The article also adds that the shareholders are responsible to the company only with respect to the capital amounts that they have subscribed to.

267. A joint-stock company may be established for any economic activity that is not prohibited by law and must have at least one shareholder at the time of its establishment and throughout the term of its existence. In other words, a joint-stock company may not continue without the presence of at least one shareholder. Additionally, a joint-stock company must have a board of directors consisting of at least one board member authorized to represent the company and a general assembly consisting of the shareholders of the company.

§4. Capital and Shares

I. Different Concepts of Capital

268. As per the TCC, a joint-stock company, whether publicly held or private, has to adopt one of the two share capital systems: (a) basic (fixed) capital, (b) authorized capital. One of the important improvements introduced by the new TCC is that it accepts an authorized capital system for both public and private companies as opposed to the TCC 1956 which accepted only a basic capital system for private companies and permitted authorized capital only for publicly held A.Ş.s. Although the TCC foresees only the two aforesaid share capital systems, CML has introduced another system for "investment funds with variable capital" which are also organized as joint-stock companies. In variable capital system, the shares are grouped as "investor shares" and "founder shares." The number and nominal value of investor shares may change and thus the capital of the company becomes variable.

A. Basic (Fixed) Capital System

269. Basic (fixed) capital means the amount indicated in the Articles of Association of the company reflecting the total nominal value of the shares subscribed by the shareholders of the company. In other words, basic capital system requires the entire capital of the company or the increased amount (where appropriate) to be fully subscribed. TCC 344(1) requires a quarter of the capital to be paid before the registration and the rest within twenty-four months following the registration. Any unpaid share capital becomes the liability of the subscribers. Accordingly, the TCC distinguishes between "nominal share capital" (i.e., the capital amount indicated in the Articles of Association), "paid-up capital" (i.e., the total amount of capital subscribed and actually paid by the shareholders) and "unpaid capital" (i.e., the total amount of capital subscribed to but not yet paid by the shareholders). The capital amount may be increased or decreased by an amendment of the articles approved by the General Assembly.

B. Authorized Share Capital[81]

270. Authorized capital is the ceiling amount indicated in the Articles of Association of the company as the amount up to which the capital may be increased by the Board of Directors. The authorized capital amount indicated in the Articles of Association is neither paid nor fully subscribed to. It is only the ceiling amount up to which the Board of Directors is authorized to increase the capital without the approval of the General Assembly. Once this ceiling amount is reached, the articles of the company is amended by the General Assembly and the board of directors is authorized with a new ceiling amount. Authorized capital system may be assumed at the time of incorporation or after incorporation through an amendment in the Articles of Association. It is also possible to leave the authorized capital system and revert to the basic capital system.

271. As per Article 20/3 of the Law on Implementation of the Turkish Commercial Code, the Ministry of Trade is authorized to determine the details and specifics of the authorized capital system and the conditions to accept or leave this system. Accordingly, the Ministry of Trade issued the "*Communiqué on the Principles of Authorized Capital System Applicable to Privately Held Companies.*" For publicly held companies, the Communiqué No. II/18.1 of the Capital Markets Board on "*Authorized Capital System*" shall apply together with the relevant provisions of the TCC.

272. In authorized capital system, there are three different types as indicated in Article 332 of the TCC which includes: (a) authorized capital, (b) initial capital, and (c) issued capital. As indicated above, authorized capital is the ceiling amount indicated in the Articles of Association. Article 332/2 of the TCC defines "initial capital" as the minimum capital required to be retained by a joint-stock company at the time of incorporation with or when converting to the authorized capital system. The "issued capital" is the current amount to which the capital is increased by the decision of the board of directors.

---

81. *See* generally H. Anaral, *Anonim Ortaklıklarda Kayıtlı Sermaye* [Authorized Share Capital in Company Limited by Shares], Ankara 1982; Hirsch/Tekinalp [*see* SB], 54, 55.

273. As per the provisions of Article 460 of the TCC, the Board of Directors may be authorized by the general assembly for a maximum of five years to increase the capital up to the ceiling amount indicated in the Articles of Association without the approval of the shareholders. Once the authorization period determined in the Articles of Association expires, the general assembly has to adopt a new decision and amend the Articles of Association for renewal of the authorization.

274. Privately held A.Ş.s can leave the authorized capital system with the permission of Ministry of Trade when they cease to qualify for the system. Even in the absence of a request by the Company, the Ministry may remove the Company from the authorized capital system if the Company loses the qualifications required for entry to the system.

275. Public companies may adopt the authorized capital system or leave the system only with the approval of the Capital Markets Board as per Article 18 of the CML and Communiqué No. II/18.1 of the Capital Markets Board on Authorized Capital System.

C. Participation Usufruct Shares

276. As per Article 36 of Share Communiqué No. VII-128.1 of the CMB, in order for a company to be able to issue participation usufruct shares ("*PUS*"), the Articles of Association of the company should include a provision permitting the issuance of PUS and the general assembly of the company should decide for such issuance. The general assembly should include determinations as to the nominal value of the PUS to be issued and rights attached thereto and identify whether the PUS will be issued through a public offering.

277. PUS may grant to its holder one or more of the following rights: (i) the right to participate in the net profit of the company by a certain percentage, (ii) the right to participate in the liquidation proceeds or (iii) preemptive rights to purchase the new shares to be issued by a non-public company at the time of a capital increase.

278. Provided that the Articles of Association of the company includes such a provision, PUS may be issued with indefinite term or at a value above the nominal value.

279. The total value of the PUS that may be issued by a company may not exceed 50% of its issued or paid-up capital. For the purposes of determination of issuance limit, the issuance value of the previous PUS issuances are taken into consideration as a deduction item.

II. Alteration of Capital Requirements

280. Unless a higher amount is not determined under particular regulations, Article 332 of the TCC requires that the minimum initial capital shall not be less than (i) TRY 50 thousand in joint-stock companies with a basic capital system and (ii) TRY 100 thousand for joint-stock companies with an authorized capital system.

III. Preferential Right of Subscription[82]

A. *Capital Increase*

281. The new TCC has improved the existing methods of capital increase in joint-stock companies while also introducing "*conditional*" capital increases as a brand-new capital increase method. As indicated above, along with the public companies, the new TCC made it possible for private companies to adopt the authorized capital system and increase their capital up to the ceiling amount indicated in the Articles of Association by a decision of the Board of Directors without the approval of the General Assembly. TCC also perfected the requirements pertaining to the prohibition and restriction of preemptive rights of the shareholders in certain capital increases and introduced fair principles.

282. The improvements introduced by the new TCC in terms of capital increases are quite significant. The conceptual innovation of permitting private joint-stock companies to adopt an authorized capital system fundamentally alters the balance of power between a company's board of directors and the general assembly by greatly strengthening the position of the former over the latter. The second crucial innovation of the new TCC is that share capital increases have been simplified, accelerated, and liberalized while government agency intervention in such events has been significantly reduced. The third innovation is that privileged shares are no longer granted with the automatic right to block all capital increases. As per the highly criticized system of TCC 1956, it was accepted that any capital increase affected, *per se*, the rights of the privileged share groups and, thus, granted the privileged shareholders the power to block all capital increases (TCC 1956 Article 392). The new TCC solves this problem by enabling the holders of privileged shares to block the capital increase (and capital decreases) only if the capital increase decision violates their rights and privileges. The fourth innovation is the strengthening of preemptive rights of the shareholders. While the former TCC 1956 lacked the appropriate protections for limitation of preemptive rights enabling the majority shareholder(s) to exercise such rights to their benefit, the new TCC introduced detailed provisions under Article 461. Preemptive right is foreseen to ensure the ability of the shareholder to protect its shareholding percentage in the company. However, preemptive rights of the shareholders may be restricted in compliance

82. *See* generally E. Moroğlu, *Türk Ticaret Kanununa Göre Anonim Ortaklıkta Esas Sermaye Artırımı* [Increasing the Share Capital of a Company Limited by Shares under the Terms of the Turkish Commercial Code], İstanbul, 1972.

with the equal treatment principle and if the benefits and requirements of the joint-stock company necessitate such action. Article 461 of the TCC has introduced four conditions for the restriction of preemptive rights: (a) the proposal to restrict or prohibit the preemptive rights has to be approved by the affirmative votes of the shareholders representing at least 60% of the total share capital in a duly convened general assembly; (b) there has to be a valid reason to justify the restriction or prohibition of preemptive rights (e.g., public offering, acquisition of a commercial enterprise, granting shares to the employees); (c) restriction or prohibition of preemptive rights should not grant an unjustifiable benefit to or create losses on anyone; and (d) the exercise of preemptive rights may not be prohibited or restricted based on an argument that the share transfers restricted as per the Articles of Association of the company. The fifth innovation is the introduction of a new type of capital increase to Turkish company law: the "conditional capital increase" (TCC Article 463). Such form of capital increase is foreseen in the TCC to facilitate the exercise of stock options that may have been granted to the employees of the company or other third parties or conversion of convertible bonds issued by the company to share certificates.

283. Under Turkish law, an increase in share capital may be examined according to the source of the contributions. Share capital may be increased through cash or capital in-kind contributions (*Increase by contribution*) or capitalization of retained earnings (*Increase through capitalization of retained earnings*). In case of capital increase by contribution of cash or assets, new shares are issued for the increased portion of share capital that is fully subscribed by the shareholders, whereas, in case of increase through capitalization of internal resources, gratis shares are issued to all existing shareholders in proportion to their shareholding in the company.

284. Capital increase through capitalization of retained earnings is a form of capital increase through internal resources. There are two other forms of capital increase that are also considered as capital increase through internal resources.

285. First, under the terms of the TCC and the tax laws, property, plant and equipment are stated in the balance sheet at historical cost. In accordance with a change in the tax legislation enacted in 1983,[83] revaluation of fixed assets, particularly property, plant and equipment, is permitted. Property, plant and equipment held throughout the financial year and related accumulated depreciations are written down in accordance with the regulations of the Ministry of Finance and Customs at a rate specified each year. This rate is in line with the official inflation rate. The rates used for revaluation purposes have generally been lower than the rate of inflation. The revaluation surplus is credited to a non-deductible reserve and is not subject to taxation. The increase in the net book value of the said assets is permitted to be added to the shareholder's equity, giving companies the option of issuing shares,

83. Law No. 2791 [O.G. No. 17936, Jan. 22, 1983] and Law No. 3332 [O.G. No. 18947 rep. Mar. 31, 1987], Communiqué of the Ministry of Finance and Customs No. 157 [O.G. No. 17933, Mar. 15, 1983].

which are called "*gratis* shares" (*bonus* shares) for the revaluation amount (*Increase by the use of an evaluation surplus*).

286. Second, under the terms of the Company Tax Law, if companies whose head offices are in Turkey use the proceeds arising from the sale of immovables (land and/or buildings) and/or shares, usufruct shares or founder shares in other companies for their capital increase, certain percentages of such the proceeds are exempt from company tax (i.e., in case of capitalization of proceeds of sale of subsidiary shares, usufruct shares and founder shares 75% of such proceeds are exempt from corporate tax and in case of capitalization of proceeds of sale of immovable assets, 50% of such proceeds are exempt from corporate tax). In order to benefit from the tax exemption, additional conditions identified under the Corporate Tax Law have to be fulfilled.

287. New TCC establishes three types of increase of share capital: (1) basic/regular, (2) authorized and (3) conditional. A regular increase may be made through a subscription of new capital or through internal funds or both.

288. It is required that the registration of the capital increase with the relevant Trade Registry is completed within three months following the capital increase decision. If the increase is not registered within three months from the decision of the general assembly (or board of directors in case of increase of authorized capital or conditional capital increase), such decisions become invalid.

289. In accordance with Article 457 of TCC, a declaration is signed by the board of directors depending on the type of capital increase. Such declaration should indicate:

- in case of cash capital contributions: (i) that the entire increased portion is fully subscribed, (ii) amounts required to be paid in accordance with law and Articles of Association are paid;
- in case of capital in-kind contributions or acquisition of an asset: (i) that the amounts to be paid in exchange of such contribution and/or acquisition are reasonable; (ii) the type and nature of the asset acquired by the company as capital in kind; (iii) the valuation method used for such asset; and (iv) an acknowledgement of such valuation as being fair and accurate;
- in case a receivable is being set off against the capital contribution: (i) an acknowledgement of the existence and validity of such receivable and (ii) its eligibility for set off against capital contribution;
- in case of capitalization of retained earnings or available funds such as the revaluation fund: (i) that the funds or retained earnings converted to capital are eligible to be disposed freely;
- in case of all capital increases that: (i) approvals are obtained from required corporate bodies and governmental institutions; (ii) all legal and administrative requirements are fulfilled;

- if preemptive rights of the shareholders are restricted partially or in full: (i) the reasons for such restriction, (ii) the amount and percentage of the restricted preemptive rights, (iii) information on the person(s) to whom such restricted preemptive rights will be made available and exercised by and at what price and for what reasons;
- if the capital is increased through capitalization of the internal resources, a guarantee as to the existence and validity of such resources;
- if there is a conditional capital increase, a declaration indicating the compliance of such condition with the applicable law; and
- information on the benefits granted and fees paid to the service providers and other persons together with a comparison of such amount with market prices.

290. There are some features of capital in a basic capital system that distinguish it from a capital increase in an authorized capital system.

291. As per Article 456 of the TCC, except for capital increases to be realized through the capitalization of internal resources, the previous share capital of a company has to be fully paid in by the shareholders in order for the company to realize a further capital increase. Such requirement applies for capital increases in both the basic capital system and authorized capital system. However, the corporate body to decide on a capital increase in a company with a basic capital system is the general assembly, whereas the board of directors is the corporate body to approve a capital increase in a company with an authorized capital system up to the ceiling amount indicated in the articles association of the company.

292. Second precondition relates to the capital loss situations defined in Article 376 of the TCC. Accordingly, if it is understood based on the last annual balance sheet of the company that the losses of the company are more than half of the sum of the capital of the company and its statutory reserves, the board of directors is required to call for a general assembly to discuss the necessary precautions. However, in case the last annual balance sheets show that the losses of the company are more than two-thirds of the sum of the capital of the company and its statutory reserves, the general assembly of the company has to either decide for a capital decrease and be satisfied to continue with the one-third of the capital or complete the lost capital portion. Thus, in case of a capital loss situation by two-thirds, the general assembly may not resolve for a capital increase but only for a capital decrease or capital completion.

293. The third precondition is set forth under Article 462(3) of the TCC. In case the balance sheet of the company reveals the existence of funds eligible to be added to and converted into capital, a capital increase may not be realized through subscription by the shareholders unless such available funds (e.g., revaluation fund) are indeed capitalized. However, it is possible to realize a capital increase through both contribution by shareholders and capitalization of the available funds at the same time and in the same ratio. In case of capitalization of the funds, the existing shareholders receive gratis/bonus shares for the increased portion of the capital pro rata to their shareholding in the company.

294. In case of a capital increase in the basic capital system, the Articles of Association of the company has to be amended to reflect the new capital amount and details of its payment by the shareholders, whereas, in the authorized capital system, an amendment to the Articles of Association shall not be required to the extent that the capital of the company does not exceed the authorized ceiling indicated in the Articles of Association as a result of such increase.

295. The provisions of TCC pertaining to the incorporation of joint-stock companies (e.g., Articles 342, 343 and 344) shall also apply in case of increase of the capital amount indicated in the incorporation Articles of Association of the Company. Accordingly, in case of capital increases realized through cash contributions, at least 25% of the total subscribed amount has to be paid in cash and in advance before registration of the capital increase with the Trade Registry and the remaining portion has to be paid within twenty-four months at the latest. For capital in-kind contributions, the provisions determining the types of assets which may qualify as a capital in-kind contribution and the valuation procedures of such assets shall apply.

296. If the Articles of Association of a Company grants the board of directors the authority to increase the capital up to the ceiling amount determined in the Articles of Association, capital increases may be realized only by the decision of the board of directors until such ceiling is reached. This authority can be given to the Board of Directors for a maximum of five years. The board of directors may also restrict the preemptive rights, issue privileged shares or shares with premium if such authority is granted to the board of directors in the Articles of Association of the company. The board of directors is required to announce in the Trade Registry and on its website the particulars pertaining to a capital increase realized within the authorized capital system, including information on any required governmental approvals and whether (i) the capital increase is realized through restriction of preemptive rights of the shareholders; and (ii) there are any privileges and/or premiums on the shares issued as a result of such capital increase together with information on the relevant procedures applicable thereto (TCC 460). Capital increases in authorized capital systems may be realized through cash contributions, contributions in kind or capitalization of internal resources.

297. Capital increases in public joint-stock companies shall be realized in accordance with the rules and regulations of the Capital Markets Board.

298. Article 465 regulates the requirements to be included in the Articles of Association of the company in case of a conditional increase as follows: (i) nominal value of conditional capital increase, (ii) numbers, nominal value and types of shares, (iii) groups which can benefit from rights to conversion and purchase, (iv) declaration that the preemptive rights of the existing shareholders are fully restricted and the amount corresponding to such restriction, (v) privileges to be given to certain share groups, (vi) transfer restrictions to apply to the newly issued registered shares. Additionally, in case bonds and similar debt instruments grating rights of conversion to shares and similar debt instruments are not primarily offered to shareholders of the company, the Articles of Association shall also include: (i) terms and conditions applicable to exercise of purchase and conversion rights (ii) principles regarding the calculation of issuance value.

299. The capital may be increased under the condition that the right to receive new shares (conversion privileges or options) are granted to employees or holders of new bonds or similar debt instruments of the company or its subsidiaries.

300. The capital will increase *ipso iure* through the exercise of conversion privileges or options. The capital contribution is either made by a deposit of funds or set off.

301. In case a bond or other debt instrument or an option issued by the company grants the right to acquire shares in a particular capital increase, the owners of such instruments shall exercise their right at the redemption value indicated in such bonds. Total nominal value of the capital increased through a conditional capital increase cannot exceed half of the capital. Payment should be at least equal to the nominal value.

a. Capital Increase in Basic Capital System

302. A capital increase is completed in the following seven stages in the basic capital system:

(1) *First Step:* the Board of Directors adopts a decision and approves its proposal for the amendment of the *capital* provision of the Articles of Association to be submitted to the approval of the general assembly and calls for a general assembly for such purpose in line with the provisions of the TCC. The new *capital* provision of the Articles of Association should reflect the total capital of the company after the increase, the increased amount and number of shares to be issued in relation to such increase, the type of the capital contribution, and, in case of in-kind contribution, its particulars and the value estimated by the expert appointed by the court.
(2) *Second Step*, in case the field of activity or the type of the company requires governmental approval for the amendment of its Articles of Association, such governmental approval has to be obtained before the voting takes place in the general assembly of the company for the increase of the share capital.
(3) *Third Step*, the General Assembly of the Company must approve the increase in share capital and the amended draft of the provisions of the Articles of Association.
(4) *Fourth Step*, the resolution of the General Assembly must be approved by the special meetings of the holders of privileged classes of shares, if necessary (TCC 454).
(5) *Fifth Step*, if the newly issued shares are not already subscribed by the shareholders in the general assembly approving the capital increase and the

amended provision of the Articles of Association does not include such details as the subscription and payment of the capital increase, the board of directors should adopt a decision outlining the principles to apply to the exercise of preemptive rights by the shareholders and grant to the shareholders at least fifteen days from its announcement in the Trade Registry Gazette for the exercise of such preemption rights.

(6) *Sixth Step*, if the newly issued shares are not already subscribed to by the shareholders in the general assembly approving the capital increase and the amended provision of the Articles of Association does not include such details as the subscription and payment of the capital increase, the shareholders may exercise their preemption rights through letters of subscription to be submitted to the board of directors and in line with the decision of the board of pertaining to the exercise of preemptive rights. Such letter should be duly executed by the shareholder and include information as to the group, number and nominal value of shares subscribed by the shareholder, payment method and term of subscription.

(7) *Seventh* and final step is the Registration and announcement of the amendment in the Trade Registry Gazette.

303. Publicly held A.Ş.s are subject to the special rules of the CML which are established by Communiqués.

b. Capital Increase in the Authorized Capital System

304. In closely held A.Ş.s, an increase of authorized capital begins with a resolution of the Board of Directors. The resolution must indicate the amount, the number, the *par value* and the types of the new shares, whether they are issued at or above *par value* and the rules regarding the exercise of the preemption rights. If necessary, governmental approvals should be obtained. The board decision is published in the Trade Registry Gazette and the website of the company, if necessary. If such capital increase affects the rights of the privileged shareholders, the amendment should also be approved by the special meeting of such privileged shareholders. In public A.Ş.s, the increase procedure is almost the same except that the shares should be electronically delivered to the purchasers as a result of the offering of the newly issued shares.

B. Preemption Rights

305. Each shareholder is entitled to purchase newly issued shares in proportion to their existing shareholding in the company.[84] The provisions of the Articles of Association set forth conditions for the use of preemption rights. The resolution of the General Meeting concerning the increase of the capital may restrict these rights partially or as a whole with the affirmative votes of the shareholders representing at

84. Any offer must be open for at least fifteen days.

least 60% of the total capital of the company and only under fair and justifiable conditions. Article 461 of the TCC refers to public offerings, acquisition of subsidiaries, enterprises or certain departments of enterprises or conversion of stock options granted to employees as reasons that may be deemed as justifiable for restriction of preemptive rights of the existing shareholders. Board of directors determines the principles to apply to the exercise of the preemptive rights and has to grant at least fifteen days to the shareholders for the exercise of such rights.

IV. Issuance of Shares at a Premium and at a Discount

306. Shares may be issued in a capital increase at *par value* or at a price in excess of the *par value* (i.e., at a premium). Issue of shares at a discount (i.e., at a value lower than the nominal value of the shares) is null and void.

V. Public Issue Requirements

307. CML and regulations govern public companies, initial and subsequent public offerings of companies, capital increases to be realized in public companies and also the capital market institutions which include, among others, intermediary institutions, portfolio management companies, collective investment funds, investment companies, real estate investment companies, independent audit companies, rating companies, mortgage finance institutions, real estate finance institutions. The general framework principles applicable to public offerings are identified under Articles 4–12 of the CML and Communiqué No. VIII/128.1 on shares and Communiqué no II/5.2 on capital market instruments.

308. As per the aforesaid regulations, public offerings are classified as the initial public offering of privately held companies through the sale of existing shares and/or through the sale of new shares to be issued in a capital increase. Also, subsequent offerings of public companies are subject to these regulations.

309. Offering circular or prospectus is the main document in the epicenter of a public offering and it has replaced the procedure of "registration with the Capital Markets Board" foreseen in the previous CML in line with the harmonization of Turkish Law with the EU Law. The new system introduced by the amendments of December 12, 2012 are inspired by the Directive 2003/71/EC of the European Parliament and of the Council of November 4, 2003 on the Prospectus to be published when Securities are offered to the Public or Admitted to Trading which is also referred to as the "Prospectus Directive."

310. CL and the CMB Communiqués Nos. II/5.1 and II/5.2 do not explicitly indicate the persons who may be held liable for the preparation of the Prospectus. Article 4/3 of the CL foresees that the names, titles and contact information of the individuals and legal entities responsible for the preparation of the Prospects have to be clearly indicated therein. This provision is supported by the Article 10 of the

CL which indicates that the issuers are liable for damages that may be caused by incorrect, misleading and incomplete information reflected in the Prospectus.

311. Professor Tekinalp is of the opinion that the board of directors of the company which is the "issuer" of the shares to be offered to the public is liable for the preparation of the Prospectus. The CL, however, also requires all other parties that were involved in the preparation of the Prospectus which may include, depending on the specifics of the case, the employees of the accounting and finance department of the company, the intermediary institution and its representatives.

312. Content requirements of the Prospectus are reflected in CMB Communiqué II/5.1. Shares may be issued through a public offering or a private placement without being offered to the public but only to a group or qualified investors.

313. There are three main methods for the sale of shares to the public which include sale through book-building (collection of demands), sale without book-building and sale in the stock exchange.

VI. Stock Exchange Introduction Requirements

314. The listing requirements of Borsa Istanbul (BIST) are set forth in the Regulation on the Principles of Borsa Istanbul A.Ş. Stock Exchange Activities published in the Official Gazette dated October 19, 2014 and numbered 29150 and further detailed in the Listing Directive of Borsa Istanbul A.Ş.

315. Trading on BIST Equity Market is carried out in three main sub-markets consisting of BIST Stars, BIST Main and BIST SubMarket. BIST Stars refers to the market where shares the market value of which is equal to or above TRY 300,000,000 according to the free float rate are listed, BIST Main refers to the market where shares the market value of which is between TRY 300,000,000 and TRY 75,000,000 according to the free float rate are listed. BIST SubMarket refers to the market where shares the market value of which is below TRY 75,000,000 according to the free float rate are listed.

316. BIST Stars, BIST Main and BIST SubMarket listing requirements are set forth in detail in the Listing Directive and consist of various criteria such as activity period, net profit, minimum free float market value, public offering ratio.

317. As per the Directive and the information available on BIST website as of February 2022, Applications filed for initial listing of shares must have been made for the whole amount of capital of the relevant company, and the company should meet the following:

(a) A minimum period of two calendar years must have passed since the foundation of the company. (For the purposes of this paragraph, periods of a company while it is in the status of any company other than the joint-stock company are also taken into consideration in calculation of two years. In the case of application of a new company founded as a holding company upon acquisition of a minimum 51% of capital shares of at least one company with an operating period of more than two years, the requirement of two calendar years is not asked for such holding company. Provided, however, that shareholder's equity of subsidiaries with at least two calendar years passed since the date of the foundation must not be below 50% of shareholder's equity of a new company founded as a holding company, and their total assets must not be below 50% of total assets of a new company founded as a holding company.)

(b) The company must meet all requirements of any one of the following groups:

	BIST Stars	*BIST Main*	*BIST SubMarket*
Market value of shares offered to public.	Minimum TRY 300,000,000	Minimum TRY 75,000,000	Minimum TRY 40,000,000
Net profit in annual financial statements of the past years audited by independent auditors.	Last two years	Last two years	Last two years
Minimum ratio of nominal value of shares offered to public to the capital.	-%15	12%	25%
Shareholder's Equity/Capital Ratio in the recent financial statements audited by independent auditors.	Over 1	Over 1	Over 1.25

(1) Shares bought by investors who purchase shares of corporations offered to public, corresponding to 10% or more of the capital after public offering, and shares purchased by Directors and General Managers of corporation or by those working in positions equivalent to or superior from general manager in terms of authorizations and duties or by top echelon managers directly reporting to them (in the position of Deputy General Manager or similar or equivalent positions) are not taken into consideration in calculation of the ratio of the nominal value of shares offered to public to the capital, and in calculation of market value of publicly held shares.

(2) Under subparagraph (a) of this paragraph, in the case of application of a new corporation founded as a holding company, except for a financial holding, upon acquisition of a minimum 51%

of shares of at least one corporation with an operating period of more than two years, the requirement of "Net profit in annual financial statements of the past years audited by independent auditors" as specified in the table hereinabove must have been met by the subsidiary of the said holding having the highest share in net total sales shown in the "Profit or Loss and Other Comprehensive Income Statement."

(3) For corporations reporting consolidated financial statements, shareholder's equity/capital ratio is taken into consideration separately for total equity and parent company's equity.

(c) Financial situation of the company must enable it to carry out its business operations in a sound manner.

(d) Shares of the company must not be restricted by encumbrances precluding the shareholder from using its shareholding rights, and its Articles of Association must not contain provisions restricting the transfer and circulation of shares to be traded in the Exchange.

(e) For causes other than the cases which may be accepted to be valid by the Exchange, the company must not have suspended its business activities and operations for more than three months during the last two years, and the company is not involved in any form of liquidation, composition or suspension of bankruptcy and being subjected to similar other cases determined by the Exchange.

(f) The company must not be subject to significant legal disputes affecting its production and other activities, and it must have been documented by a legal report issued by a lawyer not having any direct or indirect relationship with the company that the legal situation of the company in terms of its establishment and business operations and the legal situation of its shares are following the applicable laws and regulations.

318. In cases where the application for listing for Stars Market does not satisfy the conditions of "the annual profit in the independently audited annual financial statements" and/or the "equity capital ratio in the latest independently audited financial statements," which are stated in item (b) of the first paragraph of this article, the Board may decide to list the shares at Stars Market by specifying its reasons, while taking into account the submitted information about the company's operations, financial structure and use of Initial Public Offering funds, provided that other conditions are met in item (b) and given that:

- It has operating profit in the independently audited last year and the related interim financial statements.
- Market value of shares offered to public should be a minimum of TRY 500 million.
- The shareholders equity/capital ratio to be calculated by addition of nominal value of capital increased with premiums of shares to be acquired upon public offering to classified in shareholders equity in the last financial statements audited by independent auditors is required to be more than the ratio mentioned in the table in Article 8-b:
  - the public offering is made through only by capital increase or joint sales together with capital increase;
  - taking into consideration the information of the company presented, the Exchange may take into account the depreciation and the amortization amounts

that do not require cash outflows in the calculation of operating profit. In applications to be considered in BIST Stars within this article, if the "market value of shares offered to public requirement" as TRY 500 million is not satisfied after the initial public offering, the listing application is not applicable.

VII. Forbidden Reductions of Capital and Acquisition of Shares by the Corporation Itself

A. *Decrease of Share Capital*

319. The new TCC has made three important changes regarding decrease of capital which include the following:

(1) Report of board of directors disclosing the reason for the capital decrease, the method applied, and the conditions of assets has to be approved by the General Assembly, registered with the Trade Registry and announced in the Trade Registry Gazette.
(2) Decision of the General Assembly resolving the capital increase is announced in the Trade Registry Gazette three times with seven day intervals and the creditors of the company are informed that, for a period of three months following the last announcement, they are entitled to request payment of their receivables or provision of an appropriate guarantee by the Company to secure payment of such receivables.
(3) In case the Company realizes the capital decrease before the payment or guarantee of the receivables declared by the creditors, the creditors shall be entitled to initiate a lawsuit for the cancellation of the capital decrease within two years following the announcement of the registration of the capital decrease decision.

1. Types of Capital Decrease

320. The TCC provides for three types of capital decrease: (i) simple decrease, (ii) qualified decrease and (iii) capital decrease realized simultaneously with a capital increase (TCC 473–475).

321. Common principles for all types of capital decrease can be summarized as follows: (i) The capital cannot be decreased below the minimum capital amount determined by the TCC; (ii) capital decreases should be realized in a transparent manner and with the intention to protect the equity value of the company (iii) Nominal values of each share cannot be below TRY 1 for any purpose.

322. In case of a *simple decrease*, the shareholders are paid back the pro rata portion of capital amount that is decreased. In the event that a shareholder has not yet paid in full its previous capital commitments, the decreased portion may be set off against the payables of the shareholder and, if the payables by the company.

323. Save for certain differences for certain types of capital decrease, the following principles apply in general to all forms of capital decreases.

2. Steps of Capital Decrease

- *Report of the Board of Directors*: The Board of Directors of the Company shall prepare a report explaining the reasons for the capital decrease and the form of decrease to be utilized by the company. Board of Directors may not delegate or transfer such authority and duty to others (TCC 473). The board report shall constitute a road map for the capital decrease identifying the method to be applied for the decrease and distinguishing with reasons whether the decrease shall involve cancellation of shares or merging of shares. The Board Report is registered and announced upon its approval by the General Assembly.
- *Expert Report*: In the event that capital increase shall result in a repayment of certain capital portion to the shareholders (i.e., a qualified capital decrease), it has to be determined by a certified public accountant that the assets of the joint-stock company are sufficient to pay off the receivables of the creditors of the company.
- *Approval of the General Assembly*: The capital decrease decision has to be approved by the general assembly of company with the affirmative votes of the shareholders representing at least 75% of the share capital of the company.
- *Registration and Announcement*: The Articles of Association of the company as amended to reflect the capital decrease approved by the general assembly is registered with the relevant trade registry and announced in the Trade Registry Gazette. The registration request is filed with the relevant trade registry upon submission of the general assembly decision, the approval of the relevant governmental agency if the field of activity of the company requires supervision as per the applicable legislation, the report of the board of directors as approved by the general assembly, expert report and the copies of the Trade Registry Gazette evidencing that the creditors are called and invited to declare their receivables (as explained below) and other documents identified under Article 79 of the Trade Registry Regulation.
- *Invitation to the Creditors*: In case of a qualified decrease whereby the shareholders receive back a certain portion of their capital contributions, the creditors of the company have to be invited to declare their receivables. This invitation has to be published on the website of the companies which are subject to independent auditing and announced in the Trade Registry Gazette three times with seven day intervals. The invitation informs the creditors that they are granted a two months period starting from the date of the third announcement to declare their receivables and request payment or provision of a guarantee by the Company. The company is also required to send registered mails to the creditors whose addresses are known to the company. Receivables which are due are paid and which are not yet due are secured. In case the receivables are already secured, additional security shall not be required. For unsecured receivables, the creditor has to present justifiable reasons for security requests. In case of a dispute, the

creditor is entitled to initiate a lawsuit as per Article 475 of the TCC. It is also possible to initiate a lawsuit for the determination that the provision of security is not necessary.

324. There are two important aspects of *capital decrease realized simultaneously with a capital increase* that needs to be taken into consideration. In this type of capital decrease, the Articles of Association of the company is not amended since the capital is kept unchanged. Accordingly, the board of directors determines, through a statement, that the capital is kept unchanged through a simultaneous increase and decrease and that the entire share capital is fully paid. Such statement of the board of directors is then registered with the Trade Registry. The second aspect of this type of capital decrease is that it is possible to decrease the capital to zero and issue new shares for the increased portion of shares. As per Article 82/2 of the Trade Registry Regulation, in case the capital is increased to zero and then increased due to a restructuring, cancellation of the former shares needs to be registered with the trade registry. However, as per Article 473/5 of the TCC, the capital of a joint-stock company may never be decreased to the minimum capital amount required as per Article 332 of the TCC. However, Article 473/5 is not applicable in case of cancellation of all previous shares through decrease of capital to zero.

3. Reduction of Capital and the Principle of Equal Treatment of Shareholders

325. It is important to note that the principle of equal treatment is to be applied in all cases of capital decrease. The capital portions of all shareholders should be decreased on pro rata basis as a result of a capital decrease.

4. Reduction of Share Capital and Amendment of the Articles of Association

326. In cases where the capital of the company is changed as a result of a capital decrease, the required amendment in the Articles of Association of the company shall be governed by the related provisions of TCC applicable to amendments of Articles of Association.

B. Stock Buyback by the Joint-Stock Company

1. System of New TCC

327. TCC, to a great extent, has loosened the strict prohibition of A.Ş.'s stock buyback (i.e., acquisition of its own shares) or acceptance thereof as a pledge which was foreseen in the former TCC. Such change was made in line with the Second Directive of the EC, called the "Capital Directive."

328. The system foreseen in the current TCC may be summarized as follows.

329. Acquisition of own shares by the joint-stock company or acceptance thereof as pledge is prohibited as a rule.

330. However, there are various exceptions to this prohibition introduced in the new TCC. These exceptions are exhaustively listed and may not be broadened by interpretation.

2. Exceptions to the Prohibition of Stock Buyback

a. 10% Threshold

331. Joint-stock companies are permitted to conduct stock buybacks up to 10% of total capital without specifying reasons of acquisition, provided that the permission of the general assembly is obtained, and the board of directors is authorized for stock buybacks. In other words, the new TCC has recanted the prohibition of stock buybacks for all joint-stock companies for an amount up to 10% of the share capital of the company. Since the prohibition is repealed for acquisitions of up to 10% of share capital, the company is not required to dispose such shares and the joint-stock company may retain its shares acquired as a stock buyback up to the 10% threshold if the business strategies of the company require such approach. Repealing the prohibition for the 10% enables the company to protect the company against manipulations in its share price and improve shareholder value. The General Assembly may authorize the Board of Directors for stock buybacks up to a period of five years and by specifying the minimum and maximum share prices on which the stock buybacks may be exercised. In the event that the share price range specified by the general assembly becomes redundant after a while, the Board may ask the general assembly to renew and change the price range. The general assembly may specify formulas for the determination of the price range. For instance, it may indicate that the share price shall be the arithmetical average of the share price of the company for the last thirty days or 10% up or down. The reason for specifying a price range is to prevent manipulations. In the event that the buyback shares are to be sold to the employees, a different price range may be determined. It is possible to initiate a cancellation lawsuit against the decision of the general assembly authorizing the board of directors for stock buybacks. The new TCC, in line with the German Corporate Law, does not involve any restrictions prohibiting the use of shares acquired as a result of a stock buyback for commercial purposes.

b. Prevention of an Imminent and Significant Loss or Danger

332. In the event of an imminent and significant loss, the board of directors may acquire its shares without being authorized by the general assembly and without being subject to any limitations. One example of an imminent and significant loss is a hostile attack on the takeover of the company. The only tool or weapon provided to the joint-stock company to defend itself against a hostile takeover attack is the stock buyback. Despite all the warnings, the Capital Markets Board has refrained to adopt a regulation in line with the EU Takeover Directive. Another example of an imminent danger could occur if a majority shareholder or shareholder with certain management rights attempts to sell its shares in the company to a competitor. The important aspect of stock buybacks made under this exception is that such shares acquired by the company have to be disposed by the company. TCC does not specify a certain time period during which the shares should be disposed by the company. The company should realize such disposal within a time period that best fits its interests.

c. Mandatory Acquisitions

333. The joint-stock company may need to acquire its own shares as a result of a legal procedure. The following may be considered as exceptions under this heading:

- In cases of capital decrease, the company may acquire its own shares as per Articles 473 and 475 of the TCC.
- The company may end up acquiring its own shares as a result of a merger transaction if one of the parties to the merger is also a shareholder in the acquiring entity.
- As per Article 531 of the TCC, in case of existence of justified reasons, shareholders of a company representing at least 10% of the share capital (or 5% in public companies) are entitled to request the termination of the company before the Commercial Court of First Instance having jurisdiction. In such case, instead of ruling for termination, the court may decide for the company to purchase the shares of the shareholders at market value.
- As per Article 141, the merging companies may offer the shareholders the option to sell their shares in the acquiring entity at market value instead of becoming a shareholder thereof. If the shareholder wishes to exercise such option, the acquiring entity acquires its own shares.
- If the company is engaged in the trading of securities, the prohibition of stock buyback shall not be applicable.
- If the company ends up acquiring its shares as a result of an execution proceeding for the collection of its receivables, it will not be subject to the prohibition of stock buybacks provided that such acquired shares are fully paid up.
- The company is permitted to buy its own shares without any consideration provided that the shares are fully paid up.

3. The Use of Free Funds for the Acquisition of Shares

334. The purchase price of the shares to be acquired by the company may be paid through free funds available in the company. Additionally, net assets of the company remaining after deduction of the purchase price of the shares should at least be equal to the sum of the capital of the company and its reserves which are not permitted to be distributed as per the Articles of Association of the company and the applicable law.

4. Violation of Prohibition

335. In case of violation of the stock buyback prohibition, the transfer transaction shall be deemed null and void. The company is required to dispose such shares within six months following acquisition. Shares which are not disposed of until such date should be eliminated through a capital decrease.

336. If the company grants loans, advances or guarantees to a third party for the purpose of acquiring its own shares, such transaction shall also be deemed null and void.

5. Subsidiary Purchasing Parent Shares

337. The former TCC was silent on whether purchases by a subsidiary of its parent company shares be deemed within the scope of stock buyback prohibition. There were conflicting opinions on this matter in the doctrine and some companies tried to utilize such method to circumvent the prohibition. The new TCC corrected this problem and made it clear that the prohibition of stock buyback shall also be applicable to purchases by the subsidiary of its parent company shares and such purchases shall be subject to the same rules indicated above.

6. Suspension of Rights

338. As per Article 389 of the TCC, shares acquired back by the company and parent company shares acquired by the subsidiary shall not be taken into consideration in the calculation of general assembly quorums of the (parent) company. Except for the gratis shares, such shares acquired by the company shall not grant any shareholding rights and voting rights pertaining to the parent company's shares acquired by the subsidiary and the rights thereto will be suspended.

VIII. Classes of Shares

339. As stated previously, capital of a joint-stock company is divided into shares. Under Turkish law, the word "share" has various meanings. *Primarily*, it means a proportion of the share capital. *Second* it signifies one unit of the membership rights of the shareholders. As a rule, shareholders rights are vested equally on each share. A shareholder enjoys these rights according to the number of his/her shares in the share capital of the company.

340. As per Article 476/1 of the TCC, nominal value of one share shall not be less than TRKrş 1. The nominal value of one share may be increased in multiples of TRKrş 1. Shares issued in violation of this requirement shall be null and void, provided, however, that the rights of the holder of such shares to claim reimbursement of the amounts paid for such invalid shares are reserved and the issuers of these shares shall be jointly and severally liable against the holder for reimbursement.

341. As per Article 476/3 of the TCC, joint-stock companies which are in financial turmoil are permitted to decrease their nominal share value to TRKrş 1 if the nominal value is higher than such amount.

342. Another exception is provided under Article 12/2 of the CML. As per the aforesaid article, the Capital Markets Board is entitled to authorize the company to issue shares for an amount lesser than the nominal value in the event that the market price and book price of the shares is less than the nominal value. The rules and procedures to apply to such issue of shares are determined by the Capital Markets Board.

343. Like many other legal systems, under Turkish legal system, it is not possible to issue shares with fractional value or with no nominal value or denote the nominal value in a foreign currency. Although it is possible to issue shares with different nominal values, it is not possible to create privileges by assigning equal voting rights to such shares with different nominal values.

A. Bearer Shares-Registered (Nominative) Shares

344. Shares may be issued either as registered shares or bearer shares (TCC 484.1). Registered shares differ from bearer shares in terms of transfer restrictions and the registration of the holder of the share in the share certificate and company books.

345. The Articles of Association may provide that the share capital shall be divided into shares of both types and fix the proportion between them. If not specified, shares shall be deemed to be registered shares.

346. A share certificate is deemed to be a bearer certificate if it is understood based on the content or form of the certificate that the holder of certificate is entitled to exercise any and all rights arising therefrom.

347. Bearer share certificates shall be issued only after their full nominal value has been paid. Bearer share certificates issued before they are fully paid up are void. However, indemnification rights of persons acting in good faith which have suffered damages due to such invalid issuance of shares are reserved (TCC 484.2).

348. Bearer shares may be transferred by delivery of the possession of share certificate to the new holder.

349. The provisions of the TCC pertaining to the bearer negotiable instruments (Articles 658–667) are also applicable to bearer share certificates.

350. Unless the Articles of Association provide otherwise, a registered share may be converted into a bearer share or *vice versa*. This conversion requires the amendment of the Articles of Association. Under the provisions of the TCC, any resolution of the General Meeting relating to the conversion of the shares which violates the Articles of Association or the principles of good faith may be contested by shareholders or by the Board.

1. Share Ledger (Share Book)

351. A joint-stock company is required to maintain a share ledger. Although not related to accounting, share ledger is considered to be a commercial book. Therefore, share ledger shall be subject to all disciplinary rules that apply to commercial books, including those requirements that apply to the opening and closing thereof.

352. Share ledger must reflect names, titles and addresses of the holders of the registered shares, holders of the shares for which certificates are not yet issued (even if they are in the form of bearer shares) and usufruct right holders.

353. In cases where it may not be detected by the company that a share transfer is not effectuated in compliance with applicable law or a usufruct right is not duly established, such share transfer or usufruct right may not be registered in the share ledger of the company. As per, Article 499/4 of the TCC, only those that are registered in the share ledger shall be deemed as the shareholders of the company and holders of usufruct rights.

354. Shares of publicly traded companies are dematerialized and electronically registered with the Central Registration Agency which is a private legal entity established in the form of a joint stock in the form as per the provisions of Articles 3 and 13 of the CML.

2. Form of the Share Certificate

355. The TCC, via Article 486, regulates the printing and issuance of share certificates by the company. In accordance with this article, if the shares are bearer, the board of directors is required to issue and deliver share certificates to the shareholders within three months following the payment of the nominal value of the shares. Board of directors' decision to issue and deliver bearer share certificates is registered with the relevant Trade Registry and announced in the Trade Registry Gazette and also on the company's website. Upon the request of the minority shareholders, the board of directors is required to issue and deliver registered share certificates to all holders of the registered shares.

356. TCC regulates the rules applicable to the form of a share certificate in detail. According to Article 487 of the TCC, a share certificate must include the trade name, current capital amount, date of incorporation and the then registered capital amount of the Company, issuance number of the share and registration date thereof, type and nominal value of the shares, and information on how many shares are being represented by the share certificate. The share certificate must be signed by at least two authorized signatories of the Company.

357. In addition to the details above, registered share certificates must also include the name, surname or title and registered address of the holder together with details pertaining to the paid and unpaid portion of the shares being represented by the share certificate.

B. Privileged Shares (Preferred Stock)

358. The objective of the Commission preparing the TCC was to align the concept of the Privileged Shares with contemporary approaches on such matters in the European legal systems. The regime in the former TCC pertaining to the privileged shares was quite broad and did not include any limitations. The new TCC defined the term "*privileged shares*" and introduced certain limitations in relation thereto.

359. The main aspects of the "*privileged share*" system foreseen in the TCC may be outlined as follows.

360. Article 478 of the TCC defines the term "privilege" as granting to a share (group/class) a (i) superior right in terms of shareholding rights "*such as*" dividend rights, voting rights, preemptive rights or (ii) new shareholding right that is not already provided in the law. The expression "such as" gives the company the opportunity to create a wide variety of privileges which may involve preemptive rights to debentures, convertible bonds or other securities that may be issued by the company.[85]

361. Privileges may only be introduced and provided for in the Articles of Association of the company. Privileges on the shares may not be created through a board decision or the decision of the general assembly or as a result of a widespread and ongoing practice adopted by the company towards a shareholder.

---

85. Jud [11th C.Cham. Sup. Court] No. 4383/356 [Jan. 25, 1972] in: BCLR, Vol. VI, 1973, 620/21; jud [11th C.Cham. Sup. Court] No. 4286/4769, [Oct. 16, 1979], in: I. Doğanay, *Türk Ticaret Kanunu Şerhi,* 2. Bası, C. 1 ve 2 [Commentary on the Turkish Commercial Code; Vols. 1 and 2, Ankara 1981], [*see* SB], 940.

362. Privileges are attached and may be granted to the shares through the creation of a privileged share group or share class. Article 360 of the TCC provides an exception to this rule which, in addition to granting the privilege to a share group, enables granting of privileged rights to a group of shareholders and minority for representation in the board of directors.

363. In joint-stock companies, more than 50% of share capital which is held by the State, governmental entities or institutions, municipalities, unions, foundations, cooperatives ("*Special Entities*") or in the subsidiaries of such joint-stock companies in which the aforesaid institutions hold majority of the shares, privileges may only be established on shares held by the Special Entities and not the shares held by other shareholders. However, this limitation does not apply to public companies, credit and financial institutions.

364. Privileges on voting rights are subject to the limitations defined under Article 479 of the TCC. Accordingly; (i) voting privileges may be established through granting different number of voting rights to shares with the same nominal value, (ii) number of voting rights granted to one share may not exceed fifteen unless allowed by a court decision having jurisdiction if granting of a higher number of voting rights is necessary to achieve a higher standard of corporate governance or required based on a justified reason, and (iii) voting privileges may not be exercised in case of voting of shareholders in the general assembly for the amendment of the Articles of Association and release of board members or other representatives and initiation of liability lawsuits against such persons.

365. The TCC contains special provisions to protect share privileges granted in the Articles of Association of the company. As per Article 454 of the TCC, if the rights of privileged shareholders are affected, decisions of the general assembly concerning the amendment of the Articles of Association, granting the board of directors the right to increase the capital, and the decision of the board of directors to increase the capital based on such authority may not be enforced unless approved by another resolution passed at a special meeting held by the privileged shareholders in question.[86] This special meeting of the privileged shareholders may be convened by the attendance of shareholders in such group representing at least 60% of their total share capital and decisions are passed by the affirmative votes of the majority shares represented in such duly convened meeting.

366. The CML foresees certain additional rules in relation to privileged shares which may be summarized as follows.

367. Creation of any type of privileges on shares or changing the scope of an existing privilege is classified as a "significant transaction" as per Article 23 of the

86. Jud [11th C.Cham. Sup. Court] No. 2102/3083, [Jun. 11, 1979], in: BCLR Vol. X, 1979, 1037; jud [11th C.Cham. Sup. Court] No. 5838/6158, [Dec. 10, 1984], in: G. Eriş, 1st ed., *Türk Ticaret Kanunu Şerhi*, Cilt I: Ticari İşletme ve Ticaret Şirketleri, 1. Bası, [Commentary on the Turkish Commercial Code; Vol. I: Commercial.

CML which enables the shareholders that have participated in the general assembly approving such significant action but objected in the voting thereof to sell their shares back to the company and exit.

368. In the initial public offering of a joint-stock company, all privileges existing on the shares should be explained and disclosed to public in a clear and transparent manner. Disclosing the provision of the Articles of Association pertaining to the privileged shares may not be deemed, just by itself, as a full and transparent disclosure of the privileges.

C. Deferred Shares

369. Turkish system does not regulate "deferred shares" as a different share type.

D. Non-voting Shares

370. As per the system adopted by the TCC, each shareholder shall have at least one voting right even if it holds only one share (Article 434/2 of TCC). In other words, TCC foresees that each shareholder shall have at least one voting right rather than each share having one voting right. This principle regulated in TCC enables the limitation of voting rights granted to a shareholder (i.e., limitation of voting rights on shareholder basis).

371. Professor Tekinalp is of the opinion that it is not possible under Turkish Law to classify shares as shares with voting rights and no voting rights since the TCC does not regulate shares with no voting rights. Article 14/A of the former CML included a framework provision which enabled for issuance of capital market instruments and granted the authority to the Capital Markets Board to determine the rules and principles to apply thereto. Based on such authority, Capital Markets Board issued the Communiqué No:1/36 which has been annulled upon issuance of the new CML and the CMB Communiqué on Shares (No: VII-128.1). The new CML does not authorize the Capital Markets Board to determine the rules to apply for the issuance of shares with no voting rights. The aforesaid Article of the TCC which enables the limitation of voting rights of a shareholder may not be interpreted, as voting rights may be limited by the issuance of shares with no voting rights. Shares with no voting rights are issued *ex lege* with no voting rights. However, Article 434/2 of the TCC provides for a temporary freezing of voting rights attached to shares which are issued, in the first place, with voting rights.

E. Multiple Voting Rights

372. Article 478 of the TCC enables the creation of multiple voting rights as a form of a privileged share group. In other words, privileged voting rights may be created by granting different voting rights to the shares with same nominal value and must be foreseen in the initial Articles of Association of the company or adopted in the form of an amendment to the articles.

373. In contrast to the previous TCC, the new TCC provides for definite limitations in relation to multiple voting rights. Article 475 of the TCC clearly indicates that the maximum number of votes that may be granted to a share is fifteen. In the event that this limitation is exceeded, the relevant provision of the Articles of Association shall be partially invalid and only the amount exceeding the maximum limitation shall be void. However, the maximum limitation on the multiple voting rights shall not apply if there are justified reasons or if such application is required for the improvement of corporate governance. The company that wishes to benefit from such an exception has to apply to the first instance commercial court having jurisdiction in the location of the headquarters of the company and prove the existence of justified reasons.

374. As per Article 479 (3) of the TCC, multiple voting rights may not be exercised for matters that concern an amendment in the Articles of Association of the company, release of the board members or initiation of a liability lawsuit against the board members by the company.

F. Shares Issued for Cash and Non-Cash Contributions

375. "Shares issued for cash" are the shares issued as a result of a cash contribution or cash subscription. In other words, shares issued for cash are shares nominal value which may only be paid by cash. TCC Article 346 uses the term "shares for cash" and provides that the shares which may be offered to public may only be shares issued for cash. Specific laws may require certain types of companies to have only shares issued for cash. For instance, as per the Banking Law, banks are required to have only shares issued for cash and CML requires the investment partnerships and stock exchange companies to have only shares for cash.

376. Shares issued for capital in-kind contributions are referred to as "shares for non-cash contributions" (Articles 128, 342, 343, 459/2, 460/2 of the TCC). The former TCC had included a transfer restriction of two years for shares issued for capital in-kind contributions. The new TCC does not provide for such a transfer restriction and hence the shares issued for non-cash contributions may be transferred without being subject to a waiting period.

G. Shares With and Without a Nominal Value

377. As per the system adopted by the TCC, shares may not be issued without a nominal value. However, Articles 50/2 and 51 of the CML provide that shares of investment funds with variable capital do not have a nominal value.

378. Additionally, Article 347 of the TCC provides that shares may not be issued for a price that is lower than nominal value. Article 476 provides that shares of a joint-stock company should have a nominal value of at least TRY 0.1 and such amount may be increased in multiples of TRY 0.1. In case the company faces financial difficulties and the per share nominal value is higher than TRY 0.1, then such amount may be decreased down to TRY 0.1.

379. Upon the approval of the Capital Markets Board, companies traded in the stock exchange may issue shares lower than their nominal value in case the nominal value of shares is lower than the market or book value thereof. The rules applicable for such issuance are determined in the Communiqué of the CMB No: II/128.1. Professor Tekinalp is of the opinion that the aforesaid regulation permitting issuance of shares with a value lower than its nominal value is against the principle of protecting and preserving the capital of the joint-stock company which is maintained in the TCC.

380. However, in case it is foreseen in the Articles of Association or approved by the General Assembly, shares may be issued at a premium, i.e., at a price higher than its nominal value ("*Premium Shares*"). The premium amount is then added to the legal reserves in the accounts of the company. For public companies, CMB is entitled to require the public company to issue shares with premium in case the nominal value of the shares is higher than the market or book value thereof.

IX. Transfer of Shares

A. *Registration*

1. Where Share Certificates Are Issued

381. Bearer share certificates may be transferred by delivery of possession of the share certificate to the acquirer (TCC 489). Notification requirement to the Central Registration Agency was newly introduced by an amendment to the TCC which entered into force on April 1, 2021. In case of failure to notify the Central Registration Agency of the share transfer, the acquirer of the bearer share may not use the shareholding rights arising from such shares. The date of notification to the Central Registration Agency shall be dated as of when the shareholding rights may be exercised against the company and third parties. The details concerning the registration of the bearer shares with the Central Registration Agency are determined under the Communiqué dated April 6, 2021. Share certificates may be issued for bearer shares provided that they are fully paid up by their holders. As per the aforesaid Communiqué, the information pertaining to whom the issued shares will be delivered has to be reported to the Central Registration Agency.

382. Registered shares may be legally transferred by delivery of the duly endorsed share certificate to the acquirer. The transferee does not acquire the status of a shareholder upon receipt of duly endorsed share certificate but only when he/she/it is registered as the holder of the shares in the share ledger.

2. Where a Share Certificate is Not Issued

383. If certificates are not yet issued for the shares ("*Naked Shares*"), regardless of the type of the share (bearer or registered), the share transfer may only be deemed valid upon execution of a written transfer agreement (TCO 183) and registration of the share transfer in the share ledger of the company.

3. Registered Shares/Share Certificates

384. Registered shares may be transferred without restriction unless otherwise provided by law or Articles of Association (TCC 490.1). Registered shares which are not fully paid up may only be transferred with the consent of the company, unless they are inherited, acquired as per marital property law, or through execution and enforcement proceedings (TCC 491.1). Company may reject the share transfer only if the financial capacity of the acquirer is doubtful and the guarantee requested by the Company to secure the payment of the shares is not provided (TCC 491.2).

385. The acquirer of a registered share/share certificate which is not fully paid up is liable to the company for payment upon the registry of the share transfer in the share ledger of the company (TCC 501.1). The transferor of unpaid shares (previous owner) may be held liable towards the company for the unpaid portion if the company is declared bankrupt within two years from such transfer or the transferee of the shares (new owner) is deprived of exercising shareholder rights pertaining to the shares. Except for the cases mentioned in the previous sentence, the transferor of the shares shall be relieved of his/her/its obligations pertaining to the unpaid portion upon registry of the transferee in the share ledger of the company (TCC 501.3).

386. Share certificates may be issued for registered shares which are not fully paid up.

4. Transfer Restrictions on Registered Shares

387. As indicated above, unless otherwise determined in the Articles of Association of the company or law, registered shares may be freely transferred. In the system introduced by the new TCC, transfer of registered shares may be restricted but may not be prohibited in general. This is one of the important improvements introduced by the new TCC. Shares which are subject to transfer restrictions are referred to as "*Restricted Shares*" within the meaning of the Latin term "*vinculum iuris.*"

388. There may be two types of transfer restrictions: (i) restrictions arising out of applicable law; (ii) restrictions arising out of Articles of Association (voluntary transfer restrictions).

389. Transfer restrictions arising out of applicable Law.

390. Transfer restrictions arising out of applicable law include (1) restrictions applicable to the transfer of unpaid shares and (2) transfer restrictions which may be applied in case the transferor is not deemed as financially reliable by the company or the reputation of the transferor is not satisfactory.

391. As indicated above, registered shares which are not fully paid up may only be transferred upon the approval of the company. The exception to this rule is acquisitions resulting from inheritance law, marital law and execution and enforcement proceedings. The approval of the company is not sought for these types of acquisitions even if the shares are fully paid up.

392. In the event that the company does not deem the transferor of the shares as financially reliable or its reputation sufficient, regardless of whether the shares are fully paid up or not, the company is entitled to ask for a guarantee/security to be provided by the transferor as a condition for approval of the share transfer.

5. Transfer Restrictions Arising Out of Articles of Association (Voluntary Transfer Restrictions)

393. The Articles of Association of a joint-stock company may foresee transfer restrictions and require the approval of the board of directors for a share transfer to be recorded in the share ledger of the company. In the absence of such a provision, the board of directors may not refrain from registering the share transfer in the share ledger of the company, and if it refrains to register, registration of the share transfer may be requested from the court. The same rules also apply to establishing usufruct rights on the shares. Accordingly, if foreseen in the Articles of Association of the company, approval of the board of directors shall be required for registration of usufruct rights in the share book of the company since, by law, voting rights arising out of shares shall belong to the usufruct right holder.

394. The requirement for approval of the company that may be foreseen in the Articles of Association shall be in effect only until the liquidation of the company. Transfer restrictions shall be automatically lifted once the company initiates liquidation proceedings.

395. The new TCC has introduced certain limitations for the transfer restrictions that may be indicated in the Articles of Association in order to prevent the board of directors to exercise its approval right in a partial or subjective manner. Limitations introduced by the TCC may be categorized as (1) limitations to apply to quoted shares (shares that are quoted and traded in a stock exchange) and (2) limitations to apply to unquoted shares (shares that are not quoted and traded in a stock exchange).

396. In case of registered shares which are not quoted in a stock exchange, the board of directors may refuse to approve a share transfer only upon specifying a significant reason for rejection or by proposing the transferred shares to be acquired by the company or one of the shareholders based on the real (market) value applicable at the time of application to the company for the approval of the share transfer (TCC 493.1).

397. The significant reason that may be specified by the board of directors should be an objective reason related to the preservation of the shareholder environment indicated in the Articles of Association or the financial independence of the company or its field of activity.

398. In relation to the preservation of the shareholder environment several examples may be considered. For instance, Articles of Association may include a provision indicating that shares may only be transferred to (i) the descendants of the shareholders in order to maintain the family company status of the company (e.g., shares may only be transferred to the descendants of Mr. Bern Smith and Mrs. Rachel Smith) or (ii) those reside in a particular region (e.g., shares may only be transferred to pottery producers in Avanos region or shares may only be transferred to Sauvignon Blanc producers in France) or (iii) those that engage in certain type of activities (e.g., shares may only be transferred to milk producers having a certain production capacity). Provisions requiring shares to be transferred only to those from a specific ethnic group, religion, sect or political party are not tolerated under Turkish legal system.

399. Objection reasons of rejection that relate to the field of activity of the company may include transfer restrictions that require transfers to be made to those that are active in the same field of activity as the company (e.g., an architecture company may require its shares to be transferred only to licensed architects or an investment bank may require its shares to be transferred to only licensed banks and financial institutions.

400. In order to maintain the financial independence of the company, the Articles of Association may prohibit transfers which may result in the company's becoming a member of a certain Company Group. Certain opinions in the doctrine support that such rejection reason may be used by the board of directors even if not specified in the Articles of Association.

401. In the event that the important reason indicated in the Articles of Association does not justify the rejection of a particular share transfer, the board of directors may still reject the transfer proposing to purchase the shares on their real (market) value. Such proposal may be foreseen as an escape clause in the Articles of Association of the company or may be used by the board of directors even if not specified in the Articles of Association.

402. In addition, the company may refuse to approve the transfer if the transferee does not explicitly declare that he/she/it has acquired the shares in his/her/its account and on his/her/its behalf (TCC 493.3).

403. In the case of registered shares that are quoted on a stock exchange, the company may (in its articles) specify a particular shareholding percentage ratio which may not be exceeded as a result of acquisitions made off the stock exchange. Accordingly, the board of directors may reject registration in case such shareholding percentage threshold is exceeded (TCC 495.1). In addition, the company may refuse to approve the transfer if the transferee does not explicitly declare he/she/it has acquired the shares in his/her/its account and on in his/her/its behalf (TCC 495.2). In case quoted registered shares are acquired as a result of application of inheritance law, marital law or through enforcement and execution proceedings, the company is not entitled to reject the registration of the acquirer of shares in the share ledger of the company.

404. The TCC also sets out detailed rules governing how the rights associated with quoted registered shares pass from the transferor to the transferee (TCC 497). In the event that registered shares quoted in the stock exchange are acquired as a result of purchases made on the stock exchange, rights associated with the acquired shares shall pass to the transferee immediately upon acquisition. If the quoted registered shares are acquired outside the stock exchange, shareholding rights pass to the transferee upon application to the board of directors for the approval of the share transfer. As per Article 497/3 of the TCC, the new shareholder shall not be entitled to participate in the general assembly and exercise voting rights or rights associated with voting until the transfer is approved by the company, however, all other shareholding rights, including preemptive rights may be exercised immediately upon passage of the ownership status to the transferee. Transferees which are not yet approved by the Board of Directors shall be registered in the share ledger as the owner of shares with no voting rights.

B. Gift Sale

405. Turkish Law does not regulate gift sales as a special type of share transfer. On the one hand, any gift sale shall be subject to the same terms and procedures outlined above for any transfer of shares. On the other hand, gift sales may be subject to different taxation as opposed to regular share transfers.

C. Stock Exchange

406. Shares that are traded on the stock exchange are held in electronic form by the Central Registration Agency.

407. Commonly, bearer shares are traded on the BIST. However, registered shares may also be traded on the stock exchange only if the company's board of directors authorized transfer through blank endorsement which equals the transfer terms and conditions to bearer shares.

408. Principles set forth above for the transfer of bearer shares as outlined in the TCC shall also apply for the transfer of shares that are traded on the stock exchange.

D. Protection of Shareholders in Case of Tender Offer

409. Communiqué No. II-26.1 of the Capital Markets of Turkey (CMB) sets forth the rules that apply in case of tender offers (takeover bids) for public companies. Communiqué No. II-26.1 applies for both mandatory and voluntary tender offers. The Communiqué was subject to important changes on October 16, 2021 which were mainly related to mandatory tender offers and the exemptions applicable to the mandatory tender offer.

410. As per the above-referred Communiqué, in order to protect the rights of all shareholders, a tender offer is required to be made if a person or persons acting in concert acquire the control of a public company. All shares included in the same group representing the capital of the target corporation are subject to equal treatment.

411. Also, the said Communiqué details the requirements of the information memorandum that has to be approved by CMB before the launching of the tender offer. As per the latest changes on the Communiqué, investment firms are also counted as the persons that are required to sign the information form and, thus, may be held liable for the information provided along with the offerors and the signatories of the investment firms.

412. Shareholders are also protected through provisions of the Communiqué relating to the mandatory offer price. The Communiqué enables CMB to shield the mandatory tender price from extraordinary developments affecting the Turkish economy or the relevant industry or the transactions entered into during the periods used as a basis to calculate the daily adjusted average prices applicable to the tender offer price.

413. In addition to tender offers, shareholders of a company are protected in case of a squeeze out and sellout. For public companies, Communiqué No. II-27.1 of the CMB on rights of squeeze out and sellout shall be applicable. The said Communiqué foresees that the controlling shareholder becomes entitled to squeeze out all of the shareholders of a public company if it achieves (alone or together with the ones acting in concert) to hold at least 95% of the voting rights in a public company. Such right may be exercised within three months starting from the date it reaches 95%.

414. Similarly, the remaining shareholders shall have the right of selling their shares out to the controlling shareholder within the three months period starting from the date the right if squeeze-out arises. Controlling shareholder deposits the total sum required for the squeeze out of or sellout of other shareholders in the company.

415. According to the said Communiqué, the share price is paid fully in cash and in Turkish Lira during a sell-out or squeeze-out process and is determined as per the provisions of Article 7 thereof.

416. The new TCC also includes provisions applicable to private companies like the squeeze-out and sell-out rights foreseen by the CMB for public companies. The squeeze-out right is available only to the parent company in a corporation group consisting of at least three capital companies. If the parent company is the owner of at least 90% of the share capital and voting rights of a subsidiary, it is entitled to acquire the shares of the minority if the minority is preventing the company to operate smoothly or acting in bad faith or creating significant problems or acting in a reckless manner. The share price applicable shall be determined as per Article 202 of the TCC either based on the price available on the stock exchange or the price determined by the court based on the real value of the company shares or such other method.

417. Again, the TCC provides the right to the minority shareholders to sell their shares to the parent company of a corporation group in case the parent company exercises its right of control in violation of the applicable law. The parent company is not entitled to exercise its control over the subsidiaries in a manner to cause losses on the subsidiary without reimbursing such loss within the same financial year or informing the subsidiary of the date when such reimbursement may be realized. If the parent company acts in violation of such obligation, the shareholders of the subsidiary companies may apply to the court and request the court to rule for the reimbursement of the subsidiary for such loss. Upon such application, the court may rule for reimbursement or the acquisition of shares of the applicant shareholder by the parent company or such other solution as it deems fit. The shareholders of the subsidiary are also granted the right to leave the company if the control of the parent company is exercised in a manner to result in a merger, spin-off or conversion of the subsidiary or issuance of securities of the subsidiary or an amendment of the Articles of Association of the subsidiary which is not based on a rational or justified reason. Only the shareholders that casted their negative vote in the general assembly pertaining to such event may request from the parent company purchase of its shares based on stock exchange value (if available) or real value.

E. Insider Trading

418. The main legal framework concerning insider trading is set forth in CML, Communiqué No. V-2.102.1 and Communiqué No. V-2.102.1 of the Capital Markets Board. Insider trading is defined under Article 106 of the CML as a capital markets crime that is punishable with imprisonment from three years up to five years or with a judicial fine. However, if a judicial fine has been imposed due to this crime, the fine to be imposed shall not be less than twice the benefit obtained.

419. Insider trading may be committed by:

- Managers of issuers or those of their subsidiaries or their controlling corporations
- Persons who possess this information by holding a share in issuers' or in their subsidiaries or their controlling corporation
- Persons who possess this information as a result of performance of their jobs, professions and tasks
- Persons who obtained this information by committing crimes
- Persons who know that the information they possess is of the nature that could constitute insider information.

420. Insider trading shall occur if and when any one of the above-referred persons places a purchase or sale orders for capital market instruments or change the orders they have placed or cancel them and thus provide a benefit for themselves or someone else based on information directly or indirectly concerning capital market instruments or issuers which can affect the prices of related capital market instruments, their values or the decisions of investors and which have not yet been declared to the public.

421. As per Article 108 of the CML, the following cases shall not be considered as insider trading:

- Implementation of money, foreign exchange rate, public debt management policies or conduct of transactions with the purpose of stability by the Central Bank of Turkey or another authorized official institution or persons acting on their behalf.
- Repurchase programs implemented according to the Board regulations, share acquisition programs directed to employees or allocation of other shares direct to the employees of the issuer or its subsidiaries.
- Purchasing and selling capital market instruments or placing or canceling orders exclusively for the purpose of supporting the market price of these instruments for a pre-determined period, provided that these operations are performed in conformity with the regulations of the Board regarding price stabilizing transactions and market makers.

F. Debentures and Other Securities Issued by Joint-Stock Companies[87]

422. Unless otherwise stipulated by any legislation, all kinds of bonds, financial bills, asset-backed commercial papers, including the ones arranged on the basis of discount, other debt instruments, bonds having the right to purchase and exchange and all kinds of securities can only be issued by the decision of general assembly. Decision of the general assembly should include all necessary provisions and conditions regarding the security to be issued. Decision of the general assembly is executed by the board of directors. Securities can be issued in registered or bearer form and with nominal value. Nominal value is determined by the general assembly and, if authorized, by the board of directors. Prices of debt instruments should be indicated in cash and paid fully on delivery.

423. Unless otherwise regulated by law, the general assembly may authorize the board of directors to issue securities and to determine the terms and conditions thereof for a period maximum of fifteen months.

424. Total amount of debt instruments cannot exceed the sum of capital and statutory reserves. Revolution funds allowed by law to be added to the balance sheet are included in the sum.

425. The legislation of CMB is reserved for public companies.

§5. The Shareholders, Management and Control of the A.Ş.

I. Shareholder Control Mechanisms

426. A number of changes were made in TCC that take into account developments witnessed in the individual rights granted to every shareholder in recent years in the laws of countries such as Germany, France, Switzerland, and Italy but especially in U.S. and EU doctrine. These changes are intended to accomplish a variety of things like strengthening these rights, making it possible for shareholders to achieve the objectives called for and desired by the law when such rights are exercised, facilitating the exercise of these rights, and eliminating the conditions that prevent them from being exercised. One innovation introduced by TCC is its designation of the rights of participating in general meetings, obtaining information, inspection, and initiating nullification lawsuits as being "indefeasible" rights which may not be revoked. When the law's provisions governing dividend rights are examined, we see that these rights have been strengthened by the explicit adoption of the "true and fair view" principle (TCC 515) and by rules which limit such rights, prescribing strict requirements for setting aside reserve funds and specifically disallowing hidden reserves.

87. *See* generally Z. Aytaç, *Sermaye Piyasası Hukuku ve Hisse Senetleri* [Capital Market Law and Share Certificates], Ankara 1988; K. Ünal, *Menkul Kıymetler* [Securities], Ankara 1988.

427. Another individual right that has undergone a radical change is the voting right. First, the right to vote is dependent not on subscribing for shares in a joint-stock company but rather on the payment of the portion of the nominal value required in the company articles and the Articles of Association. What this means is that the owner of shares may not exercise the voting rights attached to the shares until and unless the minimum amount required by law and the Articles of Association of the company is paid (TCC 435). The amount which must be paid does not include any "premiums." This rule was introduced to prevent cash capital subscriptions from being paid for with negotiable instruments like checks and promissory notes. Another benefit of this rule is that by including a provision in its articles, a company may ensure that shares are paid for in amounts that are greater than the minimum amount and that it will be able to meet its cash needs from its own resources.

428. However, the truly radical change in voting rights is the TCC rule that allows shareholders to exercise their voting rights at the general meeting on the basis of the total value of the shares that they own. This rule not only ensures that voting rights are exercised on the basis of the nominal value of shares, but it also links voting rights directly to both the "share" and the "shareholder." The fact that voting rights are linked to the shareholder is made even more explicit in TCC Article 434(2): "Each shareholder has the right to at least one vote even if all they own is one share. The articles may however limit the number of votes to which those who own more than one share may be entitled." This TCC provision makes it possible for company articles to set limits on the number of votes that a shareholder may cast. TCC also changes the old TCC rule of "No shares without votes" to that of "No shareholders without votes." Furthermore, TCC allows preferential voting rights and, on the other side, makes it possible to limit shareholders voting rights and thus to keep major shareholders control over a company within specific limits.

429. Other innovations of TCC related to the shareholders rights shall be explained in the related sections below.

430. The rights of shareholders are categorized as (1) pecuniary (economic) rights; (2) membership and participation rights; and (3) protective rights. A distinguishing feature of the TCC is the concept of "vested interests," which are those shareholders rights which may not be taken away from the shareholder, may not be limited and may not be undermined by the resolutions of the General Meeting or the Board of Directors (TCC 452). Some of these rights are those of attendance at the General Meeting, voting, the right to dividends, the right of participation in the liquidation dividend, and the challenging of the resolutions of the General Meeting. Some of the vested rights are indefeasible; they may not be revoked or may not be limited or undermined even with the consent of the relevant shareholder. For example, the challenge of the resolutions of the General Meeting and the right of attendance at the General Meeting are indefeasible. Other rights may be limited in accordance with the law and are, therefore, called "weaker vested interests.'" These include the right to a dividend and the right to participation in the proceeds of liquidation.[88]

A. *Shareholders Meeting (General Assembly)*

1. Innovations of New TCC

431. There are various innovations introduced by the TCC pertaining to general assemblies. The new TCC: (i) sets forth, in a compact manner, the authorities and duties which are not delegable under a specific article (TCC Article 408); (ii) introduces a requirement that general assembly announcements, agendas, invitations, and related documentation be published on the company website as well as in other prescribed ways (TCC Articles 414 and 1524 (1/f)); (iii) entitles even one shareholder to call for a general assembly in situations where the company board is unable to convene (TCC Article 410(2)); (iv) sets clear and explicit rules governing the power of minority shareholders to call for a general assembly meeting (TCC Article 311(4)); recognizes the right to initiate actions of nullity against general assembly resolutions (TCC Article 447).

432. In addition to these innovations, the representation of shareholders at general assembly meetings has been shifted in the new TCC from an agency approach to a proxy system. TCC also introduces rules governing proxies of deposited shares (TCC 429).

433. The new law expands and strengthens TCC 1956's rules concerning shareholders rights of information and inspection in joint-stock companies, thereby bringing them in line with the philosophy of corporate governance (NTCC Article 437). Furthermore, if this right is violated, legal remedies are provided. The right to obtain information has been arranged in order to operate as an effective mechanism and informative content has been provided for the voting process.

434. New rules pertaining to the right to initiate special audits are introduced to make this mechanism more operable and effective.

435. The parties authorized to call for a general meeting are redefined. The auditor has no authority to call the general assembly to a meeting. Furthermore, the minority's authorization to call a meeting is determined according to specific conditions. Additionally, the competent court has been appointed in the law for the minority shareholders to apply in case their request to call a general assembly meeting should not receive a response within a specific time period.

---

88. These are discussed in more detail later: *see* paras. 331 et seq. and *see* generally Poroy/Tekinalp/Çamoğlu, [Textbook] [*see* SB], paras. 866 et seq.

436. The new TCC also introduces a requirement for the board of directors to prepare an internal directive setting forth the rules and principles of operation of the general assembly meetings and apply such directive after obtaining the approval of the general assembly. The internal directive approved by the general assembly is also registered with the Trade Registry and announced in the Trade Registry Gazette.

2. Types of General Assembly Meetings

a. General Assembly Meeting by Participation of All Shareholders

437. A general assembly meeting where all the shareholders of the joint-stock company are represented either in person or through proxy may be called a Universal General Meeting. In the event of presence of shareholders, in person or through proxy, representing the entire share capital of the company and with the approval of all such shareholders and/or their proxies, a general assembly meeting may be convened without being subject to the formalities that apply for calling for a general assembly meeting (TCC 416). Provided that the quorum of all shareholders is kept throughout the general assembly meeting, the shareholders may adopt and pass resolutions on any matter that falls within the scope of authority of the General Assembly as defined under the TCC.

b. Ordinary (Annual) General Assembly Meeting

438. The Ordinary General Assembly (OGA) meeting of a joint-stock company must be held at least once a year within three months following the end of the financial year. The matters indicated in the agenda, in accordance with Article 413, are discussed and resolutions passed accordingly. The agenda of an OGA must contain at least the following matters:

- discussion of the annual report of the Board of Directors;
- approval, amendment or rejection of the financial statements of the Company, profit and loss accounts and of proposals concerning the distribution of profit;
- release of the board of directors;
- determination of fees and allocations of the directors; and
- election, re-election or replacement of directors and, if applicable, the independent auditor.

c. Extraordinary General Meeting

439. Any general assembly meeting of an A.Ş. other than an OGA is an Extraordinary General Assembly (EGA) Meeting. EGA Meetings are held as and when required by the business of the joint-stock company. Furthermore, the directors are bound by Articles 412 and 414 of the TCC to convene an EGA at the request of the minority.

d. Special Meetings of the Privileged Shareholders

440. If an A.Ş. has issued privileged (preference) shares, the holders of these shares constitute by law an assembly, which is sometimes called a special meeting. The resolutions of the General Assembly pertaining to the following matters may not be executed or enforced unless and until approved by a special meeting of the privileged shareholders if such resolutions affect the rights of the privileged shareholders (TCC 454):

- Amendment of the Articles of Association
- Authorizing the board of directors to increase the capital of the company
- Increase the share capital of the company.

441. Special Meeting of the privileged shareholders have to be convened by the Board of Directors within one month from the announcement of the general assembly resolution affecting the rights of the privileged shareholders, at the latest. Otherwise, each holder of privileged shares may, within fifteen days from the latest day of call period, demand the convening of the special meeting of the privileged shareholders by applying to the Commercial Court of First Instance at the place of company's head offices.

442. In the event that the privileged shareholders have indeed participated to the general assembly meeting and approved the decision affecting the rights of privileged shareholders complying with the minimum quorum requirements indicated below for the special meeting of the privileged shareholders, then, convening of a separate special meeting shall not be required for the approval of the aforesaid general assembly decision.

443. The Special Meeting of the privileged shareholders is convened with the presence of shareholders representing 60% of the share capital held by the privileged shareholders and decisions are obtained by the simple majority of the participants. A Ministry Representative is also required to be present in the special meeting if the meeting is held abroad and sign the meeting minutes.

444. If it is concluded in the special meeting that the rights of privileged shareholders have been affected by the general assembly resolution, such matter has to recorded in the meeting minutes which are required to be delivered to the board of directors within ten days following the date of the meeting. Alongside of the minutes, a list of privileged shareholders that constitute the minimum quorum and that have voted against the general assembly decision has to be delivered to the board of directors together with the joint address of delivery for all such shareholders to be used in a possible cancellation lawsuit that may be initiated against the resolution of special meeting of the privileged shareholders.

445. Within one month from the date of the special meeting resolution rejecting the general assembly resolution, the board of directors is entitled to initiate a lawsuit for the cancellation of the special meeting decision and announcement of the rejected general assembly decision on the basis that the rights of the privileged shareholders are not adversely affected. This cancellation lawsuit may be initiated before the Commercial Court of First Instance located at the place of company's headquarters.

3. Convening of the General Meeting

a. Right and Duty to Convene the Assembly

i. Board of Directors

446. Both Ordinary and EGA Meetings are convened by the Board of Directors. The Board of Directors shall have the authority to call for a general assembly meeting even if its term of duty has expired.

ii. Liquidators

447. According to Article 535.1 of the TCC, during liquidation, the organs of the joint-stock company continue to exercise all their rights and duties, but their authority is restricted to acts which are necessary for the completion of liquidation process and to matters which are outside the scope of the liquidators functions. However, the liquidators shall be entitled to convene general assembly meetings in order to pass resolutions concerning matters related to liquidation (TCC 535.2).

iii. Minority

448. The minority holding at least 10% of the capital (5% in public companies) may, by a notice through notary public, require the Board to convene a General Assembly Meeting. If a General Assembly Meeting has already been called for by the Board of Directors, the minority may still demand inclusion of certain items in the agenda for discussion (TCC 411).

449. If the request of the minority is accepted by the board, the general assembly is called for a meeting to be held within minimum forty-five days, otherwise, if the board fails to convene the general assembly, the minority shareholders may directly call the shareholders to make such a request.

450. In the event that the Board of Directors rejects the request of the minority shareholders for the convening of a general assembly or inclusion of an item in the agenda or if the Board of Directors fails to respond to such request within seven business days, the same minority shareholders are entitled to apply to the Commercial Court of First Instance located at the place of company's headquarters and submit their request to the court (TCC 412).

iv. Shareholder

451. In the event that the Board of Directors of the Company may not be convened regularly or if it is not possible to establish the meeting quorum, any shareholder may apply to the court for convening of the general assembly. The decision of the court in relation to such request is final (TCC 410.2).

b. Form and Content of the General Assembly Meeting

452. The General Assembly Meeting is called in the manner provided for by the Articles of Association. In particular, notice must be given in the Trade Registry Gazette and on the website of the company at least two weeks prior to the date of the Meeting. The date on which the announcement is published in the Trade Registry Gazette and the date of the intended meeting shall not be taken into consideration for the calculation of the aforesaid two-week period. Additionally, shareholders indicated in the share book of the Company and the shareholders who have deposited one share with the company and have communicated their address have to be notified of the intended general assembly and its agenda through registered mail (TCC 414).

453. An attendance list indicating the name, address and number of shares of shareholders participating in the meeting in person or through proxy must be kept and executed by the Chairman of the general assembly meeting and the participating shareholders as well as by the Ministry Representative if present at the meeting. Companies of which share capital is represented in bearer shares have to obtain the list of shareholders from the Central Registration Agency to identify the shareholders that are entitled to attend the general assembly meeting as per Article 6 of the Communiqué on Notification to and Registration with the Central Registration Agency of Bearer Shares.

4. Location of the Meetings

454. In the absence of any provision to the contrary in the Articles of Association, the general assembly meeting shall be held at address where the head office of the A.Ş. is situated. The articles may foresee that the general assembly meetings may be held at other locations that may be determined by the board of directors.

455. General assemblies may also take place in an electronic environment. The principles governing the conduct of general assemblies convened electronically must be detailed in the internal directive of the company.

5. The Representative of the Ministry

456. The former TCC required the presence of a Ministry "Commissar" in all general assembly meetings of joint-stock companies whereas the new TCC, which uses the term "Ministry Representative" limited such requirement to those general assembly meetings convened to discuss the matters determined by the Regulation issued by the Ministry of Trade (TCC 407). The general assembly meetings in which the Representative of the Ministry should be present include: (1) all the general assembly meetings of the companies, the incorporation and Articles of Association amendments of which are subject to permission of the Ministry; (2) the general assembly meetings of the companies other than the ones mentioned under (1) the agenda of which includes capital increase, capital decrease, adoption of authorized capital system, exit from the authorized capital system, increase of the upper limit of registered capital or amendment of scope of activity, merger, division or transformation; (3) the general assembly meetings of the companies convened in the electronic environment; (4) all the general assembly meetings to be held abroad; (5) all the special meetings of the privileged shareholders to be held abroad.

6. Attendance of the Shareholders

457. The shareholders may attend in *propria persona* or they may give authority to a person by proxy. The proxy is the instrument evidencing such authority. Shareholders' names whom are included in the list of shareholders prepared by the board of directors are entitled to participate in the meeting. The Board of Directors prepares the list of shareholders based on (i) the share book of the company for registered shareholders, shareholders for whose shares, certificates are not yet issued and holders of the temporary share certificates, and (ii) the entrance cards obtained by the holders of bearer shares at least one day before the date of the general assembly, or (iii) if the Company is a public company of which shares are kept electronically by the Central Registration Agency, the list of shareholders obtained from the Central Registration Agency (TCC 415). The list of shareholders has to be signed by the chairman of the board of directors and has to be present in the room where the general assembly shall be held. The shareholders' list executed by the shareholders attending the meeting becomes the "attendance list" of the general assembly.

7. Chairing the Meeting

458. In accordance with Article 419 of TCC, if the Articles of Association do not provide otherwise, general meetings are presided over by a chairman who is not required to be a shareholder. The chairman of the general assembly meeting is elected by the shareholders participating in such general assembly meeting. If the chairman elected for the general assembly meeting deems it necessary, he/she may appoint a vice-chairman, a vote collector and a secretary who will be responsible for drawing up the minutes of the meeting.

8. Adjournment of the General Meeting

459. According to Article 420 of the TCC, upon the request of the minority of shareholders representing 10% of the share capital of the company (5% in publicly held companies), discussions in the general assembly meeting regarding the approval of the financial statements and all matters related thereto (e.g., release of board members and distribution of duties) shall be automatically adjourned for one month upon the decision of the chairman of the general assembly and without any need of approval of the shareholders. After the postponement of the discussions of financial statements and related items on the agenda for one month, a second postponement may only be requested by the minority shareholders if the Company representatives fail to provide the necessary explanations to the matters objected to or questioned in the financial statements.

9. Minutes

460. The Chairman elected to reside in the General Assembly by the shareholders is responsible for keeping the meeting minutes. The minutes have to indicate the total share capital of the company and the total number, nominal value and class of shares being represented in the meeting in person and via a proxy, together with the questions asked and answers granted and resolutions obtained in such meeting specifying the total votes casted in favor and against the related proposal. The minutes are signed by the shareholders and, if present, by the Ministry Representative. However, it is customary for the shareholders to grant the authority to sign the minutes to the chairman of the general assembly. The decisions obtained in the general assembly that are subject to registration requirements have to be filed with the Trade Registry for registration and announcement in the Trade Registry Gazette.

10. Exclusive/Non-delegable Powers of the General Meeting

461. The general assembly decides on the matters established by law and in the Articles of Association. It has, by law, the following exclusive powers which are non-transferable to other organs of the Company:

- to amend the Articles of Association;
- to appoint and dismiss the members of the board of directors;
- to determine the term of duty of board members, the renumeration, salary, bonus and premiums payable to the board members;

- to decide on the release of the board members from liability for the works and actions conducted during their term;
- to elect and dismiss the independent auditor (if the company is required to appoint one);
- to adopt decisions regarding financial statements, annual activity report of the board of directors, annual profit of the company;
- to adopt decisions regarding financial statements, annual activity report of the board of directors, annual profit of the company;
- allocation and distribution of dividends, use of the reserves of the company as an amount to be added to the capital or the distributable profit or in any other manner;
- dissolution of the company;
- wholesale of a considerable amount of the assets of the Company.

B. Majority Rule (Quorum Requirements)

462. Unless a higher quorum is foreseen in the Articles of Association of the joint-stock company, a general assembly may be held by the attendance of shareholders or their representatives representing at least a quarter of the total share capital of the Company. This quorum should be maintained during the course of the meeting. If this *quorum* is not reached at the first meeting, a second meeting is convened without being subject to a minimum quorum requirement (TCC 418). Resolutions are passed by the simple majority of votes of those present at the meeting (TCC 418.2).

463. Article 421 of the TCC establishes the requirements for meeting and resolution quorums for certain matters requiring an amendment of the Articles of Association of the company. Unless a higher quorum is foreseen in law or in Articles of Association, decisions related to the amendment of Articles of Association may be adopted with the affirmative votes of the shareholders representing the majority of the total share capital present in a general assembly meeting convened by shareholders representing at least half of the total share capital of the company. If the necessary quorum is not reached in the first meeting, the second general meeting should be convened within one month with the presence of shareholders representing at least one-third of the total share capital of the company.

464. The following decisions may be obtained only with unanimous vote of shareholders representing the entire share capital of the company and the same quorum is required for any adjourned meeting:

- transfer of headquarters of the company to abroad;
- creating main or secondary obligations for the shareholders to compensate for the balance sheet losses.

465. The following decisions pertaining to the amendment of Articles of Association may be obtained by the affirmative votes of shareholders representing at least 75% of the total share capital of the company and the same quorum is required for any adjourned meeting:

– amendment of the scope of activity of the Company in its entirety;
– creation of privileged shares and share groups;
– creation of restrictions in relation to the transfer of registered shares.

C. *Annual Accounts, Profits and Dividends and Other Pecuniary (Economic) Rights*

1. The Right to Profits

466. A shareholder has the right to a proportionate share of the net profits insofar as such profits are distributed among the shareholders according to law and the Articles of Association (TCC 507). The net profits are calculated according to the results shown by the annual balance sheet. As set forth in the Articles of Association, the holders of preferential (privileged) shares enjoy preferences in the distribution of profit over the holders of ordinary shares. For closely held A.Ş.s, minimum dividend is established by law which is 5% pursuant to Article 519. Under the terms of the CML, publicly held corporations shall distribute their profits in the framework of the profit distribution policies to be determined by their general assembly and in accordance with the provisions of the related legislations (CML 19). The details of profit distribution are regulated by the Communiqué II-19.1.

467. Unless the Articles of Association provide otherwise, participation in profit shall be calculated in proportion to the amounts of capital paid up (TCC 508). According to Article 19.3 of the CML, in contrast to the TCC, dividends are equally distributed to all shares at the end of the accounting year, irrespective of their issue and acquisition date.

468. It is the objective of the law to prevent the assets of the joint-stock company from being dissipated by means of imprudent distributions. Various provisions are, therefore, established by law for the protection of the assets of the company.

469. According to Article 523 of the TCC, dividends may not be declared until the reserves prescribed by law and the Articles of Association are set aside. Additionally, the General Assembly may decide on the creation of reserve funds other than those prescribed by law or the Articles of Association in case such may be justified in order to maintain the continued prosperity of the joint-stock company and a steady dividend distribution policy by taking into consideration the interests of all shareholders.

470. Shareholders who have unjustifiably and in bad faith received dividends or interest during the formation period are obliged to return them (TCC 512.1). The right to demand the returning of any such unlawfully received amounts to the company is subject to a statute of limitations of five years. (TCC 512.2).

2. Participation in the Proceeds of Liquidation[89]

471. The shareholder has, as a rule, the right to a proportional share in the proceeds of the Company upon the liquidation of the company. However, the Articles of Association may provide otherwise in such a manner that the liquidation proceeds can be allocated to only a person or a group of shareholders.

3. Preemption Rights

472. Each shareholder has a preemption right to participate and acquire shares in a capital increase in proportion to its shareholding ratio (TCC 461.1) in the total capital of the joint-stock company. The preemption right of shareholders may be restricted or removed only with the affirmative votes of the shareholders that represent a minimum of 60% of the total capital and in case of existence of reasons that may justify such restriction. The restriction shall apply equally to all existing shareholders. TCC has provided examples of such justifiable causes under Article 461 which include public offerings, acquisition of a business or a part thereof or new subsidiaries, and participation of the employees in the share capital of the company. Restriction of preemptive rights should not result in a loss to any shareholder or benefit any person in an unjustifiable manner.

4. The Acquisition of "*Gratis*" (Bonus) Shares

473. In case of a capital increase through the capitalization of the internal funds, every shareholder has the right to acquire the newly issued gratis (bonus) shares in proportion to their shareholding in the company (462.3 of TCC). The right on gratis shares cannot be revoked or restricted.

5. Interest During the Formation Period

474. As per Article 510 of the TCC, the Articles of Association of a joint-stock company may foresee payment of interest to its shareholders for the initial period following formation and until the company becomes fully operational with the condition that the Turkish Accounting Standards are complied with. The Articles of

89. The term liquidation dividend refers to the liquidation of net assets either as a cash dividend or property dividend. It is a weaker vested interest.

Association should also indicate the duration of such interest payments. The company shall reflect such interest expenses as expenses of investments in the form of special assets.

D. Participation Rights of Shareholders

1. Attendance

475. Shareholders may exercise their rights concerning matters of the A.Ş., such as the election of the A.Ş.'s organs, approval of the business report, and the resolutions concerning financial statements and the distribution of profits, through participation in the General Assembly (TCC 425) either directly in person or through proxy. The right of the shareholder to participate in a General Assembly may not be revoked or restricted.

2. Voting Rights[90]

476. As has been mentioned above, each shareholder carries at least one vote even such shareholder has only one share (TCC 434) in the share capital of the company. It is possible to issue shares under the Articles of Association with extra voting rights, e.g.[91] shares carrying preferential/privileged voting rights may be created, provided that it is not contrary to the fundamental principles of the law. In a General Meeting, however, held for the amendment of the Articles of Association, each share entitles its holder to one vote only (TCC 453) regardless of the extra voting rights that may have been granted.

477. Under the terms of the TCC, voting rights of a shareholder may be temporarily suspended in certain cases.[92] Pursuant to Article 436 of TCC, a shareholder cannot vote in discussions related to affairs or transactions being of a personal nature between company and himself/herself, his/her spouse, descendants or antecedents, capital stock companies under their control or personal companies in which they are partners or for matters concerning lawsuits or arbitration proceedings by the company against them. Board members and the ones authorized in management with signature authority cannot use their voting rights arising from their own shares in the decisions for the release of the board members and management.

---

90. The right to vote is one of those shareholders' rights which may not be taken away, *see* para. 330 *supra* and *see* generally Poroy/Tekinalp/Çamoğlu [*Textbook*] [*see* SB], paras. 959 et seq.
91. Poroy/Tekinalp/Çamoğlu [Textbook] [*see* SB] at 781 et seq. *See* para. 295, *supra*.
92. *Ibid.*, at. 988 et seq. and *see* generally Ö. Teoman, *Anonim Ortaklıkta Paysahiplerinin Oy Hakkından Yoksunluğu* [the Suspension of the Voting Rights of the Shareholders in a Company Limited by Shares], İstanbul 1983.

E. *Protective Rights of Shareholders*

1. In General

478. One of the developments of the new TCC related to the individual shareholding rights is the granting of new rights of legal recourse to shareholders. The most significant of these new rights are the following:

- Shareholders may initiate lawsuits to have board and general meeting decisions nullified (TCC Articles 391, 447).
- Shareholders may initiate specific lawsuits for cancellation of company mergers, divisions, and conversions or liability of managers/board members that have participated in those (TCC Articles 191–193).
- In situations where a parent company abuses its control over a subsidiary, the shareholders of the controlled company may initiate lawsuits in order to have their shares acquired by the Company at true value or to have the dispute resolved in some other appropriate and acceptable manner, and/or initiate lawsuits for the liability of the board members thereof (TCC Article 202 (1)(b-d)).
- Lawsuits to have a company terminated may be initiated in such situations when the shareholders, creditors, or public interests have been significantly endangered or compromised by actions involving illegalities in the formation of the company (TCC Articles 358 et seq.).

a. Right to Challenge Resolutions of a General Meeting (TCC 445)[93]

479. The most important right of the shareholder is to protect itself against the power of the majority which jeopardizes its rights and benefits in the Company. Under the terms of the TCC, any shareholder is entitled to challenge resolutions of the General Assembly which violate the principle of good faith, the law or the Articles of Association by bringing an action against the joint-stock company before the court (TCC 445). The statute of limitations that apply for lawsuits for the cancellation of a general assembly decision is three months from the date of the said resolution.

480. The persons who are entitled to request the cancellation of a general assembly decision are described under Article 446 of TCC. Accordingly, shareholders who were present in the general meeting and casted a negative vote and had its opposition recorded in the minutes shall be entitled to initiate a cancellation lawsuit. Also, irrespective of being present at the general meeting or casting a negative vote, shareholders claiming that (i) invitation procedures pertaining to the general assembly were not properly followed; or (ii) the agenda is not announced as required; or

93. *See generally* O. İmregün, *Anonim Şirketlerde Paysahipleri Arasında Umumi Heyet Kararlarından Doğan Menfaat İhtilafları ve Bunları Telif Çareleri* [Conflicts of Interest Between Shareholders and the Reconciling Thereof in Companies Limited by Shares], İstanbul 1962. E. Moroğlu, *Anonim Ortaklıklarda Genel Kurul Kararlarının Hükümsüzlüğü* [The Invalidity of the General Meeting Resolutions of Companies Limited by Shares], Ankara 1967.

(iii) persons or representatives who were not authorized to participate in the meeting had attended the general assembly; or (iv) their participation to the general assembly and/or exercise of their voting rights were not permitted unlawfully may initiate a cancellation lawsuit provided that such irregularities affected the adaption of the decision. In addition to the shareholders, board of directors (as a board) and each board may initiate a cancellation lawsuit if fulfillment of the general assembly decision shall result in the personal liability of the concerned board member.

481. Aside from the cancellation lawsuit, Article 447 of the TCC enables the initiation of a lawsuit for declaration of the general assembly decision as null and void.

482. The new TCC also enabled the initiation of lawsuits for the declaration of a board decision as null and void, particularly if the board decision (i) is against the principle of equal treatment of all shareholders; or (ii) does not comply with the fundamental structure of the joint-stock company or the principle of protection of capital, or (iii) violates, hinders or restricts the indispensable rights of a shareholder; or (iv) relates to a matter which is within the non-delegable authorities of other bodies or concerns the delegation of these authorities (TCC 391).

483. Under a decision of the Supreme Court of Appeals, any claim stating that a Board resolution or a general assembly decision is null and void can be brought before a court at any time and by any person.[94]

b. Right to Information

484. Under the terms of the TCC, shareholders have various information rights. Not less than fifteen days before the ordinary General Meeting, the balance sheet and profit and loss account, together with the auditors report and the report of the directors with proposals concerning the allocation of the net profit, must be open to the examination of the shareholders at the headquarters and branch offices of the company (TCC 437).

485. Right to information of the shareholder at a general assembly meeting is re-arranged in the new TCC and the limits of this right are both expanded and strictly defined. In this respect, in general assembly meetings, every shareholder may ask for information regarding transactions of the company from the board of directors and about the audit procedure and results from the auditor. The most salient features of the new right of access to information focus on six points:

- The right of access to information expands to the company's subsidiaries as well. Accordingly, shareholders have the right to obtain information about changes in

94. *See, jud* [11th C.Cham. Sup. Court] No. 4607/5042 [Jan. 16, 1981]; No. [11th C.Cham, sup. Court] 3800/3992, [Oct. 19, 1982]; [11th C.Cham. Sup. Court], No. 3370/4077 [Oct. 22, 1982] in: Eriş, 1st ed. [*see* SB], No. 1437, 1440, 1442; jud [11th C.Cham. Sup. Court] No. 66/1809 [Mar. 30, 1987]; No [11th C.Cham. Sup. Court] 2800/2391 [Apr. 15, 1988], in: Eriş, 2nd ed. [*see* SB], No. 1142/3.

the financial circumstances and assets of the subsidiaries and the relationship between the subsidiaries and the parent company and/or the shareholders and managers of the parent company.
- If a shareholder has obtained information about the company's situation, transactions, investments, or relationships from a company source outside of a general assembly, the same information must be provided to the other shareholders at the general assembly meeting.
- A shareholder may submit a demand to the general assembly or to the board of directors to be allowed to examine company records and correspondence on a certain matter(s).
- If a shareholder does not receive an answer to his/hers/its request for information or is not allowed to perform an inspection, he/she/it may initiate a lawsuit and demand from the court to order the company to provide the requested information.
- Shareholders' requests for information may only be turned down by the company if fulfilling them would risk exposure of the company's trade secrets or would endanger company interests that are needed to be protected. Even in such cases, however, the refusal is subject to court review.

c. Right to Request a Special Audit

486. The shareholder's right to demand special audit is stipulated under Article 438 of TCC. If it is necessary for the exercise of the shareholding rights and if the rights to request information and examination have been previously exercised and exhausted, each shareholder shall be entitled to request in a general assembly the investigation of a certain matter through a special audit even if such matter is not included in the announced agenda of the general assembly. If general assembly approves the special audit request, company or each shareholder may demand the appointment of a special auditor from the Commercial Court of First Instance at the place of company's head office within thirty days of the decision of the general assembly.

2. Minority (Protection) Rights

487. Another distinguishing feature of Turkish company law pertains to minority rights. These rights protect the minority against the acts and decisions of the Board of Directors and resolutions of the General Assembly which represent, as a rule, the power of the majority.

488. Under the terms of the TCC, one or more shareholders whose combined shareholding represents at least 10% of the share capital and at least a 5% capital interest in a publicly held corporation is considered to constitute a "minority." Minority rights are special rights which may be used by the minority to:

- prevent the release of the founders, directors and auditors (TCC 559) from liability with respect to establishment procedures of the joint-stock company and capital increases;
- appoint special auditors in case of rejection of the general assembly of the appointment request (TCC 439);
- call a General Assembly Meeting (TCC 411,412);
- include a discussion item in the agenda for a General Assembly Meeting (TCC 411, 412); and
- postpone discussions of agenda items pertaining to approval of the financial statements in an ordinary general assembly meeting (TCC 420).

489. The first minority right is to prevent the release of the founders, directors and auditors from their liability relating to the formation of the joint-stock company. The rule is that the above-mentioned persons may not be discharged from liability unless a period of four years has passed since the registration of the joint-stock company by shares. At the expiry of this term, the release shall be effective only upon the approval of the General Assembly Meeting. If, however, the minority objects in the General Assembly, the said persons may not be released of their liability.

490. The second minority right is to enable the minority shareholders to appoint a special auditor for the investigation of a specific matter. In case the general assembly rejects the request of a shareholder for the appointment of a special auditor, shareholders constituting the minority (10% of the capital in closed companies or 5% in public companies) or the ones holding the share's nominal value of which is minimum one million Turkish Lira may request the court to assign such special auditor within three months.

491. Shareholders representing the minority are entitled to request in writing from the Board of Directors the calling of a general assembly with the specific agenda or inclusion of a specific item in the agenda of a general assembly meeting which is already announced to be convened. The request should be sent to the Board of Directors through notary public and indicate the grounds necessitating the discussion of such agenda items in a general assembly. In the event that the Board of Directors accepts such request, it is required to call for the general assembly to discuss the requested items within forty-five days. If the Board of Directors rejects the request of the minority shareholders or fails to respond with an affirmative answer within seven business days, such shareholders are entitled to apply to the Commercial Court of First Instance having jurisdiction in the address of the company's headquarters and request the convening of the general assembly. If the court finds it necessary for the convening of the general assembly, it appoints an administrator for completing the relevant procedures. The decision of the court pertaining to the request of convening the general assembly is final.

492. The minority shareholders are entitled to request in an ordinary general assembly meeting the postponement of discussions of financial statements and other items pertaining to the financial statements which include the agenda item pertaining to the release of board members and auditors and distribution of dividends. Upon such request, the relevant items are postponed for discussion in the general assembly to be convened on the one-month anniversary of the original meeting automatically upon the decision of the chairman of the general assembly without the requirement of a general assembly decision for acceptance of the postponement request. In order for the discussions of financial statements and related items to be postponed for a second time after the first postponement, sufficient explanations should have been provided to the objected items of the financial statement which are recorded in the general assembly minutes within the scope of accountability criteria applicable to the company representatives.

493. TCC also introduces a number of new minority rights in addition to existing ones while also making changes that facilitate the exercise of already existing minority rights. Foremost among the new minority rights is TCC Articles 531, according to which a company may be dissolved by a commercial court if minority shareholders request such dissolution for just cause. Instead of dissolution, however, the court may also decide on some other solution which it deems to be appropriate in the circumstance and which is acceptable to the parties.

F. The Obligations and Duties of the Shareholders

494. The first and only obligation of a shareholder is to make the requisite capital contribution with respect to its shares. According to Article 480 of the TCC, other than the exceptions provided by law, no shareholder may be obliged by the Articles of Association to pay anything other than the price of the share or the premium (*agio*) exceeding the nominal value of the share. Save for the rights of shareholders on the liquidation proceeds, shareholders may not ask for the return of their capital contributions.[95]

495. A shareholder's default in payment of its capital contribution constitutes legitimate grounds for termination of such shareholder's shareholding in the company.[96] As per the provisions of Article 482 of the TCC, a shareholder which fails to pay its capital contribution on its due date is required to pay default interest and

95. Other obligations may be imposed on the shareholders by contracts other than the Articles of Association. However, in the case of a breach of such obligations, the consequences shall be determined by applying the principles of the law of obligations and, in most cases, shall only result in the responsibility to pay compensation. The validity of the provisions of such contracts granting advantages and rights such as issuing new shares with preemption rights, to those shareholders who fulfil their obligations under such contracts or regulating disadvantageous status, such as exempting from preemption rights, to those shareholders who do not are controversial. In order to arrive at a conclusion, the matter should be dealt with case by case. In the opinion of this author, such provisions may be valid, provided that the equal treatment principle is respected. *See* for further discussion, Poroy/Tekinalp/Çamoğlu [*Textbook*] [*see* SB] 1022a.

96. *See* generally, C. Göle, *Anonim Ortaklıklarda Nakdî Sermaye Koyma Borcu ve Bu Borcu İfada Temerrüt* [Cash Capital Contributions and a Shareholder's Default Thereof in Companies Limited by Shares], Ankara 1976.

the Board of Directors of the Company may (i) deprive the shareholders of its rights pertaining to its capital undertaking and any partial payments made in relations thereto, (ii) sell the corresponding shares to another person, and (iii) cancel the shares already issued to the defaulting shareholder. It is also possible to include a penalty clause in the Articles of Association of the Company to apply in case of defaults in capital contribution payments. In the event that the Board of Directors decides to exercise the aforesaid rights granted to it as per Article 482 against the defaulting shareholder, it has to first notify the defaulting shareholder of the fact that it will be deprived of its rights arising out of the unpaid shares and that it may be required to pay the penalty in case it fails to pay the defaulted amount within thirty days. Such notification is announced on the internet site of the Company and the Trade Registry Gazette and also sent to the shareholder in compliance with the procedures set forth in the Articles of Association of the company.

496. The notification must be sent through registered mail to the defaulting shareholder if the corresponding shares are registered shares and be announced on the internet site of the Company without being announced in the Trade Registry Gazette.

497. In case of sale of such defaulted shares to a third party, the original defaulting shareholder shall remain to be liable for any portions unpaid by the new shareholder. The A.Ş. may demand from the defaulting shareholder payment of its receivables through enforcement procedures.[97] When the procedure is completed, the A.Ş. temporarily acquires the shares of the defaulting shareholder. The shares in question must be sold.

498. As with other legal entities, the A.Ş. acts through its representative bodies ("organs"). The legal "organs" of the A.Ş. are the General Assembly, the Board of Directors and, if the company is subject to independent audit, the auditors. Additionally, the Board may appoint any number of committees and commissions, in which Directors may be members or not, for performing the functions necessary for the administration of the A.Ş., undertaking preparatory work, supervising the implementation of Board resolutions, implementing specific projects or maintaining internal control mechanisms. These committees and commissions operate under Article 366.2 of TCC. Turkish corporate law is dominated by the doctrine of separation of powers. The General Assembly is designated as the legislative body. It has the authority to adopt and amend the Articles of Association of the A.Ş. The shareholders exercise their rights in reference to the A.Ş. through the General Assembly. The General Assembly has the power to elect and remove the directors, appoint independent auditors and approve the financial statements, and determine the allocation of the profits and distribution of dividends. Although it is not an executive body, certain exceptional executive powers have been bestowed on it by law.

---

97. *See* jud [ACC Sup. Court], No. 1511/133 [Mar. 1, 1967], in: Poroy/Tekinalp/Çamoğlu [Textbook] [*see* SB] 495.

499. The Board of Directors assumes the executive function. The A.Ş. is administered and represented by the Board.

500. The audit system is completely changed with the new TCC and independent auditing is recognized which shall be explained in detail under section III (Auditors) below.

501. An important problem in determining relationships among different organs of a joint-stock company is settled in the new TCC through clearly defined limits established for the company's functions and an effective balance among the competencies specific to each organ. Among the overarching principles of TCC is that each organ is vested with a set of authorities and duties which may neither be assigned to another organ nor directly or indirectly taken from it and that each organ is obliged to exercise its authorities and perform its duties with this principle in mind

II. Administrative and Management Body (The Board of Directors)

A. Directors and Administrative Board

502. In TCC, the board of directors has been designed to be the executive organ of the company which can be easily convened and takes decisions expeditiously. The law also clearly defines the scope of authority of the board of directors. The joint-stock company is managed and represented by the board of directors in the broadest sense possible, thus, it is entitled to exercise all rights of the legal entity against third parties and, if necessary, through legal proceedings.

503. TCC now allows single-member boards, and the rule stipulated in TCC 1956, which requires a board member to be also a shareholder of the company, has been eliminated.

504. It is also possible, under the new TCC, for legal entities to become board members in a joint-stock company, whereas, as per the TCC 1956, it was not possible for a legal entity to become a board member even if it was a shareholder of the company and it could only be represented in the board by a natural person. This rule often had the effect of leaving boards in the hands of surrogate directors who lacked any accountability.

505. Under the new TCC, board meetings may now be conducted "online" and electronically. This is a matter that involves more than a mere "modernization." Facilitating the conduct of board meetings and allowing official board decisions to be taken in this way is a great convenience for all companies but especially for those in which there is a foreign shareholding interest.

506. In an effort to keep up with corporate governance principles, TCC requires joint-stock companies traded on a stock exchange to set up an "early warning risk committee" whose duty is to spot risks in advance and submit to auditors a comprehensive bimonthly report in which remedies are also proposed. In line with suggestions made by non-governmental organizations, it was decided that this committee should also be charged with risk management functions in general.

507. TCC introduces new rules governing boards liabilities, company management and liquidation of the company. These rules (TCC 553 and TCC 555 through 561) were inspired by Swiss company law (SCO Article 754 and SCO Articles 756 through 760). The Swiss model was also followed with respect to the issue of accountability, and, after a lengthy debate, the system of "*differentiated joint responsibility*" (*differenzierte Solidarität*) was also accepted.

508. As per the new TCC, members of the board of directors, their spouses, children and relatives in blood and in law up to the third degree who are not shareholders may not become indebted to and incur cash indebtedness from the company. The company may not provide surety, guarantee or securities in favor of these individuals or take over their debts. In case of violation of this restriction, the creditors of the company may pursue these individuals for the debts of the company for the amounts they are indebted to the company. Companies which are members of a "Corporation Group" may provide surety and guarantee in favor of each other.

509. The Board of Directors of the A.Ş. is empowered and authorized to manage and represent the joint-stock company on all matters, except for those exclusively reserved for the general assembly.

510. The Board of Directors may pass resolutions concerning all matters which are necessary for the implementation of the business objectives and ultimate direction of the business of the joint-stock company.

1. Distribution of Duties and Delegation of Authority

511. As per Article 366 of the TCC, the board of directors elects one chairman and one vice-chairman each year from among its members. The Articles of Association of the company may foresee that the chairman and/or vice-chairman of the board of directors be elected by the general assembly of the company. The board of directors is also entitled to establish committees and commissions from among its members or third parties for supervision of the operations of the company, execution of the board decisions or conduct of the internal audit of the company.

512. The TCC introduces the following non-delegable and inalienable authorities and duties for the board of directors:

- to manage the company at the highest level and provide instructions to such effect;
- to determine the organizational chart of the company;

- to establish the necessary mechanisms for financial planning required by the accounting, financial audit and management of the company;
- to appoint and dismiss the managers of the company or persons with similar ranks and signatories authorized to represent and bind the company;
- to supervise and oversee whether the individuals granted with management powers comply with the law, Articles of Association and internal directives of the company;
- to keep and maintain the share books and minute books of the general assembly and the board of directors;
- to prepare and submit to the general assembly of the company the annual activity report and corporate governance declaration;
- to make the necessary preparations for general assembly meetings and execute the decisions obtained in such general assembly meetings; and
- to notify the courts in case of insolvency of the company.

513. While the former TCC did not strictly differentiate between the management powers of the board of directors and the day-to-day technical management of Company, the new TCC introduced this distinction. Other than the non-transferrable duties of the board of directors as discussed above, the management authority of the Board of Directors may be transferred to one or more board members or third parties in its entirety provided that such is permitted in the Articles of Association of the company and the board issues an internal directive for delegation of the management authority. This internal directive should define the organizational and management structure of the company with clear reference to reporting requirements and seniority of the company officers. In the event that the management authority is not delegated through an internal directive, each board member shall have the right and duty to exercise such authority (TCC 367).

514. If otherwise is not provided in the Articles of Association of the company or the board does not consist of only one member, any two members of the board of directors may represent and bind the company by their joint signatures.

515. As per Article 371 of the TCC, to the extent that at least one board member retains the authority to represent the company, the board of directors may delegate representation authority.

2. Number and Eligibility of Directors

516. In accordance with the TCC, the board may consist of a single member. This is both a reform and development. The new TCC also eliminated the requirement of a board member to be a shareholder, and thus, board members may be appointed from outside of the company. The former TCC did not allow a legal entity to become a board member and it required a representative to be appointed on its behalf. However, in accordance with the new TCC, a legal entity may be elected as a board member. As per Article 359 of the TCC, in case of election of a legal entity to the board of directors, such legal entity member appoints one real person to represent it in the board meetings. The real person representative is registered with the Trade Registry and announced in the Trade Registry Gazette along with the legal entity board member.

517. The law does not impose any conditions in relation to the citizenship and domicile of the board members and it does not introduce any education requirements.

518. Article 363 of the TCC foresees that the membership of a board member shall automatically terminate in case of bankruptcy and limitation of his/her legal capacity or if he loses the qualifications of being a board member as may be defined in the Articles of Association of the company or the applicable laws.

3. Nomination, Election and Dismissal

a. Nomination and Election

519. At the time of the formation of the company, the first board members of the joint-stock company are nominated and named in its Articles of Association. Following the formation, the shareholders of the company may elect and appoint board members in either an Ordinary or Extraordinary General Meeting.

520. If a board member dies, resigns or is otherwise incapacitated prior to the expiry of his term of office, the remaining board members can elect a temporary successor for the vacant position. The board member elected for the vacant position shall be submitted to the approval of the general assembly in its first upcoming meeting.

521. The names, addresses and nationalities of the directors must be registered at the *Trade Registry*. Any subsequent changes that may occur in relation thereto should also be registered with the Trade Registry.

b. Term of Duty

522. Directors are elected for a maximum term of three years (TCC 362) and may be re-elected thereafter unless otherwise provided in the Articles of Association of the company.

c. Dismissal

523. As per Article 364 of the TCC, the members of the board of directors may always be removed from duty by a decision of the general assembly even if they had been appointed by the Articles of Association. The general assembly may remove the board members from duty if there is a related item on the meeting or, even if a related item does not exist, in case of a justified reason. The right for indemnification of the directors who have been discharged is reserved.

B. Powers of Management and Representation

1. The Administrative Rights of the Board Members

524. Each board member may: (1) through a written notice delivered to the chairman of the board of directors, require the convening of a meeting; (2) during the course of a board meeting (and outside the meeting but with the pre-approval of the chairman) require the managers and authorized representatives of the company to provide all information concerning the conduct of business and specific transactions (TCC 392); (3) request the submission to the review of the board any and all books or records, documents and agreements of the company.

2. The Remuneration of Board Members

525. Under the terms of the TCC, provided that the amount is determined by the Articles of Association or a general assembly decision, board members may be paid *honorarium, renumeration, salary, bonus, premium or a portion from annual profit* (TCC 394) for their services. According to Article 511 of the TCC, members of the board of directors may receive shares from the profit of the company to the extent that required allocations have been made to the statutory reserves and that a dividend of 5%, or such higher amount as the articles may prescribe, has been paid to the shareholders. Furthermore, Directors are bound to refund bonuses unduly paid or received in bad faith. The action for recovery expires five years after such a bonus has been received.

3. Management

526. The A.Ş. is managed by the Board of Directors. The word “management” is not defined in the Commercial Code. It indicates the performance of the executive duties in a joint-stock company, such as making policy decisions with respect to products, services, prices, wages, labor relations and the election and removal of officers and executive personnel.

527. The Board exercises its administrative functions when duly convened as a Board. It is a requirement of the TCC that every year, at the commencement of its term, the Board must elect a chairman and a vice-chairman to act in his absence (TCC 316). The Board may appoint a Secretary from among the Directors or from outside the Board, although it is not common to appoint a Secretary in practice.

528. The chairman and vice-chairman do not have any casting votes. The chairman is *primus inter pares.*

529. The Board may appoint, from its members and from outside the Board, one or more committees to supervise the conduct of business, to prepare the agenda for the Board, to report to the Board on questions of importance—in particular, the preparation of the balance sheet—and to supervise the execution of its resolutions.

C. Duties of Board Members and Applicable Restrictions

530. Board members are required to perform their duties with due care and confidentiality and safeguard in good faith the interests of the company. As per Article 395 of the TCC, board members may not, without the approval of the general assembly, transact with the company either directly or on behalf of third parties. In the event of a breach of this obligation, the joint-stock company may claim that the transaction made is null and void. Also, as per Article 396 of the TCC, board members may not, without the approval of general assembly, directly or on behalf of third parties, operate in a business field that falls within the scope of activity of the company and may not become a shareholder with unlimited liability in a company that operates in such field. In the event that one of the directors breaches the obligation regarding non-competition, the A.Ş. may, at its discretion, claim damages from the director in question or, in lieu of damages, consider the transactions as having been made on behalf of the company and demand that the benefits arising out of agreements enacted with third parties are the benefits of the company. As discussed earlier, board members who are not shareholders of the company and their blood relatives and in-laws up to the third degree may not become indebted to the company for any cash amounts. The company may not provide any guarantee, surety or security in their favor.

531. Finally, under the terms of the TCC, board members cannot participate in discussions regarding matters that may give rise to a conflict of interest between the company's interests and personal interests of the (i) board member, (ii) his/her descendants or ascendants, (iii) spouse, (iv) blood relatives or in-laws up to and including the third degree. This restriction shall also apply to the situations where participation of the board member in the discussions may constitute a violation of the good faith principle.

D. Liability of Directors[98]

98. *See generally* E. Çamoğlu, *Anonim Ortaklık Yönetim Kurulu Üyelerinin Sorumluluğu* [Liability of the Board of Directors of Companies Limited by Shares], İstanbul 1972; S.K. Mimaroğlu, *Anonim Şirketlerde İdare Meclisi Üyelerinin Hukuki Mesuliyeti* [The Civil Liability of the Board of Directors of Companies Limited by Shares], Ankara 1967; T. Atan, *Anonim Şirketlerde İdare Meclisi Azalarının Hukuki Mesuliyeti*, [The Civil Liability of the Board of Directors of Companies Limited by Shares], Ankara 1967. R Poroy/Ü. Tekinalp/G. Tekinalp, "La Responsabilité Civile des Organes

1. Features

532. It is a Director's duty to exercise reasonable care in the management of the A.Ş.'s affairs. Directors are liable for damages if they do not duly perform their duties.

533. The first feature of this civil liability is that the Board of Directors can be held liable for losses and damages of the company and shareholders and company's creditors if they breach their obligations arising from law and Articles of Association. A Director who proves, however, that he/she is not at fault for the occurrence of losses cannot be held liable. In particular, Directors who (i) voted against the transactions/actions which caused the said damage and had their objections recorded in the minutes of the board meetings and advised the internal auditors of the associated risks in writing, or (ii) were not present in the deliberations concerning the transaction for a valid reason may not be held liable. Furthermore, if duties of a board member have been delegated to third parties in accordance with Article 367 of the TCC, only the delegated person(s) can be held responsible. The Board of Directors and/or board members transferring their duties and authorities to others may be held liable only if they did not act diligently while appointing the persons to whom they have delegated their duties and powers. Nobody can be held liable for violations of law and/or Articles of Associations or such other irregularities which are out of his/her control.

534. The second feature of the Director's liability is that this liability is a contractual liability, i.e., its source is the contract which exists between the joint-stock company and each Director. The director may be held liable if he/she is in breach of such contract.

535. The contractual obligations (including fiduciary duties) of the Directors include the following: (i) to manage the A.Ş.'s affairs;[99] (ii) to perform all the duties that are attributed to directors by law, Articles of Association or in separate contracts executed with the company; and (iii) not to commit any illegal acts. If the joint-stock company suffers losses and damages as a result of the acts and actions of the members of the board of directors, it can recover the entire amount of its losses from any of such members.

536. The third feature of this civil responsibility is that in case there is more than one director that may be held liable for the same loss, each one may be held liable severally and jointly with the others to the extent the damages may be attributed to such person depending on the level of his/her fault and circumstances affecting the specific case (TCC 557). The right of recourse among the directors is determined by the court according to the degree of fault of each Director.

Sociaux en Droit Turc", and Y. Karayalçın, "La Responsabilité des Organes en Droit Turc des Sociétés" in: *Die Verantwortlichkeit im Recht*, Türkisch-Schweizerische Juristenwoche 1980 in Zürich und Bern, Band 1, 2, 297–347 and 275–296.

99. *See* para. 400, *supra* and Poroy/Ü. Tekinalp/G. Tekinalp, *ibid.*

2. Causes of Liability

537. The Directors may be held liable for the following:

- incorrect and incomplete payments made by founders and shareholders;
- distribution of incorrect (false) dividends;
- failure to maintain A.Ş.'s records duly and properly;
- failure to comply with and perform the required actions for the fulfillment of the decisions of the General Assembly without a valid reason; and
- violation of duties bestowed to board members by law or by the Articles of Association knowingly. In case of delegation of such duties to third parties or one or more board members, only the delegates may be held responsible.

3. Plaintiffs of the Liability Lawsuit

538. A legal action against a defaulting director may be brought by the A.Ş., as well as by any shareholders.

539. According to Article 555 of TCC, in case the company suffers losses due to the actions of the board members which constitute a violation of their duties, the company and each shareholder can demand such losses to be compensated to the company. In other words, even in cases where the liability lawsuit is initiated by a shareholder for the losses incurred by the company, the compensation is always paid to the company and not to the shareholder.

4. Statute of Limitations

540. Liability lawsuits against directors may be initiated within two years from the date on which the injured party has knowledge of the damage and of the person responsible, therefore, and, in any case, within five years from the date on which the action giving rise to liability is committed by the board member (TCC 560).

541. If the action is based on a criminal act, and the criminal law provides for a longer statute of limitations, such a longer period shall also apply to the limitation period for the action of the civil claim.

5. Effects of Release of the Directors from Liability

542. The joint-stock company cannot initiate a liability lawsuit against the members of the board of directors if the directors have been released of liability by a decision of the General Assembly. Also, the shareholders who have voted in favor of the release of the directors or who have acquired the shares with knowledge of the release of the previous owner (shareholder) of the shares may not initiate liability lawsuits against the released directors for matters that fall within the scope of such release. However, the shareholders that have not participated in the general assembly or voted against the release of the board members directly initiate liability lawsuits against the board members within six months after the date of release decision of the general assembly.

E. Board Meetings

543. Members of the Board can only exercise their powers collectively by adopting resolutions at Board meetings.

544. Unless a higher majority is determined in the Articles of Association of the company, the board of directors is convened with the presence of the simple majority of the total number of board members and resolutions are obtained by the simple majority of the votes existing in a meeting that has been duly convened.

545. In the event that none of the board members request for convening of a physical meeting, board resolutions may be obtained through written approval of the majority of the total board members, provided that the written decision proposal of a board member is shared with all board members and the approvals of the majority of the board members are affixed on such proposal. It is not necessary for the approvals of the board members to be on the same page so long as different pages executed by the required majority of the board members are kept together and affixed to the board minutes book.

546. Board decisions may be deemed valid so long as they are in written form and signed by the board members constituting the requisite majority.

547. The Board meets whenever necessary upon invitation by the chairman. Each member may require, in writing, the chairman to call a meeting of the Board (TCC 392.7).

548. The TCC does not make any provision regarding the form of the notice to be given. Such rules are usually set forth in the Articles of Association of the A.Ş. It is an imperative general rule that notice of a Board meeting should provide all directors with sufficient time to enable them to attend. The agenda is certainly an integral part of the notice. It is usually specified by the chairman or his/her deputy. Notice of a Board meeting must specify when and where it is to be held. The form and period of the notice are usually fixed by the Articles of Association.

549. A Board meeting cannot take place unless a quorum of the Directors is present. Under the terms of the TCC, except as otherwise provided in the Articles of Association, the presence of the majority of the directors is required (TCC 390.1).

550. Each Director has one vote at a Board meeting. According to a mandatory rule of the TCC, Directors are not allowed to vote for each other, nor are they allowed to appoint a proxy (TCC 390.2).

551. Under the terms of the TCC, resolutions are passed by the majority of the Directors present at the meeting unless the Articles of Association otherwise provide. If there is an equality of votes, the resolution is not passed. The chairman does not have a casting vote in case of equal votes in the affirmative and negative.

552. A joint-stock company must keep minutes of the proceedings of its Board meetings. The minutes have to be signed to show both the participating members and the ones approving the resolution.

F. Representation of the A.Ş.

553. The A.Ş. is represented by the Board (TCC 365). The Articles of Association determine whether and how the representation of the A.Ş. shall be divided among the Directors. Unless otherwise provided in the Articles of Association of the company or the board of directors consists of only one member, the joint-stock company is represented by the joint signature of any two board members.

554. As mentioned above, as per Article 371 of the TCC, to the extent that at least one board member retains the authority to represent the company, the board of directors may delegate representation authority to one or more executive board members or third parties as managers. Limitation of the representation power of the board of directors may not be enforceable against third parties acting in good faith, provided, however, that representation authority limitation are introduced through joint signature requirement or whereby representation power is restricted to the transactions of only the headquarters or the branches of the company shall be valid if registered with the trade registry and announced in the Trade Registry Gazette. The board of directors may appoint non-executive board members or employees of the company as commercial representatives with limited representation powers through an internal directive to be registered with the trade registry and announced in the Trade Registry Gazette.

III. Auditors (Auditing of A.Ş.)

A. Basics

555. The most radical change brought upon by the TCC, which was subject to a wide scope reform in 2011, is the system change with respect to the independent audit and accounting standards of capital market companies in line with the language of international markets. We may refer to this as change of mentality. While the old Commercial Code considered auditors as a legal statutory body of joint-stock companies, it did not require auditors to have the appropriate training for the job or even any type of education. Limited liability companies, however, were entirely exempt from audit obligations. The scientific commission in charge of drafting the new TCC, chaired by Tekinalp, put great importance on an independent audit of joint-stock and limited liability companies structured by independent and modern principles, preparation of financial statements and other financial charts in line with IFRS and bringing forth an investment climate identical to that of the EU. Unfortunately, shadowed by the information pollution created by the Turkish Union of Chambers and Exchange Commodities, the umbrella organization in the trade, industry, agriculture and service sectors of Turkey, the reform was partially degenerated four days prior to its effective date by the Law No. 6335 prepared by the commission chaired by Ali Babacan, who was Vice President at the time. Without a doubt, the negative impact of Babacan as a politician has been marked in the history of Turkish law.

556. Considering that the audit system governs 20,000 (in 2011) private and public companies, with approximately 780,000 limited liability companies while the number of public companies being merely 600, it becomes harder to argue that only public companies should be audited in line with EU practices.

557. The article titled "*Moving to modernity*" published at that time in the International Financial Review states:

> The reaction of business circles to such transparency was vociferously negative. Some even labeled it "corporate voyeurism." Statute 6335 did not entirely abolish the corporate website requirement but limited independently audited companies. It also circumscribed the scope by dispensing among other items (…) financial statement auditing reports. These changes are incompatible with the principle of transparency and information valued by society (by Ünal Tekinalp, Chairman of the Commission responsible for drafting the new Commercial Code, IFLR, September 2012, Vol XXX17, p.56).

558. In accordance with the new system, the Council of Ministers was authorized to determine of companies who shall be subject to independent audit requirement. The Council of Ministers fulfilled the requirements of Article 398(4) of the CC by issuing the "Decision on Determination of Companies Which Shall be Subject to Independent Audit Requirement" (2012-4213/BKK). While the aggregate number of Joint Stock Companies and Limited Liability Companies, at the time, were estimated at TRY 1 million, with the decision, the number of companies which shall be audited in accordance with CC was set as 4,000.

559. In line with the Decision of the Council of Ministers numbered 2012-4213, companies which shall be subject to independent audit requirement shall be determined via three methods.

1. Benchmark (Economic Power Thresholds) Method

560. According to this method, companies which, alone or together with their affiliates and subsidiaries, meet at least two of the benchmarks, or in other words, the economic markers, specified in the relevant decision as "aggregate assets," "annual net sales" and "number of employees" shall be subject to independent audit requirement.

561. In this method, the key determinant is that at least two of the above-referred economic thresholds are exceeded. Otherwise, the type of the capital partnership, the sector it is active in, its field of activity or the significance of its operations does not have an effect on such determination.

2. Method Based on Consideration of "Institutions Concerning Public Interest"

562. The second method does not take into consideration the economic magnitude or power thresholds but instead, it considers whether the institution is included in the List No. 1 annexed to the Decision of the Council of Ministers. List No. 1 includes (from item 1 through item 6) names of capital partnerships identified as per the laws they are subject to, their field of activity, the governmental institutions of which they are a member and operational licenses they hold. Partnerships that are identified in List No. 1 are named as "institutions concerning public interest" (ICPI) under Article 2(1)/ğ of Decree (Having Force of Law) No. 660 relating to the "*Organization and Duties of the Public Oversight and Audit Standards Authority.*" Capital partnerships which are identified as ICPI as per the aforesaid provision are "*Public companies, banks, insurance, re-insurance and retirement companies, factoring companies, financing companies, financial leasing companies, asset management companies, retirement funds, issuers and capital market institutions and institutions that are deemed by the Authority to concern the public due to their field of activity, transaction volumes, number of employees and such other criteria.*" The term "ICPI" have been used since 2006 in the regulations and directives of EC and EU concerning audit of the partnerships corresponding to joint-stock companies in Turkish law. The term "Public" used in ICPI should not be interpreted as the "State" and/or "State-owned economic institutions" but instead as "community," "community interest" or even as "investors."

3. Hybrid Method

563. This method may be interpreted as the determination of the companies subject to independent audit requirement based on List No. 2 annexed to the Decision of the Council of Ministers numbered 2012-4213. The companies which are indicated in the aforesaid decision and which exceed at least two thresholds of the economic magnitude and power are identified again in the said decision.

B. Interpretation of the Provision Requiring the Appointment of the Auditor

564. Article 399(1) of the TCC refers to the obligation to appoint the auditor each year by indicating that "it is required that the auditor is selected for each activity (financial) year and, in any case, before the end of the financial year during which it shall perform its services." The referred part of the aforesaid article does not seem to serve its purpose. Because the selection of the auditor before the end of the financial year during which it shall perform its services means that the auditor may be elected any time before the end of the financial year and even just two to three days before the year-end. Such an approach may not be acceptable. Besides, such an interpretation would result in a contradiction with Article 399(6). As per this provision, in case the auditor is not selected until the fourth month of the financial year, the auditor shall be appointed by the court upon application.

565. The above-mentioned conflicting situation requires examination of the source law pertaining to the first sentence of Article 399(1) and determination of the interpretation of the source law doctrine.

C. The Objective of the Obligation Requiring the Selection of the Auditor Before the End of the Financial Year

566. The objective of the obligation requiring the selection of the auditor before the end of the financial year is to enable the auditor to get acquainted with the company or corporate group that it will audit, make necessary preparations, have information about the inventory and plan its services. It is necessary for the auditor to have the opportunity of examining the company beforehand. Therefore, the system enabling the Public Oversight Authority to inspect/audit the auditor via the internet or in its location and the auditor to fill in the form published by the Authority on the internet each month are in a logical relation with the obligation requiring the selection of the auditor before the end of the financial year. Such system is applied in many countries and was included in Provisional Article 3 of TCC which was abolished by Law No. 6335. If the aforesaid provision was not abolished, the first information form to be published by the Authority on the internet would aim to determine whether the auditor had (i) audited the inventory of the company in line with the generally accepted practice, (ii) made its audit planning and (iii) discussed the possible problems with the company directors.

D. Audit Agreement

567. "Audit Agreement" is mentioned under Article 399(8) of the TCC. It is understood based on the text of the aforesaid provision that the "audit agreement" refers to the agreement to be executed between the board of directors and the auditor. As per Article 399(1), "after election (by the general assembly) board of directors registers with the Trade Registry and announces in the Trade Registry Gazette and its website the auditor to whom the auditing duty is given." In other words, it may be concluded that, through the election of the auditor by the general assembly, the auditor is only "determined" as per Article 400/1 of the TCC either as a real person or legal entity, however, such determination does not automatically result in the appointment of the auditor which shall be made by a service agreement to be executed between the auditor and the board of directors of the company.

568. The importance and weight of the auditing agreement in Turkish Law is a lot more than what is conceived in general. The significance of the auditing agreement may be understood based on the "Turkish Auditing Standards" which constitutes the basis of our auditing system. Independent Audit Standards ("IAS") 200 relates to the "Independent Audit Agreement." IAS 700 and 706 and IAS 200 which regulates the Independent Audit Agreement in detail, make it clear that the election by the general assembly of the auditor is merely a "determination." Taking into consideration IAS 200 and the aforesaid authority granted to the board of directors, the general assembly may not give instructions to the board of directions as to the terms and conditions of the Audit Agreement or grant (delegate) authority for execution of such since the authority does not belong to the general assembly in the first place. The Board of Directors should act within the limits determined by IAS 200 while executing the Independent Audit Agreement.

569. The absence of an audit agreement does not result in the invalidity of the election of the general assembly. Public Oversight Board may compel the parties to execute such an agreement as well as penalize the auditor.

570. Article 399(1) of the TCC may be applied in two ways. *The first way* is that the board of directors comes to an agreement with an auditor it deems fit and, subject to the condition that the auditor is elected by the general assembly, submits to the approval of the general assembly the agreement it wishes to execute with the auditor. *The second way* is that the board of directors negotiates with the auditor elected by the general assembly and executes the audit agreement as per TCC 399 if an agreement may be reached. If an agreement may not be reached, submits to the approval of the general assembly of other auditor(s) with which an agreement may be reached.

571. Audit agreement is a service agreement which is also considered as an agreement for work.

E. Appointment of the Auditor

572. An auditor may be appointed either (i) through the election of the general assembly and execution of the audit agreement between the board of directors and the auditor; or (ii) by the court under the conditions set forth by the TCC; or (iii) by the board of directors as per TCC 399(6).

1. Election by the General Assembly and Execution of the Audit Agreement by the Board

573. The principal method assumed by the TCC for the appointment of the Auditor is the election of the auditor by the general assembly and execution of the audit agreement between the board of directors and the auditor. Unless a higher quorum or majority is not determined in the Articles of Association of the company, the general assembly shall make its election as per the quorum and majority set forth under TCC 418.

2. Appointment by the Court

574. If the joint-stock company or the corporate group does not have an auditor, the auditor is appointed by the Commercial Court of First Instance upon application of the board of directors or any board member or shareholder. The respondent in such a lawsuit is the legal entity of the joint-stock company. The lawsuit for the appointment of the auditor may be initiated under the following circumstances:

- if an auditor is not appointed by the company by the fourth month of its financial year (TCC 399/1);
- if the auditor elected by the general assembly rejects the appointment;
- if the auditor terminates the audit agreement executed between the board of directors and the auditor due to a change of its conditions by the general assembly; or
- if the corporate decisions concerning the appointment of the auditor are terminated, they become invalid or canceled.

575. The application to the court for appointment should also request the court to resolve the sample audit agreement, auditor fees and expenses. The sample agreement provided in IAS may be benefitted from for such purposes.

3. Appointment by the Board of Directors

576. As per TCC 399/6, the board of directors shall immediately appoint a temporary auditor if the previously appointed auditor notifies the company of cancellation of the audit agreement.

F. Cancellation of the Audit Agreement by the Auditor

577. The auditor may terminate the audit agreement under three conditions. Such conditions are: (1) there are valid reasons (just cause) for termination; (2) a lawsuit is initiated against the auditor for termination of its auditor position in the company; (3) the general assembly alters the conditions of the audit agreement that had been executed between the board of directors and the auditor.

578. The auditor may terminate the audit agreement only in the existence of valid reasons and justifiable grounds. Article 399/8 of the TCC does not define or specify what constitutes a valid reason. However, it determines the conditions which may not be considered as valid reasons for termination. As per the aforesaid provision, (a) disagreement on the content of the auditor's opinion, (b) limitation of the audit work and (c) refrainment by the auditor to provide an opinion. Appointment of another person or legal entity as the auditor of the company, failure and default of the company to perform its major obligations under the audit agreement, failure of the company to perform its obligations (to supply documents and information) within the time limits provided under the law, commitment of a crime by the company against the auditor and, especially, prevention of the audit works through physical abuse constitute valid reasons for the termination of the audit agreement by the auditor.

579. In the event that a lawsuit is initiated against the auditor for termination of its auditor position, the auditor may terminate the audit agreement. This provision enables the auditor who is under the threat of a court case to defend itself through a counter or independent lawsuit.

580. As mentioned above, the auditor is entitled to terminate the audit agreement it had executed with the board of directors if the terms thereof are altered by the general assembly.

G. Lawsuit for Dismissal of the Auditor and Appointment of a New Auditor

581. Articles 399(4) and 399(5) of the TCC provides the exception to the strict rule which prohibits dismissal of the auditor through termination of the audit agreement without cause or due to reason which is not recognized by law. The characteristics of the lawsuit that may be initiated for the dismissal of the auditor are as follows: (1) The lawsuit should be initiated for both the dismissal of the current auditor and appointment of a new one. The board of directors is not entitled to appoint a new auditor to replace the dismissed auditor. (2) The dismissal lawsuit may be initiated if the auditor does not have or loses his/her/its impartiality or fails to perform his/her/its duties due to constant illness or work overload. (3) The respondent of the dismissal lawsuit is the auditor and the plaintiff is the board of directors of the company. However, the dismissal lawsuit may also be initiated by the minority. However, in order for the minority shareholder(s) to initiate the dismissal lawsuits, two conditions should exist. First condition is that the minority shareholder(s) should have objected to the appointment of the auditor in general assembly and registered its objection in the meeting minutes. The second condition requires the minority shareholder(s) to be a shareholder in the company starting from at least three months prior to the date of the general assembly electing the auditor. The minority constitutes at least 10% of the total capital in companies which are not public and 5% in public ones. The minority should initiate the dismissal lawsuit within three weeks following the announcement of the election of the auditor in the Trade Registry Gazette.

H. Scope of the Audit

582. The matters which are subject to audit are exhaustively determined in the TCC. IAS 220 also adopts the same approach. The audit standards, in general, and especially paragraphs 18–20, supports such a conclusion. Auditor may not exclude any of the matters which are determined in the law from the scope of the audit. The matters subject to audit are as follows:

- financial (stand-alone) tables of the company;
- the inventory and accounting of the company and its internal control mechanism to the extent provided by the Turkish Accounting Standards;
- consolidated financial tables of the company and the corporate group;
- whether the company is in compliance with Turkish accounting standards, applicable laws and provisions of the Articles of Association pertaining to financial tables (in practice, the auditor does not comply with this requirement and especially does not audit and reflect in its report whether the necessary precautions that are required to be taken in certain stages are taken by the Company as per TCC 376);
- whether the risk assessment committee is established for public companies traded in the stock exchange and for closed companies (and public companies which are not listed in the stock exchange) for which establishment of the risk assessment committee was requested by the auditor;
- whether the company is in compliance with the principle of a fair and true view of the financial affairs of the company.

583. Auditing of the "internal control" requires some discussion. The TCC has a positive approach to this question. Because: (1) As per TCC 398(4), the auditor "*audits whether the board of directors* has *established the system and the authorized committee provided for under TCC 378 and if such a system and committee exist prepares a separate report detailing its structure and activities and submits such to the board*"; (2) for companies which are not publicly traded, the auditor also reports to the board of directors if it determines that establishment of an internal control system and the committee is necessary; (3) IAS 610/11 does not impose an obligation on the outside independent auditor with respect to "internal control" if such a mechanism exists in a company besides the risk assessment committee. Additionally, TCC does not impose on the auditor the obligation to audit the information technology systems of the company. The Public Oversight Board may require the retaining of an expert in the company for such purposes as per IAS 220/A11 and A12.

584. TCC requires the auditor to act diligently and comply with professional standards and ethics during the performance of the audit services. Reference to both professional standards and ethics imposes a mandatory obligation on the auditor with universal power and recognition.

585. The auditing foreseen under the TCC extends to the entire financial year during which the auditor is required to follow up on the developments in the company and the corporate group as per the Turkish Accounting Standards and, if and when necessary, remind and caution the board of directors the required standards. The practice that is intended to be prevented by the TCC is the preparation of a format report without visiting the joint-stock company for the entire year.

IV. Workers Participation (Via Two-Tier Board Structure or Auditor Appointment)

586. Turkish Law does not foresee a two-tier board structure whereby employees become part of the management through a mandatory body. However, in practice, various companies form internal committees that consist of executive officers/employees of the Company. These committees usually adopt decisions that would serve as a proposal to the Board of Directors. Since a two-tier board structure is not foreseen, decisions adopted by such committees shall not have a formal effect enforceable against third parties.

§6. The Dissolution and Liquidation of a Joint-Stock Company

I. Grounds for Dissolution

587. Under Turkish law, the dissolution of a joint-stock company may be examined from the following standpoints:

- whether it comes to an end *ipso iure*; or
- whether it comes to an end by means of a decision of the court or by means of a resolution of the General Meeting.

A. *Dissolution* Ipso Iure

588. The grounds for dissolution *ipso iure* are divided into two categories:

(1) grounds established by law; and
(2) rounds established in the Articles of Association of the company limited by shares.

1. Grounds Provided by Law

589. The joint-stock company shall dissolve *ipso iure* based on the following grounds provided by law:

(a) Expiry of the Term of the Company (TCC 529.1a): The joint-stock company dissolves at the end of the term if it is established for a definite term and does not become a company with indefinite term through de facto continuance of its activities beyond the term.
(b) Realization of the Company Objective (TCC 529.1b): The joint-stock company terminates in case it realizes its objectives or if such objectives become unattainable. According to the Court of Appeal, the company limited by shares may be dissolved by the transfer of its complete assets.[100]
(c) Bankruptcy of the Company (TCC 529.1e): In the event that a court decision is granted for the bankruptcy of the company, the company shall also dissolve.
(d) Occurrence of Other Dissolution Events foreseen in Law (TCC 529.1f): There are various other events provided elsewhere in law which result in the dissolution of the company. As per (i) TCC 152.3, in a merger transaction, the transferred entity dissolves; (ii) TCC 159.1, in a complete division, original entity dissolves; (iii) TCC 376.2, the joint-stock company dissolves in case the company loses two-thirds of its capital (calculated by inclusion of the legal reserves) and the shareholders do not resolve for completion of capital or decrease it to one-third of the original amount; and (iv) Article 20.1 of the Law on Implementation of the TCC, the company shall dissolve if it fails to increase its capital to the minimum requirements foreseen under TCC 332 within the time limit foreseen thereunder.

2. Grounds Provided in the Articles of Association

590. As per TCC 529.1c, the joint-stock company shall dissolve upon the occurrence of events provided in the Articles of Association.

591. The Articles of Association of the company may include certain events or conditions which shall result in the dissolution of the company. These events or conditions may relate to the business affairs of the company or may be unrelated. For instance, Articles of Association may indicate that the company terminates upon the finalization of a specific construction project undertaken by the company. Alternatively, the articles may indicate that the company shall dissolve upon the death of a certain shareholder.

B. Other Dissolution Cases

1. Upon the Decision of the General Assembly

592. As per TCC 529.1d, the general assembly of the company may resolve for termination with the qualified quorum foreseen under TCC 421.3 which requires the

---

100. *See* jud [11th C.Cham. Sup. Court] No. 1278/1669 [Mar. 25, 1985] in: *ibid.*, para. 1548.

affirmative votes of the shareholders representing at least 75% of the share capital of the company. Voting privileges shall not be taken into consideration in such calculations.

2. Dissolution (Termination) in Case of Absence of Legal Organs

593. As explained above, the legal organs of a joint-stock company include the General Assembly and the Board of Directors. In the event that any of these mandatory organs are or become absent, a termination lawsuit may be initiated for the dissolution of the stock company.

594. TCC 530 requires the absence of the general assembly or the board of directors which may be deemed to have occurred if one of these organs may not convene for a long period of time. Such failure should continue for a long period of time which should not be shorter than three years.

595. The termination lawsuit may be initiated by any of the shareholders, creditors or the Ministry of Trade.

596. The court provides a reasonable time to the company for the correction of the irregularity and decides for termination if the absent organ may not be formed during such time.

3. Dissolution (Termination) for Just Cause

597. The joint-stock company may be terminated by the decision of the court in case of existence of justified grounds. As per TCC 531, minority shareholders representing at least 10% of the share capital (or 5% in public companies) may apply for termination to the Commercial Court of First Instance having jurisdiction at the address of the head offices of the company.

598. The new TCC enabled termination (dissolution) of both limited liability companies (TCC 636) and joint-stock companies (TCC 531) based on justified grounds while bestowing the court to rule for alternative solutions.[101] The termination lawsuit is constitutive in nature and the parties to the lawsuit are the minority and the company.

599. The authority of the court to decide on alternative solutions rather than termination is quite broad. Regardless of the request of the plaintiff, the court may decide, instead of termination, spin-off of a certain business of the company, purchase of the shares of the minority, distribution of dividends from legal reserves or

---

101. *See* Poroy/Tekinalp/Çamoğlu, Law of Corporations, II Volume, Updated and Rewritten 15th Edition, 2021, 347–359 [*see* SB], 121–124, 61–63.

inclusion of the minority to the management of the company through representation in the board of directors. The authority of the court to decide on alternative solutions is absolute.

600. Transferring the business and resources of the company or siphoning off funds of the company, violation of audit and inspection rights of shareholders, condemnation of the minority to dividend deprivation, mismanagement of the company by incompetent individuals (*Grumser* decision dated May 12, 2000) are some examples that may constitute justified grounds for termination of a joint-stock or limited liability company. Through the renovations introduced by the new TCC, termination (dissolution) lawsuits have now become a part of Turkish corporate law.

C. Consequences of Dissolution and Liquidation

601. In the event that the company dissolves due to any reason other than bankruptcy or the decision of the court, the board of directors is required to apply to the relevant Trade Registry for the registration and announcement of the dissolution of the company.

602. Except otherwise provided in law (e.g., merger and division), the dissolved company enters into liquidation (TCC 533.1) under the supervision of the liquidation officers. However, the relations between the shareholders and the joint-stock company and the liabilities of the organs of the company towards the shareholders continue. However, the joint-stock company is required to add to its title the term "under liquidation."

603. The legal entity status of the joint-stock company continues through the liquidation process and its organs (general assembly and board of directors) continue to function. However, duties and powers of these organs are now limited only to such acts and actions that are required for the conclusion of the liquidation but may not be directly and properly conducted by the liquidation officer due to their nature (TCC 535).

604. Such restriction should be interpreted as a limitation on the legal capacity of the company organs.[102] For instance, the general assembly shall not be entitled to amend the Articles of Association if such amendment is not necessary for the purposes of liquidation. However, it may exercise its powers provided under TCC 408.2f and initiate liability lawsuits and appoint an auditor. The same rule also applies to the powers and authorities of the Board of Directors. The board continues to represent the company on matters other than those that relate to liquidation and are conducted by the liquidation officer and initiates lawsuits against the general assembly decisions for their cancellation or declaring them null and void.

---

102. *See* the decision of the Swiss Federal Court: BGE 117 III 39.

605. Liquidation officers may be appointed by the Articles of Association or the decision of the general assembly. If such an appointment does not exist, liquidation is handled by the board of directors of the company. Liquidation officers may be a shareholder or third person. In cases where the termination of the company is decided by the court, the liquidation officer is also appointed by the court.

606. Upon appointment, liquidation officers prepare and submit to the approval of the general assembly the initial inventory and balance sheet to reflect the financial status of the company at the start of liquidation.

607. The creditors of the company that are reflected in company books and records or determined as per other means are invited by registered mail (if their addresses are known) and through three announcements made in one-week intervals in the Trade Registry Gazette, the website of the company and as per the related provisions of the Articles of Association (if any) to report to the liquidation officers of their receivables from the company. In the event that any of the known creditors of the company fail to report to the liquidation officers, the company pays their receivables to an account to be determined by the Ministry of Trade. For receivables which are not yet due or disputed, the company may either provide appropriate guarantees to the creditors and acknowledge that the shareholders shall not be paid before the satisfaction of such receivables or pay the relevant amounts to the notary public to be transferred to the relevant creditors on their due dates. In case the company wishes to pay the creditors any undue receivables, the liquidation officers are required to apply a discount on the receivable amount at the discount rate applied by the Turkish Central Bank to short-term loans. The creditors are not entitled to reject such early payment.

608. TCC enables the company to revive the company from liquidation in only two cases where the company is liquidated: (1) due to expiry of the term and (2) as a result of the decision of the general assembly. In order to rescind the liquidation, the company should not have started the distribution of the liquidation proceeds to the shareholders. The general assembly should vote for rescinding of liquidation by a majority of at least 75% of the share capital of the company. Such decision of the general assembly to rescind liquidation should be registered with the Trade Registry and announced.

609. Any amounts remaining after payment of the debts of the company and the capital portions of the shareholders shall be distributed among the shareholders pro rata to their shareholding in the company or as per the privileges foreseen in the Articles of Association.

610. Liquidation proceeds may not be distributed before the lapse of a period of six months following the third and last announcement made to the creditors, provided, however, that the court may permit an earlier distribution if it decides that the receivables of the creditors are not in any danger.

611. Upon finalization of liquidation, the liquidation officers apply to the relevant Trade Registry for the deregistration of the company's title. Deregistration of the company is registered and announced.

§7. Mergers and Takeovers

612. Detailed explanations have been provided in relation to mergers, takeovers and protection rights of the shareholders under paragraphs 128-135, 334 and 411–419.

§8. Holding Companies and Subsidiaries

613. Holding companies are not defined in the TCC. The former TCC defined "holding companies" as companies whose objective consists only of participation in other companies. However, holding companies are subject to certain requirements based on the regulations of the Ministry of Trade.

614. As per the provisions of the Communiqué pertaining to the Capital Increase by Joint Stock and Limited Liability Companies up to the newly determined Minimum Capital Amounts and the Determination of Types of Joint-Stock Companies of which Establishment Requires the Pre-Approval of the Ministry dated November 15, 2012, the establishment of holding companies are subject to the pre-approval of the Ministry of Trade. Again, the same Communiqué foresees that the amendment of the Articles of Association of holding companies requires the pre-approval of the Ministry if such amendment is pertaining to a capital increase or capital decrease.

615. TCC includes a special requirement with respect to the legal reserve requirement of holding companies. In principle, joint-stock companies are required to set aside 5% of net annual profits as general legal reserves until such amount reaches 20% or the paid-up capital. After such threshold is reached and 5% of net profits are distributed to shareholders as first dividend, 10% of the amounts to be distributed to ones that are entitled to receive a portion of the net profits is added to the general legal reserves. These requirements pertaining to the setting aside of general legal reserves do not apply to holding companies whose main scope of business is to participate in other companies as an equity holder.

616. Also, it is possible to consider that the holding company and its subsidiaries as a corporate group which shall be subject to the requirements applicable to corporate groups as per the provisions of the TCC. In which case, the holding company shall be treated as the parent company in terms of corporate group provisions of the TCC and shall be required to exercise its control over the subsidiaries in a manner to protect the subsidiaries. In other words, as per Article 202/1 of the TCC, the parent company may not abuse its control over the subsidiary in a manner to create losses for the company. Additionally, the holding/parent company should exercise its voting rights in the general assembly of the subsidiaries pertaining to structural changes (e.g., merger, spin-off, liquidation, issuance of securities and material changes in the Articles of Association). As per Article 209 of the TCC, the parent company (holding) is responsible for protecting the reputation of the corporate group.

§9. Taxation of a Joint-Stock Company

I. Corporate Tax

617. The revenues of joint-stock companies are subject to corporate tax like the other capital-based companies as clearly stipulated under Articles 1 and 2 of the Corporate Tax Law No. 5520 ("*CTL*").

618. Joint-stock companies which have a principal place of business or headquarters in Turkey are taxed based on their entire revenues generated in and outside of Turkey. However, companies which do not have their principal offices or headquarters in Turkey shall be taxed only based on their revenues generated in Turkey.

619. Corporate tax is calculated based on the net profits generated by the joint-stock companies within a fiscal year. Provisions of Income Tax Law No. 193 (*ITL*) pertaining to the commercial revenues shall apply while determining the net profit. Article 59 of the ITL shall also apply with respect to the calculation of the net profits of corporations generated from agricultural activities if any.

620. The base amount to be taken into account in determining corporate tax is calculated by subtracting the sum of privileged earnings and previous year's losses, if any, from the sum of non-deductible expenses and net commercial revenues.

A. *Deductible Expenses*

621. The following items listed in Article 8 of the CTL may be deducted from the commercial revenues while determining the net profits:

- expenses pertaining to the issuance of securities;
- incorporation and organization expenses;
- expenses incurred in relation to general assembly meetings and expenses pertaining to mergers, transfers, spin-offs, termination and liquidation;
- in commandite partnerships, the capital of which is divided into shares, the dividends distributed to the commandite partner;
- dividends distributed by participation banks in relation to the participation accounts; and
- for insurance companies, technical reserves pertaining to the insurance policies are in effect as of the date of financial statements.

B. Deduction of Losses

622. As per the provisions of Article 9 of the CTL pertaining to the "Deduction of Losses," the following items may be deducted in determining the corporate tax, provided that such items are stated for each year separately in the corporate tax statements and other required procedures are completed:

- Losses declared in the previous year's tax statements provided that they are not carried for more than five years (losses of the entitles acquired as per Article 20/1 of the CTL which do not exceed their equity amounts as of the date of acquisition and losses of the entities that are spun off as per Article 20/2 of the CTL within the scope of a "complete spin-off" which do not exceed the equity amounts that are taken over may also be deducted).
- Losses that relate to the activities of the company outside of Turkey except for those that relate to revenues that are exempted from corporate tax in Turkey.

C. Other Deductions

623. In addition to those listed above, the following items may also be deducted from the revenues of the corporation as per Article 10 of the CTL, provided that such items are stated for each year separately in the corporate tax statements and other required procedures are completed:

- Entire amount of sponsorship payments made to amateur sports and 50% of the sponsorship payments made to professional sports within the scope of Law No. 3289 on Organization and Duties of the General Directorate of Youth and Sports dated May 21, 1986 and Law No. 3813 on Organization and Duties of The Turkish Football Federation dated June 17, 1962.
- Up to 5% of the relevant year's revenue may be deducted in relation to documented donations and contributions made to public administrations with general and special budgets, special provincial administrations, municipalities and villages, foundations and associations working for the public benefit for which tax exemption has been granted by the Presidency and institutions and organizations that are engaged in scientific research and development activities (collectively "*Deductible Institutions*").
- Entire amount of cash and in-kind donations and contributions or expenses made to Deductible Institutions in relation to construction or maintenance of schools, health institutions, student hostels, kindergartens, orphanages, hospices, nursery and rehabilitation centers, sanctuaries built under the supervision and consent of the local authorities, institutions providing extended religious education under the supervision of Directorate of Religious Affairs and youth centers, youth and scouting camps of the Ministry of Youth and Sports.
- Expenses made by Deductible Institutions or expenses supported by or deemed eligible to be supported by the Ministry of Culture and Tourism.
- Entire amount of documented cash and in-kind donations made to the donation campaigns started by the President.

- Entire amount of documented cash and in-kind donations and contributions made to Turkish Red Crescent Association and Turkish Green Crescent Association (except those made to their commercial institutions).
- Up to 10% of the declared revenues may be deducted in relation to amounts set aside as venture capital as per Article 325/A of the Tax Procedural Law No. 213.
- 50% of the revenues generated from architecture, engineering, design, software, medical reporting, accounting recording, call center, product testing, certification, data storage, data processing, data analysis services provided in Turkey to persons and workplaces located outside of Turkey and to companies of which the main place of business is located outside of Turkey and revenues generated by entities active in vocational training in the fields determined by the Ministry of Finance after having sought the opinion of relevant ministries and by entities providing services to persons that are located outside of Turkey under the approval and supervision of the relevant ministry (in order to be able to benefit from this deduction, invoices or similar documentation should be issued to the name of the client located outside of Turkey)
- 100% of the annual gross salaries made to the mentally or psychologically disabled people employed by protective workplaces established as per Law No. 5378 on Disabled Individuals.
- Cash capital increases in the amount of paid or issued capital registered in the trade registry of capital companies, except for institutions operating in the finance, banking and insurance sectors and state economic enterprises, within the relevant accounting period, or 50% of the amount calculated until the end of the relevant accounting period, taking into account the "weighted average annual interest rate applied to TRY-denominated commercial loans opened by banks" for the year in which the discount was benefited by the Central Bank over the portion of the paid capital in newly established capital companies that are covered by cash (this deduction is benefited separately for each subsequent period starting from the fiscal period in which the corporate decision regarding the capital increase or the Articles of Association in the first establishment phase was registered. In case of a capital decrease in the following periods, the decreased capital amount is not taken into account in the calculation of the discount).

D. Non-deductible Expenses

624. Article 11 of the Corporate Tax Law sets forth the expenses which may not be deducted when determining corporate earnings. These are:

- Interest paid or calculated over shareholder's equity.
- Interest, exchange differences and similar expenses paid or calculated over thin capitalization.
- Profits are distributed implicitly by transfer pricing.
- Any type or form of reserves (including all reserves set aside from net profits in accordance with the Turkish Commercial Code, laws of incorporation, Presidential decrees or by-laws, formation documents or agreements and general provisions set aside by banks in accordance with Banking Law).

- All corporate tax calculated in accordance with this Law, all monetary fines, tax penalties, all penalties paid in accordance with Law No. 6183 on the Procedure For Collection of Public Receivables dated July 21, 1953, default interest and charges and default interest paid in accordance with the provisions of Tax Procedure Law.
- Losses resulting from the issuance of securities below the nominal value, save for margins determined by Laws or based on the authorities vested by laws, and commissions and similar expenses paid in relation to such securities.
- Expenses and amortization of yachts, cruisers, boats, speed boats and similar motor sea vessels and aircrafts such as planes and helicopters leased or registered in the name of the company, which are not associated with the main operations of the company.
- Losses arising from indemnification of monetary or moral damages caused by criminal acts of the company, its shareholders, managers or employees, excluding contractual penalty clauses.
- Losses arising from indemnification of monetary or moral damages caused by acts committed through the medium of the press or radio and television broadcasts.
- 50% of advertisement expenses for all types of alcohol and alcoholic beverages, tobacco and tobacco products. The President shall be authorized to increase this ratio up to 100% or decrease it down to zero.
- The portion, as determined by the President, up to 10% of the aggregate expenses and cost elements under the name of interest, commission, carrying charges, dividends, exchange differences or other similar names pertaining to foreign assets used by the company excluding those which are included in the investment costs of companies whose equity is exceeded by the foreign assets used apart from credit institutions, financial institutions, financial leasing and factoring companies and financing companies, exclusive to the part in excess. The President shall be authorized to determine the above-referred ratio based on different sectors and the Ministry of Finance shall be authorized to determine the terms and conditions applicable to the enforcement of this paragraph. This ratio has been determined by the decision of the President dated February 3, 2021 and Law No. 3490 as 10% effective as of January 1, 2021.

E. Principle of Declaration

625. Corporate tax shall be imposed upon the taxpayer's declaration. The declaration shall include the results of the relevant accounting term.

626. All taxpayers shall submit a declaration for the entire earnings subject to taxation. However, the declarations for state-owned economic enterprises without a legal entity status and economic enterprises owned by associations or foundations shall each be submitted, as a separate declaration, by the governing state-owned legal entity, association or foundation.

627. The corporate tax declaration shall be submitted and paid by the taxpayer to the tax office of such taxpayer until the expiry of the fourth month following the month in which the accounting term has ended.

F. Tax Period and Assessment

628. The taxing period for corporate tax is the accounting term. The taxing period for those who have been assigned a special accounting term shall be that special accounting term.

629. For taxes paid by way of deduction and in cases where no additional annual declaration is submitted, the periods relevant to the tax deduction shall be construed as the taxing period.

630. Corporate tax shall be assessed by the tax office where the declaration is submitted.

G. Corporate Tax and Provisional Tax Rate

631. Corporate tax shall be 20% of the company's earnings.

632. Corporate taxpayers shall pay provisional tax in accordance with the terms set forth under the Corporate Tax Law and in the amount of the applicable corporate tax of the current period (which, for limited taxpayers, shall be limited to commercial and agricultural earnings), which shall be deducted from the applicable corporate tax of the current taxing period. Rules applicable to full taxpayers shall be applicable, ad verbum, to limited taxpayers.

II. Value Added Tax

633. In Turkey, the following shall be subject to value added tax (VAT):

- Commercial, industrial and agricultural operations and services and deliveries within the framework of independent business operations.
- Import of any goods and services.
- Services and deliveries arising from other operations are listed under Article 1 of Law No. 3065 on VAT (Law).

634. The transactions being realized in Turkey means the goods being located in Turkey at the moment of the delivery or the services being rendered or benefitted from in Turkey.

635. Joint-stock companies shall be responsible for VAT as of their registration with the trade registry.

636. In accordance with Article 9 of the Law, in cases where the taxpayer does not have a residency, workplace, registered headquarters or business center in Turkey or other cases where deemed necessary, the Ministry of Finance may, in order to secure tax receivables, hold those, who are party to the transaction subject to taxation, accountable for the payment of the tax.

637. In Turkey, the general VAT rate is 18% and the reduced VAT rates are 8% and 1%.

638. Deliveries and services which are exempt from VAT have been listed in detail under Articles 11–17 of the Law.

A. Tax Deduction

639. Article 29 of the law regulates Tax Deduction. Accordingly, Unless provided hereunder as otherwise, taxpayers shall be entitled to deduct the following from the VAT calculated based on their taxable transactions:

- the VAT indicated in invoices and similar instruments issued in connection with services or deliveries acquired for themselves;
- VAT paid in connection with imported goods and services;
- the VAT indicated under invoices or similar instruments pertaining to assets of taxpayers, which have changed from lump-sum or compensatory taxation system to real taxation system, which, in accordance with the inventory list, are existing at the commencement of the accounting term.

B. Principle of Declaration and Taxing Period

640. Unless provided hereunder as otherwise, VAT shall be imposed upon written declaration of taxpayers.

641. For joint-stock companies, the taxing period for VAT shall be the one-month terms of the applicable calendar year. The Declaration for VAT shall be submitted until the twenty-sixth night of the month following the taxing period and paid until the twenty-sixth night of the month in which the declaration has been submitted.

III. Other Taxes and Fees

642. Depending on their transactions and field of operations, joint-stock companies may be subject to additional tax and/or payment obligations set forth under other laws, including particularly Special Consumption Tax, Stamp Tax and Fees.

Chapter 2. Commandite Partnerships Limited by Shares

§1. Distinguishing Features

643. A commandite partnership limited by shares, which is called a *"Sermayesi Paylara Bölünmüş Komandit Şirket"* (SPBKŞ) in Turkish, is a mixed type of Commercial Enterprise, composed of the characteristics of both the A.Ş. and the commandite partnership (i.e., limited partnership). The capital of an SPBKŞ is divided into shares, and one or more partners are jointly and severally (i.e., jointly and individually) liable to the full extent of their property for the company's obligations in the same manner as partners in a collective partnership (general partnership). The other partners are in the same position as the shareholders in an A.Ş. Under the terms of Article 124 /2 of the TCC, the SPBKŞ is recognized as a capital company.

644. As per Article 564 of the TCC, in the event that the capital is not divided into shares but into parts which merely regulate the extent of the participation of several partners, the provisions relating to Commandite Partnerships (TCC 304–328) are applied.

645. The first feature of the SPBKŞ is its Board. The unlimited partners form the Board of Directors. In this respect, the SPBKŞ can be qualified as an A.Ş. (ex officio) administered and represented by law by its unlimited partners. The provisions regarding the duties and responsibilities of the Board of Directors of an A.Ş. also apply to the unlimited partners.

646. The second feature of the SPBKŞ is that, in the absence of any other clause in the Articles of Association of the partnership, the auditors are responsible for obtaining resolutions of the general assembly.

647. The SPBKŞ is regulated very briefly by the TCC (Articles 564–572). In certain respects, the provisions applicable to commandite partnerships apply to SPBKŞ, such as the relationship of the unlimited partners to one another and the relationship of the unlimited partners to the limited partners and to third persons. Furthermore, the administration and representation of the SPBKŞ, as well as the retirement of the unlimited partners from the partnerships, is governed by the provisions of the TCC regarding limited partnership. In other respects, the provisions of the TCC applicable to joint-stock companies apply to commandite partnerships limited by shares unless otherwise provided for by Articles 564–572 of the TCC.

648. As a corporate body, the SPBKŞ acts under its trade name. The name of an SPBKŞ must contain the first and family name of at least one partner with unlimited liability, as well as indicating the type of partnership (TCC 42). It is forbidden to mention the names and the family names of the limited partners in the trade name of the SPBKŞ. Like joint-stock companies, an SPBKŞ may be founded for any economic purpose or objective which is not prohibited by law.

649. The capital of SPBKŞ is determined in the Articles of Association and divided into shares as the joint-stock companies. Since the provisions of TCC are applicable to the capital of joint stock-companies, it also applies to the commandite partnerships limited by shares; it would be possible for a commandite partnership limited by shares to adopt an authorized (registered) capital system.

§2. Formation

I. Comparison with the Formation of Joint-Stock Companies

650. Articles 566–569 of the TCC regulate the formation of the commandite partnerships limited by shares. These provisions relate to the form and minimum scope of the Articles of Association, founders and formation general assembly. The scope and form of the Articles of Association of a commandite partnership limited by shares shall be subject to Article 399 of the TCC which is the provision applicable to the Articles of Association of joint-stock companies. However, as opposed to the joint-stock companies, benefits from the profits of the partnership may not be granted to board members and others. Incorporation procedures are the same as the incorporation procedures of joint-stock companies.

II. Founders and Procedure of Formation

651. As per Article 568/1 of the TCC, the signatories of the Articles of Association and the ones who have contributed non-cash capital to the partnership shall be deemed as founders. The minimum number of founders required for commandite partnerships limited by shares is five. These partnerships may not be founded by or survive with a single partner. At least one of the founders has to be liable without limitation for the liabilities of the partnership ("unlimited partner"). The number and value of the shares of the partners with limited liability ("limited partners") who are also founders have to be recorded in the Articles of Association of the company.

652. The Articles of Association has to be signed and executed by all founders. The foundation of the SPBKŞ is not subject to the approval of the Ministry, however, same registration and announcement requirements of joint-stock companies shall apply for the SPBKŞ.

III. Organization

653. The SPBKŞ has a corporate structure and is considered as a capital partnership.

A. Management

654. As per Article 570 of the TCC, the unlimited partners of the SPBKŞ shall be considered as managers/directors and be subject to the same scope of duty and liability provisions as the board of directors of a joint-stock company. The SPBKŞ does not have an elected Board of Directors.

655. As evident in Article 570 of the TCC, on the one hand, the unlimited partners are declared by law as the managers/directors of the SPBKŞ and they have both the power and the duty to represent and manage the company. On the other hand, an unlimited partner may reject to act as a manager since the TCC does not include a provision which prohibits such rejection or resignation. In case all the unlimited partners resign from management duty, a lawsuit for the liquidation/termination of the company may be initiated based on the absence of the required corporate organ.

656. The limited partner of an SPBKŞ or a third party may not be appointed as the manager/director of the partnership. However, limited partners or third parties may be appointed as commercial representatives. Such appointment has to be registered with the Trade Registry and announced in the Trade Registry Gazette.

B. General Assembly

657. The limited and unlimited partners of the SPBKŞ constitute the general assembly of the partnership. The provisions pertaining to the general assembly of the joint-stock companies shall also apply for the SPBKŞ. However, such general reference may be misleading to the reader since there are some provisions which may not apply to the general assembly of the SPBKŞ due to the legal nature of this partnership. For instance, the provisions concerning the election and dismissal of the board members and special audit may not be applied for SPBKŞ. Professor Tekinalp is of the opinion that the provisions pertaining to the cancellation and nullity of the general assembly decisions of the joint-stock companies shall also apply in the case of SPBKŞ.

C. Audit

658. The provisions for joint-stock companies concerning auditors also apply for the SPBKŞ.

IV. Changes among the Partners

659. The provisions for the A.Ş. concerning the transfer of shares of the joint-stock companies shall apply.

660. The transfer of registered shares may be performed by handing over the endorsed share certificates to the acquirer.

V. Dissolution and Liquidation

661. As per the reference of Article 565/2 of the TCC, the provisions of TCC concerning the liquidation of the joint-stock companies shall also apply for the SPBKŞ. However, the application of Article 531 of the TCC which enables the minority shareholders holding at least 10% of the share capital of the joint-stock company (5% for public companies) to request from the court the dissolution of the company based on a valid reason may not be applied for SPBKAŞ since the concept of minority shareholding does not exist in commandite partnerships limited by shares. The company is terminated by the resignation, death, incapacity or bankruptcy of all unlimited partners (TCC 476.2). Furthermore, the dissolution of the SPBKŞ is governed by the provisions for the dissolution of the A.Ş. A dissolution by resolution of the SPBKŞ requires the consent of the unlimited partners.

Chapter 3. Limited Liability Companies (*Limited Şirket*)

§1. Distinguishing Features

662. In new TCC, rules applicable to the Limited Liability Companies (*"Limited Şirket"* (L.Ş.), have undergone a substantial reform. Although its hybrid nature which combines the characteristics of both the Collective Partnership and the A.Ş., still continues to a certain extent, under the new TC, its characteristics have become more similar to "Joint Stock Companies (*Anonim Şirket* (A.Ş.))." Diverting from the approach of former TCC of 1956, new TCC states that "the limited liability company may be formed by "one or more real or legal persons" (TCC Article 573.1). In the new TCC, L.Ş. has turned into a limited liability partnership which provides opportunity to determine share groups, give privileges to certain share groups, issue dividend right bonds, which has a board of managers operating like the board of directors of A.Ş.; which can address needs of information society through independent audit (if required, according to criteria determined by the Councils of Ministers), its financial tables prepared according to Turkish Accounting Standards and websites, in which interests of partners and third parties are protected with effective provisions. Therefore, new L.Ş. may be defined as a minor-scoped A.Ş.[103] Under new L.Ş. the disposal of capital share has been limited by law but such limitation is not mandatory; the rules for withdrawal and exclusion of partners from the partnership are regulated as a structural procedure and personal contributions of the partners has importance. Some of the features of new L.Ş. are peculiar to New TCC: *First*, the law provision requiring management and representation of the partnership by the partners has been abolished (TCC Article 623.1). *Second*, TCC's provisions regarding L.Ş. has become mandatory unless otherwise is stated in the law (TCC Article 579). As with the other new features introduced by new TCC, a partner may hold more than one capital share and based on the reference in TCC Article 644 (1) lit (b) to TCC Article 358 shareholders are not allowed to take out loans from L.Ş. unless they pay their due debts arising from allocated capital share and unless profit of the partnership together with its voluntarily allocated reserves of the partnership covers past year's losses[104]. Again different from the Former TCC, shareholders are not required to pay their capital shares at once. The provisions applicable to the payment of capital shares in the joint-stock companies are also applicable to the payment of capital shares in the L.Ş. However, as per Law No. 7099 on "Amendment of Certain Laws for Improvement of the Investment Environment" dated March 10, 2008, the requirement of payment of one-fourth of the share capital undertaking in advance has been removed for limited liability companies. Provisions applicable to joint-stock companies regarding the liability system, the maximum and minimum number of partners, economic aim of the partnership, accounting, formation, protection of the capital and content requirements of the Articles of Association (partnership agreement) shall also apply for the limited liability companies.

---

103. Compare. MEIER-HAYOZ/FORSTMOSER (2007), § 18, N. 15; § 10, N. 86.
104. *See* TEKİNALP/ÇAMOLU (2012), Açıklamalı, Notlu ve Karşılaştırmalı 6102 Sayılı Yeni Türk Ticaret Kanunu ve Ticari Mevzuat, Güncelleştirilmiş 14. Bası, m. 358 altındaki notlar.

663. The L.Ş., which is popular for small and medium-sized businesses, can be formed for any economic purpose, e.g., for trading, manufacturing, or other business with other economic objects. A partnership with limited liability may not, however, operate in the banking, insurance, financing, financial leasing and factoring fields. In many respects, the principles applicable to A.Ş.s and to General Partnerships also apply to L.Ş.s.

664. One of the characteristic features of an L.Ş. is the limited liability of the shareholders. The liability of the shareholders is limited to the amount of their capital contributions. They are not obliged to perform any other obligation other than as stated in the L.Ş.'s Agreement (Articles of Association) and are not personally liable for the debts of the partnership. The obligation to pay L.Ş.'s public debts (e.g., tax liabilities) has been imposed on the shareholders by Article 35 of Law No. 6183 Regarding the Procedure of Collection of Public Receivables. However, this approach contradicts the TCC system (TCC Article 573.1 and 2). The said provision (Article 35 of Law No. 6183) reads as follows, "Shareholders of a limited liability company are directly liable from (payment of) public receivables which cannot be, partially or as a whole, collected from the company or is not likely to be collected, pro rata to their shares in the capital of the company, and can be subject to legal proceedings for collection pursuant to this law. In case a shareholder transfers its shares in the company, the transferor and transferee are jointly liable from the payment of the public receivables that has arisen before the transfer. If the shareholders in the period during which the receivables have arisen are different from the shareholders at the time when the payment is due, all of such shareholders shall be jointly liable from are the payment of the public receivable pursuant to the first paragraph."

665. The following are certain novelties introduced by the new TCC in relation to the limited liability companies:

(a) Share certificates representing the capital of the limited liability company may now be issued (New TCC Articel 593.2) either to serve as proof of ownership or in the form of registered share certificates. However, registered share certificates of a limited liability company may not be converted to bearer shares as the new TCC does not allow the issuance of bearer shares in limited liability companies.
(b) Article 531 of the former TCC which allowed recourse to the former owners of shares of a liability company for the amount of unpaid receivables of the company against the current owner of the shares has been revoked.
(c) Financial structure has been strengthened by the introduction of additional payment obligations (New TCC Article 603) and secondary/subordinate performance obligations. Additional payments may be used to recover the loss declared on the balance sheet or when the partnership needs equity or requires the monetary support of the shareholders. Secondary/subordinate performance obligations enables the company to realize its objective of the company.

(d) L.Ş. is subject to financial reporting (TCC Article 610) and Independent audit (TCC Article 397.4 and 635) provided that it falls within the criteria published by the decree of Council of Ministers.
(e) Withdrawal from shareholding has been subjected to more detailed rules and the right to participate in withdrawal has been introduced (TCC Article 639), payments to be made in case of withdrawal from shareholding are clarified by new rules (TCC Article 141).
(f) Transfer of shares has become easier and it is possible to determine the details and rules of transfer of shares in the Articles of Association (partnership agreement) (TCC Article 577.1, lit a).
(g) Share Groups and privileges may be created (TCC Article 576.1, lit c). However, limited liability companies may not adopt an authorized (registered) capital system.
(h) Right of first refusal, call option and put option rights may be provided for in the Articles of Association (partnership agreement).
(i) Casting vote and veto rights may be conferred upon some of the partners as a personal right (TCC Article 577, lit. e).
(j) Managers are required to treat all the partners equally (TCC Article 628).
(k) Annulment and cancellation of the general assembly decisions have been regulated in the law (TCC Article 622) for limited liability companies.
(l) Article 549, 550, 551, 553, 554–561 regarding liabilities of the founders, board members, directors, liquidation officers and auditors of joint-stock companies and penalties applicable under Article 562 (8)–(10) for violation of certain liability provisions (TCC 549–551) have become applicable to limited liability companies as well.

666. The second distinguishing feature of the L.Ş. is its basic, predetermined capital. Therefore, an increase or decrease of capital requires the observance of formal procedures. The third feature of the L.Ş. is that the law sets forth a number of principles relating to the protection of the basic capital.

667. In comparison, there are some features of the L.Ş., that distinguish it from an A.Ş. These concern the shareholder status in the limited liability company; for example:

- prohibition of competition applicable to shareholders;
- withdrawal rights of the partner from shareholding;
- exclusion of a partner from shareholding in an L.Ş.; and
- termination of the Articles of Association on substantial grounds.

§2. Formation

668. The L.Ş. is subject to immediate formation; the TCC excludes gradual formation. The L.Ş. is set up immediately in five stages.

669. The first stage is the preparation of the L.Ş.'s Agreement (Articles of Association) and its certification. The L.Ş.'s Agreement must specify the date of the agreement, the trade name and the place of the head office of the L.Ş., its purpose, the amount of its capital, nominal value of the shares, number of shares issued, privileges and share groups, if any, the name, citizenship and domicile of the managers and the procedure for the announcements to be made by the partnership. (TCC Article 576). The formation occurs at the instant when the partners unconditionally undertake to pay the capital in its entirety and sign the partnership agreement.

670. The second stage is payment of the undertaken capital. Based on reference in TCC Article 585 to provisions regarding A.Ş., TCC Article 344 which requires payment of at least 25% of nominal value of allocated shares before the registration and of remaining amount within twenty-four months following the registration of the partnership applies to L.Ş.s as well. However, as indicated above, Law No. 7099 on "Amendment of Certain Laws for Improvement of the Investment Environment" dated March 10, 2008, abolished the requirement of payment of one-fourth of the share capital undertaking in advance for limited liability companies. The agreement may be signed by the founders before the director or the deputy director of the trade registry at which the partnership will be registered (TCC Article 575).

671. The capital of the limited liability company must be at least TRY 10,000. The Council of Ministers has the authority to increase this amount up to tenfold (TCC Article 580). The shareholders can contribute cash or property. The nominal value of the capital shares has to be at least TRY 25 and cannot be decreased to "0". However, if the financial situation of the partnership requires so nominal value of the shares may be decreased below this level (TCC Article 583.1). The nominal values of the shares vary. In any case, nominal value must be multiples of twenty-five (TCC Article 583.2). Shares may be issued with premium. The voting right that will be conferred upon a capital share is calculated based on the nominal value of such shares (TCC Article 618).

672. A partner/shareholder may hold more than one capital share (TCC Article 583). Capital contribution may be made in cash or in kind. As per Article 578 of the TCC, provisions pertaining to the joint-stock companies shall apply for capital in-kind contributions in limited liability companies. A capital contribution in kind and its value must be specified in the L.Ş.'s Agreement (Articles of Association). Article 128 of TCC aims to provide security for the capital contribution in kind. Subparagraph 2 of Article 586 of the new TCC used to require an audit report prepared specifically for the contribution in kind to be submitted to the Trade Registry for registration, however, through Law No. 6335, this requirement has been revoked. Therefore, only Article 128 provides security to a certain extent. However, if the requirements are laid down under Article 128 are not complied with, a legal gap may occur with respect to the capital contribution in kind. In order to avoid such a situation, trade registry directorates should perform their duties with due care.

According to regular practice, the value of the capital in-kind contribution is determined by an expert appointed by the court. The same rule is applied to those assets which are acquired by the L.Ş. from the shareholders or third persons during the formation.

673. The maximum number of shareholders/partners in a limited liability company is fifty (TCC Article 574).

674. If the number of partners/shareholders drops down to one, the transaction that leads to this result should be notified to the managers and the managers are required to have such situation and the name, the place of residence and nationality of the relevant single partner registered with the Trade Registry and have these details announced. However, the partnership may not acquire its own shares in a way to result in the company to be its own single shareholder (TCC Article 574).

675. The third stage is the occurrence of the pre-partnership which does not have a legal personality.

676. The fourth stage is the preparation of the relevant documents until registration.

677. The fifth stage is registration with the Trade Registry which creates the legal personality (TCC Article 586, 588.1. Persons who act on behalf of the L.Ş. in the course of its establishment are personally liable to third parties).

§3. Organization

678. As with the A.Ş., the L.Ş. also acts through its representative bodies “organs”). The legal organs of the L.Ş. are the general assembly and the managers.

I. General Assembly Meeting

A. In General

679. The general assembly of the shareholders/partners is designated as a legislative body, namely, it has the authority to adopt and amend the L.Ş.’s Agreement (Articles of Association). Furthermore, the shareholders/partners exercise their rights concerning matters of the L.Ş., such as the election of the managers and approval of the financials in the general assembly. Finally, the general assembly has the power to elect and remove the managers, approve the external auditors (if any) and financial statements, and decide on the treatment of profits of the company. It is not an executive organ; however, exceptionally, certain executive powers have been provided to it.

680. Under new TCC, the duties and powers of the general assembly are classified as delegable and non-delegable. Some of the duties are non-delegable because they are statutory duties (subparagraph 1 of Article 616 of TCC), some duties may become non-delegable only if they are cited in the partnership agreement to be non-delegable (subparagraph 2 of Article 616 of TCC).

681. Statutory non-delegable powers and duties of the general assembly (TCC Article 616.1) are as follows:

(a) Amendment to partnership agreement (Articles of Association).
(b) Appointment and dismissal of the managers.
(c) Appointment and dismissal of auditors.
(d) Approval of the financial tables and annual reports.
(e) Approval of year-end financial tables, dividend distribution, determining bonus payments to be made out of the company income.
(f) Determining remuneration of the managers and releasing them from liability;
(g) Approval of share transfers.
(h) Applying to the court for exclusion of a partner from L.Ş.
(i) Authorizing the managers for the company to acquire its own shares or approving such an acquisition.
(j) Winding-up of L.Ş.
(k) Adopting resolutions regarding the matters on which L.Ş. partnership agreement the general assembly is specifically authorized (ex. TCC Articles 589.1 and 591.2) or which are presented to general assembly's approval (TCC Article 625.2).

682. Powers that may become non-delegable based on the partnership agreement:

(a) Issues that are subject to approval of general assembly resolution according to the partnership agreement of L.Ş.
(b) Exercise of right of first refusal, preemption right, call and put options.
(c) Establishing pledge on shares of the company.
(d) Issuing internal regulations regarding secondary performance obligations.
(e) Permitting managers to enter into transaction that may constitute competition with the company.
(f) Removal of a shareholder from L.Ş. based on the reasons cited in the partnership agreement of L.Ş.

B. Quorum and Resolution

1. Ordinary Decisions

683. Except for the material decisions indicated in the TCC (as explained below) and unless otherwise stated in the law or the L.Ş.'s Agreement (Articles of Association), no quorum requirement is applied and resolutions are adopted by the simple majority of votes represented at the meeting unless otherwise provided (TCC 620).

2. Unanimous Consent

684. Any amendment to the Partnership Agreement (Articles of Association) after the establishment of the company that enables inclusion of reasons for the removal of a shareholder from the company in the Articles of Association (TCC 621.3).

3. Material Decisions

685. Material decisions which require qualified meetings and decision quorums of the general assembly are listed under Article 621 of TCC. Save for the exception under the Article 621/3 explained in the above paragraph, new TCC does not require unanimous votes. However, Article 621 requires the approval of two-thirds of the participants in a general assembly meeting which should also represent at least simple majority of the total share capital of the company with voting rights. In other words, double majority is sought for the execution of such matters ("*Double Qualified Majority*").

The Partnership Agreement may introduce other additional matters to require a unanimous vote or certain qualified decisions and/or meeting quorum requirements. However, according to Article 621(2) of TCC, if the qualified quorums and decision majority requirements foreseen in the law are intended to be increased to higher quorums in the partnership agreement, such provisions may only be included in the articles upon the approval of shareholders representing such qualified majority.

686. The following resolutions require Double Qualified Majority as per TCC 621(1):

(a) Changing scope of business of the company.
(b) Issuing shares with privileged voting rights.
(c) Restriction, prohibition or simplification of transfer of shares.
(d) Capital increases.
(e) Restriction or revocation of preemption rights.

(f) Changing the address of the headquarters of the company.
(g) Granting permission for the managers to be exempted from loyalty and/or non-competition obligations.
(h) Application to court for removal of a shareholder from the company based on a justified reason or deciding for removal based on a reason indicated in the Articles of Association of the company.
(i) Winding-up of the company.

C. Convening of the General Meeting

687. The ordinary General Meeting must be held at least once a year within the three months following the end of the financial year (TCC 617.1). However, there are not any legal consequences tied to the violation of such requirement, thus, general assembly meetings held after the three-month period are also valid.

688. As per TCC Article 617/3, provisions applicable to joint-stock companies with respect to an invitation to general assembly meeting, agenda, preparations for the general assembly, meeting minutes, unauthorized participation in the general assembly, rights of the minority concerning the invitation to general assembly meeting and inclusion of an item in the agenda are also applied for limited liability companies by way of comparison and without regard to the requirements concerning the attendance of Ministry Representative to the general assembly meetings.

689. Invitations to the general assembly meetings have to be sent at least fifteen days before the meeting date (TCC Article 617.2). The Partnership Agreement may prolong such period or shorten it to a minimum of ten days.

690. An extraordinary General Meeting of the general assembly is held as and when required by the business of the L.Ş. (TCC 617.2). The provisions regarding convening the general assembly meeting of A.Ş. are applicable to L.Ş. by analogy. Both ordinary and extraordinary General Meetings are convened by the managers (TCC Article 617.1).

691. Under certain situations outlined in the TCC, the following parties are entitled to call for a general assembly meeting: minority (TCC Article 617.3), court-appointed administrator (TCC Article 617.3 by reference to Article 412) and liquidators (TCC Article 643).

692. L.Ş. can also be convened without any invitation procedures if 100% of the share capital of the company is represented at the meeting. In such cases, provisions of TCC 416 regarding the convening of general assembly meetings without invitation in a joint-stock company shall apply.

693. According to Article 1527(2) of TCC, provided that the Partnership Agreement contains a provision allowing electronic general assembly meetings, therefore, general assembly meetings may be held electronically and some or all of the partners may attend the meeting and cast their votes online.

694. As a diversion from the rules applicable to A.Ş., the new TCC provides for an opportunity to adopt general assembly decisions without holding a physical or electronic meeting in joint-stock companies. Unless requested by a shareholder that a physical meeting is held, general assembly resolutions may be adopted by a presentation of a resolution proposed by a shareholder and obtaining written approvals of other shareholders to such proposal. Submission of the said proposal to the approval of all shareholders is a requisite for the validity of such general assembly decision (TCC 617/4). By analogy to Article 390/4 of the TCC, signatures of the shareholders do not need to be affixed on the same paper.

695. The minority, whose interests in the L.Ş. amount to at least 10% of the basic capital, may, by notice in writing stating the justified grounds, require the managers to convene a general assembly (TCC 411). If a general assembly has already been called, the minority may demand inclusion in the agenda of the matters which they wish to discuss. If the Board does not accept the request within seven days, the shareholder may apply to court.

696. A General Meeting may also be convened by the liquidators in order to pass resolutions regarding matters connected with a liquidation.

II. Manager(s)

A. In General

697. Managers assume the executive function and authority in limited liability companies. The L.Ş. is managed and represented by its managers. The scope of, and limitations on, the power of the managers are subject to the provisions of the TCC pertaining to joint-stock companies. Managers are entitled to adopt and implement decisions on any matter regarding management of the company provided that the general assembly is not exclusively empowered to resolve such matter according to the law and/or partnership agreement (TCC Article 623.3). Additionally, in the event that legal entities are appointed as managers of the L.Ş., individuals empowered to represent the legal entity shall be registered at the Trade Registry. Furthermore, the L.Ş.'s Agreement can lay down provisions regarding a Board of Managers, which are subject to the same principles as are applicable to an A.Ş. In many respects, the principles regarding the duties of director(s) of an A.Ş. apply to an L.Ş., such as duties related to the protection of basic capital (TCC 633), duties regarding financial statements and accounting (TCC 610), and, finally, the principles relating to the extent and restriction of the representation of the L.Ş.

B. Appointment

698. The principle is that managers of a limited liability company are appointed upon election by the general assembly. The first manager(s) of a newly established L.Ş. is appointed by indicating their names in the partnership agreement (TCC Article 576.1, lit.d). When the duration of duty of a manager ends, the general assembly elects a new manager. The new TCC has departed from the principle of shareholders being natural managers of the company which was required in the former TCC.

699. Manager(s) are usually natural persons. However, the new TCC allows legal entities to be appointed as managers as well. If, a legal entity is appointed as a manager, such legal entity is required to appoint one real person to represent it as the manager of the limited liability company. Such representative of the legal entity manager is registered with the Trade Registry and announced in the Trade Registry Gazette as per Article 623/2 of the TCC.

700. Provisions of the TCC pertaining to the scope and limitation of representation authority of the board members in joint-stock companies and determination of the authorized signatories shall also apply, by way of comparison, for managers of limited liability companies (TCC 629/1). As per Article 623/1 of the TCC, management and representation of the company may be delegated to one or more shareholders who are also managers or to all shareholders or to third parties by the partnership agreement. However, at least one of the shareholders is required to be a manager in the company.

701. Management and representation of L.Ş. shall be regulated by partnership agreement (TCC Article 623). The partnership agreement shall stipulate matters determining certain specifics concerning the managers such as the number of managers, whether they are required to be shareholders and duration of duty.

702. There may be one or more managers in a limited liability company. As per Article 624 of the TCC, in case there is more than one manager, one of such managers is required to be appointed as the chairman of the board of managers by the general assembly without taking into account whether the manager is a shareholder or not. Decisions of managers are adopted by a board by the majority votes of managers. The chairman has a casting vote in case of a tie in votes, however, the partnership agreement may foresee otherwise.

703. As per Article 629(2) of the TCC, in a limited liability company with a single shareholder, regardless of whether limited liability company is represented by such single shareholder, all agreements between the single shareholder and the company has to be in writing in order to be valid. However, such requirement does not apply to ordinary and everyday matters that shall be determined based on the relevant market conditions.

704. The directors may be foreign citizens.

705. Some provisions in Turkish Criminal Code prevent persons who are convicted of certain crimes from being a manager of an L.Ş., such as declaring a fraudulent bankruptcy. Crimes that lead to revocation of title of a manager also prevent them from being appointed by a director.

C. *Dismissal*

706. General Assembly may always dismiss the managers or restrict their powers (TCC Article 630.1).

707. Shareholders may decide on the dismissal of a manager even if the agenda of the general assembly meeting does not include such an item. The manager may claim compensation based on his service agreement with the company (if any) in case the dismissal is in violation of such agreement.

708. Each shareholder is entitled to apply to courts for dismissal or limitation of the management and/or representation powers of a manager based on a justified reason (TCC Article 630.2). The TCC does not require the shareholder first to apply to the general assembly in order to be able to file such request with the court.

709. The law has given examples of justified grounds for dismissal from duty or limitation of powers. Such examples include breach by the manager of his obligation to act diligently and prudently while performing his management or representation duties, breach of loyalty obligation, breach of other obligations that may arise out of other laws or regulations and the partnership agreement and losing the ability to perform his management or representation powers.

D. *Non-delegable Powers and Duties of the Managers*

710. Managers are authorized to perform all actions and transactions which are not left to the exclusive authority of the general assembly by law or the partnership agreement (TCC Article 625.1).

711. Managers may not delegate the following powers and authorities or recant from such:

(a) High-level management of company and giving instructions to this effect.
(b) Determination of management organization of the company within the framework of the law and partnership agreement.
(c) Developing accounting, financial audit and the financial planning of the company, if necessary, for the management of the company.
(d) Monitoring whether the persons to whom certain parts of company management are delegated act in accordance with law, Articles of Association, internal directives and instructions of the managers.

(e) Except for small-sized limited liability companies, establishing a committee for the early identification and management of risks.
(f) Preparation of company's financial tables, annual activity reports and, if necessary and part of a corporate group, preparation of financial tables and activity reports of the corporate group.
(g) Preparation of the general assembly meetings and execution of decisions adopted in the general assembly meetings.
(h) Notifying courts if the company becomes insolvent.

E. Scope of Representation Power

712. The provisions of TCC concerning the scope of representation authorities of the board of directors of a joint-stock company also apply to limited liability companies (TCC Article 629). Based on the third paragraph of Article 629 of TCC, Articles 367 and 371 of the TCC pertaining to delegation of management and representation powers of managers shall apply for the appointment of persons who are acting based on a service agreement as commercial representatives in a limited liability company.

F. Obligations of Managers

1. Duty of Diligence, Duty of Loyalty

713. According to Article 626 of TCC managers and all persons in the management of the company are under the obligation to perform their duties diligently and to act in line with the interests of the partnership and in compliance with the equal treatment principle (TCC Article 627).

714. *"All persons in the management of the company"* means all members of the management team of the company other than the managers. Such reference to the management team includes commercial representatives, persons who have the authority to sign on behalf of the partnership and the persons implementing the decisions.

715. Article 626 of TCC states that managers are required to act diligently and if they fail to comply with this obligation, they will be considered to be in default. In other words, there is a direct relationship between the degree of diligence exercised and fault. The degree of diligence sought is "the diligence to be exercised by a prudent manager" within the sense of Article 369 of TCC pertaining to joint-stock companies. Article 626/3 of the TCC also states that the managers are subject to the same type of loyalty obligation towards the company as the shareholders.

2. Non-Compete Obligation

716. In principle, directors are prohibited from conducting activities in competition with the partnership. This prohibition may be revoked by a general assembly resolution. Notion of "activities in competition with the partnership" has a broad scope and includes not only transactions directly conducted by the managers but also transactions carried out indirectly through companies owned by the managers or in the name of third parties but at the account of the managers.

3. Notification Obligations

717. Managers are under the obligation to notify the general assembly and/or courts under the following circumstances:

(a) In case of loss of capital of the partnership, Article 376 of TCC applicable to joint-stock companies shall also apply to limited liability companies. Accordingly, in such cases, managers are required to call for a general assembly meeting and introduce improvement suggestions for the approval of the general assembly. In case it is understood that the company is insolvent and unable to pay its debts, the managers are required to file a request with the courts for the bankruptcy of the partnership.
(b) TCC's provisions regarding "corporate group-group of companies" impose on the managers certain notification obligations which include application to the trade registry in case of certain changes in the shareholding structure of the company (TCC 198) and financial reporting to the parent company (TCC 199).
(c) Managers are required to notify all other shareholders immediately if a shareholder requests to leave the partnership based on a clause in the partnership agreement or initiates a lawsuit to such effect based on justified reason (TCC Article 639.1).

4. Liability

718. Liability of managers and auditors of a limited liability company is subject to the same provisions applicable to A.Ş.'s board members and auditors (TCC Article 644.1-a). Shareholders decide whether or not to release the directors from their liabilities. The power to release the directors is a non-delegable power of the general assembly (TCC Article 616.1-f).

719. As per Article 632 of the TCC, the limited liability company shall be responsible for damages to third parties arising out of tort that is committed by the persons authorized to represent and manage the company during the performance of their duties.

III. Auditor and the Right to Request Special Inspection of the L.Ş.'s Affairs

720. According to Article 635 of TCC, the provisions regarding the auditors and shareholder's right to request special inspection applicable to joint-stock companies shall also apply for limited liability companies.

§4. Legal Status of the Shareholders (Partners)

721. The provisions regarding the legal status of the shareholders combine the characteristics of both collective companies and joint-stock companies.

I. Rights of the Shareholder

722. The rights of shareholders are categorized as:

- financial (pecuniary) rights;
- participation rights; and
- protective rights.

A. Financial (Pecuniary) Rights

723. Pecuniary rights are the rights to dividends, participation in the proceeds of liquidation, preemption rights, the acquisition of gratis shares and interest during the formation period. In many respects, the principles relating to pecuniary rights are the same as the principles relating to the A.Ş. (TCC 608, 609, 610, 611).

B. Participation Rights

724. Participation rights are those of attendance at the general assembly, voting, and management rights. Attendance at the general assembly is one of the shareholder rights which may not be revoked. Unless the L.Ş.'s Agreement provides otherwise, voting rights are determined by the amount of the capital contribution; every TRY 25 grants one voting right to its owner (TCC 618.1). Any clause of the L.Ş.'s Agreement revoking the right to vote is considered null and void. The managing partner, however, for whom a resolution of release from liability (discharge) is to be passed is not entitled to vote for the said resolution. Voting rights must be used in the general assembly. The exception to this rule is established in Article 536.2 of the TCC; i.e., in L.Ş.s having twenty or fewer partners, the L.Ş. Agreement may substitute votes in writing for votes at the meeting. Under the terms of the TCC, if the L.Ş.'s Agreement does not provide, to the contrary, all partners may and shall jointly manage and represent the L.Ş.

C. Protective Rights

725. Protective rights include the following:

- To examine and obtain information (TCC 614): Partners may request information as regards the entire business and accounts. In case any partner is prevented from exercising these rights partner can plead to exercise these rights by obtaining a court order. Furthermore, partners may exercise the right to request a special audit by analogy to provisions applicable to A.Ş.s (TCC Article 635). In principle, these rights are exercised at general assembly meeting but they may be exercised also outside the general assembly (TCC Article 614) and may be assisted by an expert. If the general assembly rejects the request or if the partner is not invited to the meeting, the shareholder may file such a request with the courts.
- To request from courts cancellation of a resolution of the general assembly: Each partner has the right to challenge a resolution of a general assembly. According to Article 622 of the TCC, the provision for A.Ş.s concerning the cancellation and nullity of the general assembly decisions shall also apply to the limited liability companies.
- To convene the general assembly: by reference given in 617, relevant articles regarding A.Ş.'s also apply to L.Ş.'s (TCC Article 411–412).
- To withdraw from the shareholding of the L.Ş. (TCC Article 638)..
- To demand the expulsion of a shareholder from a partnership (TCC Article 640).
- To demand the termination of the L.Ş. for a justified cause (TCC Article 636.3).

II. Duties of the Shareholders

726. The first duty of every shareholder is to make the requisite capital contribution in respect of his interest. If he fails to do so, the L.Ş. may declare him to have forfeited his membership. Provisions regarding payment of capital contribution set forth for joint-stock companies also apply to limited liability companies. Different from joint-stock companies, additional payment obligations may be imposed on the shareholders of a limited liability company in the partnership agreement (Articles of Association). The boundaries of such additional requirements are drawn by Article 603 of TCC which sets forth the limited conditions under which such additional payment obligations may be requested. Also, ancillary obligations which may serve the realization of the company's objectives may be foreseen in the Articles of Association of the company (TCC Article 606).

727. Shareholders are required not to disclose the trade secrets of L.Ş.; this obligation may not be revoked by a general assembly resolution or partnership agreement. Shareholders may not act in the detriment of the partnership's interests, especially if such an act provides a personal advantage to them. Provisions prohibiting the shareholders from competing with the company may be introduced in the partnership agreement.

III. Share Book and List of the Shareholders

728. A share book must be maintained by the manager(s) (TCC Article 594). The share book contains the names and addresses of the shareholders, the shareholding amount of each shareholder in the capital of the company, nominal value of the shares held by a shareholder, as well as share transfers made by and to each shareholder and details as to any pledges or usufruct rights that may exist on the shares.

729. The director(s) are personally and jointly liable for losses caused by the negligent or incorrect maintenance of the share book.

730. As a novelty introduced by new TCC, certificates representing the shares in L.Ş. can now be issued. Share certificates may be issued as registered shares or only as certificates merely evidencing the shareholding in the company. Share certificates should include information as to the following:

- additional payment obligations and secondary obligations are foreseen in the partnership agreement, if any;
- non-compete obligations intensified or made applicable to all the shareholders by the partnership agreement, if any;
- right of first refusal, first offer, call option and put option rights that are foreseen in the partnership agreement, if any.

731. A share certificate which does not include the above information shall be deemed invalid. Additionally, in case of a share transfer, the share purchase agreement should include details as to all the rights mentioned in the above paragraph.

IV. Acquisition of Shares of a Limited Liability Company

732. Former TCC included provisions which made share transfers in limited liability companies quite difficult whereby the approval of shareholders representing three-fourths of both the total capital of the company and the total number of the shareholders in the company were sought for a share transfer to be valid and effective. The new TCC has eased such conditions applicable to share transfers in limited liability companies to a certain extent while still keeping formal and more intensified perfection requirements compared to the joint-stock companies:

733. The approval of the general assembly is no longer a must for a share transfer to be valid if the partnership agreement permits. It is now possible to eliminate the approval requirement completely and indicate in the partnership agreement that the share transfers shall not be subject to the approval of the general assembly (TCC 595.2).

734. If the approval of the general assembly is not eliminated by the partnership agreement and if a specific majority is not foreseen therein, simple majority approval of the transfer in the general assembly shall be sufficient and a qualified majority as was foreseen in the former TCC shall not be sought.

735. It is also possible to indicate in the partnership agreement that share transfers are prohibited completely (TCC 595/4) or restricted with certain limitations and requirements (TCC 621/1.c).

736. As per Article 595/7 of the TCC, if the general assembly does not reject a share transfer within three months following its notification to the company, the share transfer shall be deemed to have been approved.

737. If the general assembly does not approve a share transfer, the transferring shareholder may request its exit from the company if there are justified causes.

738. Share transfer agreements concerning the shares of a limited liability company has to be in writing and the signatures of the parties should be notarized. If the approval requirement is not eliminated by the partnership agreement, share transfer becomes valid upon approval of the general assembly. Following the general assembly's approval, transfer is registered with the Trade Registry by the manager(s) of the limited liability company. However, registration with the Trade Registry is not a perfection (validity) requirement. If the company does not apply to the Trade Registry within thirty days, the transferring shareholder may directly apply to the Trade Registry and request the deregistration of his/her/its name from the registry records pertaining to the transferred shares. In such case, the Trade Registry provides the company with a certain period to notify the Trade Registry with the details of the new owner of the shares (TCC 598).

739. If the shares are transferred as a result of inheritance law or by virtue of the marital property law or are acquired through mandatory execution proceedings, approval of the general assembly shall not be sought for the transfer to become valid and all rights and obligations pertaining to the shares shall pass on the acquirer at the time of the transfer (TCC 596). However, general assembly is entitled to reject the new owner of the shares as a shareholder in the company within three months following the date it becomes aware of such acquisition. In such case, the limited liability company is required to offer to purchase the shares held by the acquirer on their actual value in the name and on account of (i) the company itself, (ii) a shareholder of the company; or (iii) a third party (TCC 579). The value is determined according to the market value of shares calculated after deduction of the shares and taking into consideration the goodwill value. If the parties fail to agree on the actual value of the shares such determination shall be made by the court. The court decision is final (TCC 597.1).

740. If shares are held jointly by two or more owners, rights arising from such shares are exercised through a representative appointed by such owners who are jointly and severally liable for all primary and ancillary obligations arising from the shares.

V. Acquisition or Acceptance as Pledge by the Company of Its Own Shares or Establishing Usufruct Rights

741. Limited liability company may purchase its own shares provided that (i) the company has sufficient equity that may be freely used by the company to purchase the shares and, (ii) total nominal value of the shares to be purchased does not exceed 10% of the total share capital of the company (TCC 612/1). The 10% limitation is increased to 20% for acquisition of shares of a shareholder exiting or being removed from the company as per a provision of the partnership agreement or a court decision. In such case, shares exceeding 10% are required to be disposed by the company or terminated as a result of capital decrease within two years following their acquisition by the company.

742. The limited liability company is required to set aside reserves in the amount corresponding to the purchase price paid for the acquired shares. Voting rights and other rights attached to the shares acquired by the company shall freeze during the term they are held by the company. Also, additional and ancillary payment obligations pertaining to the shares may not be claimed during such term they are held by the company.

743. The provisions of the TCC pertaining to the transfer of shares shall also apply for establishing usufruct rights on the shares of a limited liability company (TCC 600/1). Accordingly, a written agreement should be executed between the parties and their signatures should be notarized (TCC 600/3).

744. The partnership agreement may require the approval of the general assembly to establish a pledge on the shares. In such case, the provisions pertaining to share transfer shall be applicable and the general assembly shall be entitled to reject the pledge only based on a just cause (TCC 600/2).

VI. Exit, Participation to Exit and Removal from the Partnership

A. Exit of a Partner from the L.Ş.

745. A shareholder can exit from the limited liability company in any one of the following cases:

(i) Sale and transfer of entire shareholding in the company in compliance with the provisions of Article 595 of the TCC as explained above.
(ii) Acquisition of shares through inheritance law, marital property law or mandatory execution (TCC 596).
(iii) Exercise of an exit right explicitly provided in the partnership agreement (TCC 577) through a written notification served to the company by the shareholder. If the partnership foresees certain conditions for the exercise of the exit right, the general assembly may reject the exercise of such right if such conditions are not fulfilled or met.

(iv) Exit from the company based on a court decision given as a result of a shareholder's request if such request is based on valid and justifiable reasons (TCC 638).

B. Participation to Exit

746. New TCC has introduced a new provision which enables a shareholder to join when another shareholder is exiting the company. As per Article 639, the managers of the company are required to inform all shareholders if one of the shareholders exercises its exit right provided in the partnership agreement or initiates a lawsuit for exit based on just cause.

747. Within one month of the notification of exit, each shareholder is entitled to (i) inform the managers that he/she/it shall participate in the exit if the conditions set forth in the partnership agreement for exit are also applicable to him/her/it; or (ii) join the exit lawsuit through initiation of a lawsuit based on just cause.

748. If the managers fail to notify the shareholders of an exit request to lawsuit, they shall be liable for the damages incurred by the shareholders and the shareholders may also request for the annulment of the exit proceedings concluded or conducted. The legal action may be addressed not only to the directors but also to the partnership.

749. Shareholders participating in the exit proceedings shall be subject to equal treatment pro rata to their shareholding in the company.

750. The notification requirements and participation to exit shall not apply in cases where a shareholder is removed from the company based on a justified reason provided in law or under the partnership agreement.

C. Removal from the Partnership

751. The partnership agreement may foresee the conditions under which a shareholder may be removed from the partnership by the decision of the general assembly. The company is also entitled to initiate a lawsuit for the removal of a shareholder from partnership based on a justified reason (TCC 640).

752. TCC 574/3 provides that the company may not acquire its shares to result in the sole shareholding of the company. By way of analogy, it may be concluded that the limited liability company may not remove a shareholder if it remain as a single shareholder as a result of such removal. Likewise, the shareholders may not remove the company from shareholding.

753. A shareholder can be removed from the partnership in the following circumstances:

(a) A shareholder may be removed from the partnership by a general assembly resolution adopted with qualified majority based on the grounds set forth in L.Ş. Agreement as of the date of resolution. The general assembly resolution aiming to add a new ground for removal in the partnership agreement can be adopted only by unanimous votes of the partners representing the entire share capital. The partner to be removed may participate in the general assembly meeting and voting on removal. Therefore, a qualified majority may be foreseen or voting right of the partner may be restricted with respect to removal voting in the L.Ş. Agreement. The partner may lodge a claim to cancel the general assembly decision within three months. Otherwise, the resolution becomes final (TCC 640). The grounds set forth in the L.Ş. Agreement do not need to be objective or justifiable reasons. For example, to be aged younger than 60 may be an applicable ground to exclude a partner.

(b) A shareholder may be removed from partnership through application of provisions of TCC 636/2 which enables the court to rule for the removal of a shareholder requesting the termination of the company based on justified grounds instead of granting a decision for the dissolution of the company. In such case, the shareholder may be removed from partnership upon payment of the real and actual value of his/her/its shares in the company. Since the philosophy of the Commercial Code is to ensure, if possible, the survival of the partnership, TCC 636/2 grants the court such opportunity to rule for the continuance of partnership instead of its dissolution through removal of the requesting shareholder from partnership. In fact, according to the philosophy of ensuring the survival of the partnership, the court would reject the case for dissolution if another course is available which may cure the problem at hand and satisfy the shareholder. As per the provisions of TCC 636/2, the court is entitled to rule for solutions other than removal of the shareholder instead of granting a decision for the dissolution of the company.

(c) L.Ş. is entitled to request from the courts the removal of a shareholder from partnership based on the just cause (TCC 640 lit. 3). The reasons for just cause are not required to be determined in the Partnership Agreement since such right arises directly from the provisions of Article 640/3. The general assembly should adopt a resolution for application to the court for removal of the shareholder from the partnership.

(d) Another reason for removal of a shareholder is the shareholder's default in payment of its capital contribution obligations. In such case, provisions of Article 585 of the TCC applicable to joint-stock companies shall also apply to the limited liability company.

754. The general assembly decision pertaining to both application to the court for removal of the shareholder and removal based on a reason identified in the partnership agreement is counted among the major decisions identified under Article 621 of TCC which require the approval of two-thirds of the votes present in a general assembly meeting which should also represent the majority of the total share capital of the company. If such a double majority cannot be achieved, the shareholders that had requested the removal of a shareholder may apply to the courts for dissolution of the company or for their exit from the company provided that they can establish that such requests are based on justifiable grounds.

755. If the general assembly decision with the qualified majority indicated above is obtained in favor of removal of a shareholder, one of two consequences ensue. The *first* would be the assumption that the removed shareholder agrees with the decision. In this case, the shareholder shall demand payment of the real value of his shares in the company. The *second* possible consequence would be the assumption that the removed partner does not agree with the decision. In this case, the L.Ş. may request the court to remove the partner in question.

756. In this second assumption, the shareholder needs to notify his objection to the company. The company shall then be entitled to apply to the courts for the removal of the partner based on just cause if there are legitimate grounds. If the court finds the arguments to be justified, it shall decide on the removal of the shareholder from partnership. Otherwise, the court shall reject the case and, consequently, the partner shall remain in the partnership.

757. The shareholder may also file a case for the cancellation or annulment of the general assembly deciding on the removal of the shareholder as per the provisions of Article 622 of the TCC. If the court rejects the case for cancellation or annulment, the removal decision of the general assembly shall become final.

758. When the removal process is completed, the company acquires, by law, the shares of the removed shareholder on actual value.

D. Consequences of Exit/Removal

1. Exit Payment

759. The general principle pertaining to exit payment is provided under Article 641 of the TCC which indicates that the shareholder shall be entitled to receive the actual value of his shares in case of his exit or removal. Right to exit payment is a right that may not be waived which is also made available for shareholders removed from the partnership. The partnership agreement may foresee specific methods for calculation and determination of the exit payment and divert from TCC foreseeing the payment of the actual value. For instance, partnership agreement may cite that the exit payment shall be calculated based on the value indicated in the books of L.Ş. or any other method accepted by business economics rather than the actual value of the shares.

760. Depending on the circumstances, L.Ş. may prefer one of the following alternative ways set forth under TCC 642 for the exit payment:

(a) *Acquisition of the share by using the available equity of the company:* L.Ş. may acquire the exiting/removed shareholder's share by using its equity freely disposable at its option at the actual value or at another amount agreed upon with the shareholder. According to TCC 612.2, L.Ş. may sell its own shares up to an amount equal to 20% of its capital if the shares are acquired from exiting or removed shareholder.
(b) *Sale of Shares to a Shareholder or a Third Party:* In certain cases, one of the shareholders or third party may be willing to purchase the shares of the exiting shareholder. In principle, exit payment should be equal to actual value of the shares, however, the parties to the sale transaction may negotiate and agree on a different price. The agreed purchase price or the actual value of the shares are then paid to the exiting/removed shareholder as an exit payment by the purchaser of the shares.
(c) *Capital Decrease for the Exit Payment:* If the freely disposable equity of the partnership is not sufficient for the exit payment and if the other shareholders or third parties are not willing to purchase the exit shares, the limited liability company may decrease its capital to generate funds for the exit payment. If the exit payment amount cannot be fully paid, the unpaid portion of the exit payment shall become a payable/debt of the limited liability company. The company may not distribute dividends or make bonus or premium payments to its managers before reimbursement of the exit payment in full. If the company has registered profits, the exit payment automatically becomes reimbursable.

761. The effective date of the exit/removal of the shareholder varies based on the method of exit/removal. If the exit/removal of a shareholder is based on a court decision, the shareholder shall be deemed to be removed from or have exited the company as of the date of court decision without it being finalized. Upon the decision of the first instance court, the exiting/removed shareholder may no longer be considered as a shareholder by the company and may not attend the general assembly meetings or vote. If the Court of Appeals overturns the decision of the first instance court, the exiting/removed shareholder shall obtain all shareholding rights with retrospective effect.

762. If the shareholder is exiting the company at his own will and based on a provision of the Partnership Agreement, the exit shall become effective on the date of receipt of the exit notification by the company. If the exercise of exit right is challenged by L.Ş. before courts and the exiting shareholder loses the lawsuit, he/she shall be reinstated as a shareholder as of the date of the first instance court decision. On the contrary, if the exiting shareholder wins the lawsuit at the first instance court, exit shall become final upon the finalization of the court decision.

763. The same principles apply also for the removal of the shareholder from the partnership.

2. Calculation of the Share Value

764. Removal or exit of a shareholder dissolves the relationship between the partner and the L.Ş. and terminates the rights and liabilities provided for and imposed by the law and the partnership agreement. On the one hand, the exiting shareholder shall no longer be bound by such obligations pertaining to shareholding in the company such as loyalty or non-compete obligation or other liabilities which are imposed on him due to *afectio societatis*. On the other hand, the exiting shareholder has a significant claim from the company which is the exit payment. Exit payment is calculated pro rata to the shareholding of the exiting partner in the total share capital of the company and should be based on the actual value of the company shares. Depending on the company value, the exit payment amount may become a substantial payment obligation for the company.

765. Actual value of company shares shall be determined based on the balance sheet of L.Ş. and the assets of the company shall be valued at their possible sales prices as of such date. All assets of the company, including intangible assets such as goodwill shall be taken into account. Payables of the company shall be deducted from the total asset value calculated in this manner. Both exit payment amount and the calculation method and formula of the company value and exit shares can be freely determined. If parties cannot reach an agreement on the actual value, i.e., on the calculation method or probable sales prices, or value of the assets such as goodwill, the date to be taken into account for the sales prices, rates of discount and interest, actual value of the exit shares shall be determined by the competent commercial court (TCC 597.1). The court decision on the actual value of the exit shares is final. The shareholders may freely determine the details of exit, company value, payment conditions and all other matters applicable to the exit in a separate agreement or in the Partnership Agreement. However, an agreement in which the shareholder declares that he has forfeited his right to collect a withdrawal payment is not valid.

766. The right to demand exit payment becomes effective at the moment when the exit or removal of the shareholder occurs in the internal relationship of the company.

VII. Liability of the Shareholders

A. In General

767. In an L.Ş., the liability of a shareholder is limited to the amount of such shareholder's capital contribution and other ancillary and additional obligations that may have been agreed upon in the general assembly or the foundation Articles of Association of the company (TCC 602). Neither other shareholders nor the L.Ş. or the creditors of the L.Ş. may raise claims against the shareholder outside the aforesaid scope. Shareholders are released from liability upon payment of their capital subscriptions and fulfillment of ancillary or additional obligations, if any, indicated in the articles of the company.

768. In principle, shareholders are not personally liable for L.Ş.'s debts. If a creditor has a claim against the L.Ş., the claim must be satisfied from the assets of the company.[105] However, there are some exceptions to this general principle as will be explained in more detail under section B below.

B. Exception

1. Company Acquiring Its Own Shares

769. Where the partnership acquires or receives pledges on its own not fully paid up shares in a valid form, the partners are jointly liable for the unpaid portion of the share capital.

2. Liability for Public Receivables

770. As per Law No. 6183 on the Procedure of Collection of Public Receivables, shareholders of a limited liability company shall be liable, in proportion to their shareholding in the company, for the unpaid portions of public debts which are not or may not be fully paid by company in proportion to their shareholding in the company.[106] The aforesaid law contradicts with the TCC principle which accepts that the shareholders of a limited liability company may not be held liable for the debts of the company (TCC Article 573.1 and 2).

§5. Accounts of the Partnership

771. The provisions concerning the balance sheet and reserve funds of an A.Ş. apply to limited liability companies as well. By reference provided under TCC 644 (1) lit b, TCC 358 regarding limitations applicable to loans made to shareholders of a joint-stock company also apply to shareholders of a limited liability company. As per TCC 358, shareholders may not obtain loans from the company unless they have paid their capital contributions in full and the profits of the company, together with the legal reserves, are sufficient to reimburse the previous year's losses.[107]

---

105. Creditors cannot claim the balance of the contribution directly from partners, *see* jud [15th C.Cham. Sup. Court], No. 5614/5491 [May 23, 1968], in: Olgaç [note 13], 279 [ACC Sup. Court], No. 160/230 [Apr. 7, 1971], in: Ankara Barosu Dergisi [*Ankara Bar Association Review*] [1971], 984.
106. O.G. No. 8469, Jul. 25, 1953.
107. Bkz. TEKİNALP/ÇAMOLU (2012), New Turkish Commercial Code No. 6102 and Commercial Legislation With Explanations, Notes and Coparisions, Revised 14. ed, Notes under Art. 358.

§6. Dissolution and Liquidation

I. Grounds for Dissolution

772. The grounds for dissolution are provided in Article 636 of the TCC. The TCC, however, also recognizes other grounds for dissolution, which are set forth in other provisions of the TCC. The latter have previously been explained.

773. According to Article 636 an L.Ş. can be dissolved upon:

- occurrence of one of the dissolution events determined in the partnership agreement, if any;
- the resolution of the general assembly obtained by the affirmative votes of two-thirds of the votes represented in the meeting provided that such votes also represent at least the simple majority of the total share capital of the company;
- being declared as bankrupt;
- occurrence of any other dissolution events that may be determined in applicable laws.

II. Liquidation

774. The provisions concerning the liquidation of the joint-stock companies shall also apply to limited liability companies.

Part II. Partnerships

Chapter 1. Ordinary Partnership (*Adi Şirket*)

§1. Distinguishing Features

775. In defining an Ordinary Partnership (which is called "*Adi Şirket*" (AdŞ) in Turkish), the first paragraph of Article 620 of the TCO takes the "partnership" concept as the starting point and, thereafter, defines it as two or more persons who enter into a contract to attain a common object by joint endeavors or means. According to the second paragraph of Article 620 of the TCO, a partnership which does not carry the characteristics of a partnership that is regulated by law shall be deemed as a AdŞ.

776. Since an AdŞ is formed by several people for achieving a common purpose by combining their endeavors and skills under a contractual commitment, its foundation and operation have not been regulated under legal forms or conditions. Although most partnerships are formed pursuant to a partnership agreement, a partnership may also arise as a result of the conduct of the parties.

777. The partners of an AdŞ may be natural or legal persons. The partners are usually considered to be in a very close relationship based on trust, confidence and mutual reliance.

778. The objective of an AdŞ must be a common purpose, and this purpose must be an economic purpose. Due to its highly flexible structure, it is very suitable for joint ventures and consortiums. An AdŞ is also a suitable form for a silent partnership.

779. The provisions of the TCO on AdŞs are also applicable to non-profit associations which have not acquired the status of a legal person.

780. An AdŞ is not a legal entity. It cannot sue or be sued, but its partners can sue or be sued. While it is possible to sue both partners at the same time for a claim, it is also sufficient to sue only one partner since all partners of an ordinary partnership are jointly and severally liable for the obligations of the partnership. In principle, an AdŞ constitutes joint ownership (*condominimum plurium in solidum*) where each partner's ownership extends over the entire property of the partnership.

However, the partners may agree among themselves to adopt the system of joint co-ownership (*communio pro partibus indivisus*) where each partner's portion of the property is specified.

§2. Formation

I. In General

781. As explained previously, an AdŞ can be formed without any statutory formalities. It is based upon an agreement. The AdŞ's Agreement may be made in written form or orally; it can be expressed or implied, but, for proof, written form should be preferred. If the partnership agreement contains provisions relating to matters that are required to be in a specific form mandated by applicable law (such as the transfer of real property or the assignment of industrial rights and mining licenses), the partnership agreement should also comply with such perfection requirements.

782. An AdŞ Agreement cannot be registered with the Trade Registry, however, subject to certain conditions, a specific tax number may be obtained for the ordinary partnership.

II. Limitations on Freedom of Contract

783. In many respects, the principles of the TCO regarding limitations on freedom of contract apply to the AdŞ Agreement. AdŞ's Agreements against law, public order and ethical rules are void (TCO 26, 27). Additionally, a partner who has entered into an AdŞ Agreement under the effect of a material error (TCO 30–35), being willfully deceived or frauded by the other party (TCO 36), or under effective duress by the other partner(s) or a third party (TCO 37) is not bound by such a contract and may declare it void within one year.

§3. The Relationship Between Partners

I. Management and Control

784. Under the terms of the law, the administration of the partnership and the administrative powers of a partner are distinguished from the representation of the partnership and the representative power of the partner. The administrative powers of the partners are an internal authority. Every partner may and should take part in the management and representation of the partnership's affairs and has individual management power (TCO 629) on ordinary transactions (TCO 625). The management authority may, however, be conferred on one or more of the partners, or even on third persons, by the AdŞ's Agreement or resolution (TCO 625). In case the partnership is managed and represented by all or some of the partners, each managing partner has the authority to conduct transactions without the participation of other managing partners, however, each managing partner has a veto right against an intended transaction by another partner before the completion and finalization of such transaction.

785. In the event that administrative powers are conferred on one or more partners by resolution, he may be dismissed, or his powers may be limited by a further resolution. If this power is conferred by the AdŞ's Agreement, it may not be revoked or limited except on justifiable grounds.

786. Each partner is obliged to employ in the affairs of the AdŞ the same diligence and care which he normally exercises in his own affairs (TCO 628). If a managing partner receives compensation for his work, he may be held liable under the provisions pertaining to the representation agreement.

787. The managing partner is responsible to his fellow partners for losses resulting from his default. In such cases, the partners may sue the said partner jointly or separately (*actio pro socio*).

II. Partnership Resolutions

788. Under the terms of the law, partnership resolutions are passed by the unanimous consent of all partners. The AdŞ's Agreement may, however, set that resolutions may be passed by a simple majority of votes. Absent agreement to the contrary, the partners have equal votes (TCO 624).

III. Contributions of Partners

789. An AdŞ requires no minimum capital. According to Article 621.1 of the TCO, however, each partner must furnish contributions, consisting either of money, property, or services. Although the commentators[108] consider this provision as an *ius dispositivum*, it is generally accepted to be a mandatory rule. Unless otherwise agreed, the contributions shall be equal and of such amounts as are required by the objects of the partnership (TCO 621).

790. The partners may sue jointly or separately (*actio pro socio*) a defaulting partner to enforce his obligation to contribute (TCC 627.1).

IV. Profit and Losses

791. Each partner is obliged to share with the other partners any profit attributable by its nature to the partnership (TCO 622). In the absence of an agreement to

108. *See* Becker H., Das Obligationenrecht, Berner Kommentar, Bd. IV/2: Die einzelnen Vertragsverhältnisse, Berne 1934, Art. 531, No. 1.

the contrary, the partners share profits and losses equally without regard to the type and amount of their respective contributions (TCO 623). Different arrangements may be made in the AdŞ's Agreement.

792. Under the terms of the TCO, provision of a partnership agreement indicating that a partner shall be entitled to profits without being liable for losses is invalid unless foreseen with respect to a partner which only contributes labor to the partnership (TCO 623). The AdŞ's Agreement, or resolutions, may also provide for a salary and/or interest to be paid to the partners.

793. According to Article 627 of the TCO, each partner of an ordinary partnership shall be responsible to another partner for the expenses incurred and liabilities undertaken by such partner in relation to the affairs of the partnership.

V. Inspection Rights

794. Each partner, even the ones without management and representation power, is entitled to obtain information about the operations of the partnership, examine its books and records and take copies thereof. Any provisions which eliminate these inspection rights are null and void (TCO 631).

VI. Non-competition

795. No partner may engage in activities, on his behalf or on behalf of third parties that may hinder or harm the objectives of the partnership (TCO 626).

§4. Representation and Liability

796. A partner that enters into a transaction with a third party in his name and on account of the partnership shall be personally liable against and be entitled rights from such third party. In the event that one of the partners enters into a transaction with a third party in the name of the partnership and/or all other partners, such other partners may only be held liable against or be entitled to rights from such third party under the provisions of law concerning representation. The partner to whom the management rights and duties are bestowed shall be deemed to have the authority to represent the partnership or all other partners towards third parties. However, representation power of a managing partner with respect to substantial transactions should be granted with the unanimous vote of all partners and such matter should be clearly indicated in the representation certificate. (TCO 637).

797. Partners are subject to unlimited and joint liability towards third parties for the obligations and the debts of the partnership, provided that the acting partner acts on behalf of the partnership and the other partners. In such a case, the creditors may demand the fulfillment of their obligations from any of the partners.

798. There is no joint liability among partners of an ordinary partnership with respect to losses arising from tort. However, according to Article 50.1 of the TCO, where several persons have jointly caused the damage, be it as instigators, principals or accessories, they are jointly liable to the damaged party.

§5. Changes among the Partners

799. An AdŞ is a contractual relationship based on trust, confidence and mutual reliance. Therefore, any changes in membership, such as retiring from the partnership or joining the partnership after its foundation, require the consent of all the partners.

800. A partner can be removed from partnership as per the law or by the AdŞ's Agreement. According to Article 639/2 of the TCO, the partnership shall dissolve upon the death of a partner unless the partnership agreement includes a provision foreseeing that the partnership shall be continued with the heirs. Furthermore, under the terms of Article 639/6 of the TCO, the partnership can be dissolved by notice from the partners if such notice is provided for in the AdŞ's Agreement or where the partnership has been entered into for an indefinite duration or for the life of one of the partners. This is another example of the legal and *ipso iure* termination of the partnership. In both cases, the partnership can be continued by the remaining partners or by the new partners, provided that the remaining partners unanimously accept that the partnership shall continue.

801. In case of just cause, the partnership may be terminated as per a court decision pertaining to a dissolution request.

802. A retiring partner remains personally and jointly liable with the other partners for all debts incurred before, but not after, his retirement.

§6. Dissolution

I. Dissolution Ipso Iure

803. An AdŞ is dissolved *ipso iure* in the following cases:

- if the object for which the AdŞ has been formed has been attained or has become unattainable (TCO 639.1);
- the death of a partner dissolves a partnership, unless the AdŞ's Agreement specifically provides to the contrary (TCO 639.2);
- unless otherwise provided under the partnership agreement, upon the appointment of a legal custodian for a partner or a partner's bankruptcy or cashing of the share of the partner in the partnership as a result of a mandatory enforcement proceeding (TCO 639.3); or
- upon the expiry of the term determined for the partnership (TCO 639.5).

II. Dissolution by the Partners

804. An AdŞ is voluntarily dissolved:

– by mutual agreement of all partners (TCO 639.4);
– upon termination notice by one of the partners, if such right has been reserved in the AdŞ's Agreement (TCO 535.6); or
– upon termination notice by one of the partners, where the AdŞ's Agreement has been entered into for an indefinite time period or for the duration of the life of a partner (TCO 535.6).

III. Dissolution by Court Judgment

805. An AdŞ may be dissolved for justified reasons by the judgment of a court granted upon application by a partner (TCO 535.7).

Chapter 2. Silent Partnership

806. A silent partnership is a contractual relationship between a main partner and a person who is an undisclosed partner (silent partner) of a business, where a sum of money is provided in return for participation in the profits and losses of the business. Silent partnership is an internal partnership. The main partner enters into agreements with third parties in his own name and he alone acquires rights and obligations against such third parties.

807. Special provisions were made by the former TCC regarding silent partnership (Articles 518–526). These provisions were abolished by the present TCC. According to the present legislation, silent partnership is an AdŞ, and the principles and provisions applicable to AdŞs are applicable to silent partnerships.

Chapter 3. Collective Partnership (*Kollektif Şirket*)

§1. Distinguishing Features

808. The Collective partnership ["*Kollektif Şirket*" (K.Ş.)] is a type of partnership where the element of *affectio societatis* plays an important role. The difference between the K.Ş. and the AdŞ is that the former is a legal entity, conducting its operations under a trade name and that it is set up to operate a commercial business. As it is recognized as a legal entity, the K.Ş. is registered with the Trade Registry (TCC 215). Moreover, all admissions of new partners, partner's leaving the partnership either on their own accord or by compulsory removal, transfers of a partner's share, increases or decreases of share capital, and the appointments of representatives or liquidators must also be recorded at the Trade Registry. In view of the significance of the personal element (such as the close relationship of trust and mutual reliance) in the characteristics of this partnership model, a partner's decease, bankruptcy, or his being placed under legal custody– if the articles of the partnership do not include a provision to the contrary—may entail the dissolution of the partnership. Moreover, even a personal creditor of a partner may demand, if necessary, the dissolution of the partnership with a view to collecting his claim.

809. The legal provisions pertaining to a K.Ş. emphasize particularly that the regulation of internal relations is not of a mandatory character. Only the provisions concerning external relations, i.e., provisions regarding the liabilities of the partners and proceedings to be instituted by the partnership's creditors against the partners, are of mandatory character.

810. The K.Ş. model is especially suited for retail or wholesale trades, international trade, and service businesses (e.g., real estate brokerage, laundries, dry-cleaning etc.).

§2. Formation

811. Execution of a partnership agreement among the partners is required for the formation of the K.Ş. Signatures of partners should be certified by a notary public or the partnership agreement should be executed by the partners before the Trade Registry director or assistant director (TCC 211). The partnership agreement should also be registered with the Trade Registry (TCC 215). The K.Ş.'s Agreement should include, as a minimum, the points mentioned in Article 213 of the TCC. Otherwise, the collective partnership shall not be duly formed and thus will be treated as an ordinary partnership (AdŞ).

812. The K.Ş. Agreement must contain:

- name, place of residence and nationality of each partner;
- determination that the company is a collective partnership;
- trade name of the K.Ş. and its place of domicile;

- objectives of the partnership;
- amount of capital which each partner has agreed to contribute, amount of contribution in cash and contribution in kind, determination whether labor is contributed as capital and, if so, the nature and scope of the said labor; and
- name of the representatives of the K.Ş. and whether they are authorized to represent the company with sole or joint signature.

§3. Relationship Between Partners

I. Management and Control

813. Each partner is entitled to and liable for the management of the company. However, management duties and authority may be delegated to one or more of the partners or to each one of them by the partnership agreement or the majority decision of the partners (TCC 218.1).

814. All general partners have an equal vote in the management and control of the partnership. There are three different categories of decisions in relation to the management of the K.Ş.

A. Decisions Relating to Ordinary Affairs

815. Article 223 of the TCC sets forth the scope of management of the company and defines the affairs that fall under the management of the company to be limited with ordinary actions and transactions that are required to be conducted for the realization of the objectives of the company. The managers of the Company shall be authorized to settlement, waiver, acknowledgement and arbitration subject to the condition that such authorities are limited to matters that relate to the ordinary affairs of the company.

B. Decisions Relating to Extraordinary Affairs

816. TCC 223 also determines that matters that are outside the scope of ordinary actions and transactions shall require the unanimous approval of the partners. The law provides examples, in a non-exhaustive manner, of such extraordinary matters which include making donations, providing surety or guarantee in favor of a third party, appointing commercial representatives and, if not within the scope of company business, sale or purchase of the real estate, providing guarantees on the real estate or establishment of a commercial enterprise pledge.

II. Resolutions

817. As per TCC 226, all resolutions pertaining to any form of amendment of the Articles of Association shall require the unanimous vote of all shareholders. All other decisions may be obtained by majority vote if a different majority requirement is not foreseen under the law or the Articles of Association of the company.

III. Contributions of the Partners

818. Although the law does not set a minimum capital requirement for the formation of a K.Ş., the Articles of Association of the company must designate the nominal amount of company's share capital. Partners usually contribute cash, property or personal services to the K.Ş. or their commercial reputation (TCC 127). In the absence of provisions to the contrary in the K.Ş.'s Agreement, the general provisions of the TCC pertaining to the contribution of partners in a commercial enterprise shall apply. (TCC 127–133).

IV. Profit and Loss

819. TCC 227 sets forth the details pertaining to the distribution of profit and loss among the partners. Accordingly, manager partners are required to prepare and sign the financial tables of the company at the end of each financial year and submit such for the approval of the partners. The financial tables become final upon the approval of the majority of the shareholders. In the same meeting where the financials of the company are approved, the partners also decide on the distribution of profits. Within three months following the date of profit distribution decision of the partners, each partner shall be entitled to initiate a lawsuit for the cancellation thereof if such decision is not in compliance with the applicable law, Articles of Association of the company, decisions of the company or the principle of good faith.

820. The partners are also entitled to delegate another partner or a third party authorized to determine the portion of the profit to be distributed. Such delegation may be made as per the Articles of Association or a decision of the partners. The partner or the third party delegated with such authority shall be required to make a fair determination for profit distribution in compliance with the good faith principle.

V. Inspection and Audit Rights

821. Even if a partner does not have any management authority in the company, he/she shall still be entitled to obtain information on the affairs of the company, inspect and examine the books and records of the company and draw financial tables for his/her use based on such information. Any agreement to the contrary is null and void (TCC 225).

VI. Non-competition

822. Unless otherwise provided for in the K.Ş.'s Agreement, the TCC states that no partner may, without the consent of his co-partners, deal in a business of the same nature as that of the partnership, either on his own account or on account of a third party; nor may he participate in such an undertaking as unlimited partner (TCC 230).

823. In the event that a partner breaches the obligation of non-competition, the K.Ş., at its discretion, may claim compensation from him or, in lieu of compensation, consider the transactions concluded by the said partner in his own name as having been made on behalf of the K.Ş. and demand that any profits resulting from transactions concluded for the account of third persons be handed over to the K.Ş. This right is barred by a statute of limitations of three months following the knowledge of the competing transaction concluded by the partner or his/her shareholding in a competing entity and, in any case, one year following the date of the conclusion of the said transaction (TCC 231.2). Also, partners of the K.Ş. whose rights are infringed may still request a dissolution of the company (TCC 231.3).

§4. Representation and Liability

824. Since a K.Ş. is a legal entity, it acquires rights and incurs liabilities in relation to transactions and acts concluded in its name by its authorized representatives. It can sue and be sued. The K.Ş. is primarily liable for the partnership's obligations and debts (TCC 237.1). However, if an enforcement proceeding conducted against the company does not yield any proceeds or the K.Ş. has dissolved due to any reason, the creditors may pursue the partner(s) or the company together with the partner(s). Also, the creditors may request a preliminary injunction to be placed on the personal assets of the partner(s).

825. A new partner becomes jointly liable with other partners for the liabilities and undertakings of the K.Ş. regardless of whether such liabilities were incurred before he/she joined the partnership (TCC 236.2).

§5. Changes among Partners

I. In General

826. A K.Ş. is a contractual relationship based on trust, confidence and mutual reliance. Therefore, any changes in shareholding requires the amendment of the K.Ş.'s Agreement and the unanimous approval of all partners. Additionally, when a partner dies or is placed under guardianship or becomes bankrupt, or if the interests of a partner in the company is attached and sold through mandatory execution proceedings, the partnership is dissolved *ipso iure*.

II. Termination of Partnership

A. *Special Situations*

1. Death of a Partner

827. In the event that the partnership agreement does not include a provision enabling the continuance of K.Ş. following the death of a partner, the partnership may still remain to exist upon the decision of the heirs and the remaining partners. In the event that one of the heirs does not wish to stay a partner in the K.Ş., the remaining partners shall be entitled to force the heir to exit the partnership through purchase of the shares corresponding to the inheritance portion of such heir. In the event that one of the remaining partners does not wish to continue with the partnership following the death of a partner, the K.Ş. shall terminate.

828. In the event that the partnership agreement includes a provision enabling the continuance of the partnership following the death of a partner, the heirs of the deceased partner are free to continue with the K.Ş. or reject being a partner therein. If the heirs wish to become a partner, the remaining partners have to accept such request. However, if the heirs wish to continue as a *commendator* partners in the company, the remaining partners are not required to abide by such request.

2. Bankruptcy of a Partner

829. Unless otherwise provided for in the partnership agreement, a bankrupt partner may be forced to exit the partnership through purchase of the shares by the remaining partners. The value of the shares of the bankrupt partner is paid to the bankruptcy administration and the collective partnership continues among the remaining shareholders.

830. Under the terms of the TCC, the withdrawal of a partner from the K.Ş. requires the consent of all the partners. If the partners refuse to give such consent, the partner in question may not sue the other partners or the K.Ş. Different arrangements may, however, be made in the K.Ş.'s Agreement, such as withdrawing by notice or withdrawing if certain conditions are not met.

3. Forced Exit due to Justified Reasons

831. As per Article 255 of the TCC, in situations where a partner may be forced to exit the partnership due to reason attributable to such partner, the remaining partners may decide by unanimous vote for the removal and continuance of the partnership with the remaining partners. The partnership agreement may foresee that the removal decision may be granted by a majority vote.

832. The removal decision of the remaining partners has to be delivered to the removed partner through a notification sent via the notary public. The removed partner shall be entitled to initiate a cancellation lawsuit against the removal decision within three months following such notification.

833. If the voting for the removal of a partner does not yield a removal decision, each partner shall be entitled to initiate a lawsuit for the removal of the partner and calculation of his exit fee.

4. Termination by Notice

834. In a collective partnership established for an indefinite period, each shareholder is entitled to request the termination of the partnership through a termination notice. However, if the remaining partners do not wish to terminate the partnership, they may decide for the removal of the partner requesting termination from the partnership.

5. Consequences of Exit

835. In case of a shareholder exiting the partnership either on his own will or through a forced exit, the remaining partners are required to register such change with the Trade Registry and announce such in the Trade Registry Gazette. Exit of a partner shall be enforceable against third parties only after its registration and announcement and the exiting partner shall remain liable for the transactions conducted by the partnership until the date of registration and announcement.

836. Unless otherwise foreseen in the partnership agreement, the price for the shares of the exiting partner shall be calculated based on the partnership value as at the date of exit request of the partner, removal decision of the company (whichever is applicable) or, in case of dispute, the closest date to the exit decision of the court. Such exit payment may be paid to the exiting partner only in cash and at the time indicated in the partnership agreement. If the partnership agreement does not include any provisions as to the timing of exit payment, payment has to be made at the date of the first balance sheet to be issued by the partnership following the exit. However, the exiting shareholder may not receive any payment until all the works undertaken by the partnership before the date of the exit are concluded.

837. The exiting partner participates in the rights and obligations arising out of the works undertaken by the partnership before the date of the exit. Although the exiting partner is not entitled to prevent the conclusion of the works by the remaining partners in a manner advantageous to the company, he is entitled to request from the partnership provision of information on the accounts of works concluded within a financial year and the status of the continuing works as at such date.

B. Other Termination Cases

838. As per the provisions of TCC 243, collective partnerships terminate in the following cases:

- bankruptcy of the partnership even if it results in the announcement of a concordat;
- the loss of capital by two-thirds or more and the lack of decision by the partners to compensate the lost capital or to decrease the capital;
- merger of the partnership with another company; and
- upon a court decision given as per the request of a partner due to failure to register the company within fifteen days following the notarization of the partnership agreement;
- upon a court decision given as per the request of a partner based on justified reasons which include (i) disloyalty of a partner to the partnership in the management of the company or preparation of the accounts; (ii) failure of a partner to perform his primary obligations and duties; (iii) abuse of partnership's name or assets for the benefit of a partner; (iv) a partner losing his capacity to duly perform his obligations due to an illness or another reason; (v) failure of a partner to pay his capital portion within the required time period despite of a notification sent to such effect.

839. The above situations are in addition to the termination reasons indicated in Articles 639 and 640 of the TCO which include, among others, a lapse of the time period for which the partnership was established.

840. TCC also sets a legal presumption which indicates that a partnership continuing its activities beyond the term indicated in the partnership agreement shall be deemed as a partnership with indefinite period.

841. As per TCC 248, creditors are entitled to object to the prolongation of the time period for which the partnership was established. Any creditor is entitled to make such an objection through a notification sent via the notary public within fifteen days following the announcement of the extension of the period. Objection should be based upon a court decision or a similar document, or a final enforcement proceeding.

842. A creditor of a partner is entitled to place an attachment to the liquidation proceedings that shall fall upon the indebted partner and request the termination of the company from the courts. In the event that the partnership or the partners pay the receivables of the creditor, the termination lawsuit shall be discontinued.

§6. LIQUIDATION

843. The K.Ş. is liquidated by liquidators, who may be partners or third parties, and who must act jointly. The liquidator must be notified to the Commercial Registry and the words "in liquidation" must be added to the trade name of the K.Ş.

844. The liquidation of a K.Ş. involves the process of collecting the assets, satisfying the creditor's claims and distributing whatever is remaining.

845. In the case of the bankruptcy of the partnership, the liquidation of the K.Ş. is carried out by the Board of Bankruptcy under the supervision of the court.

Chapter 4. Commandite (Limited) Partnership (*Komandit Şirket*)

§1. Distinguishing Features

846. Under the terms of the TCC, a commandite (limited) partnership ["*Komandit Şirket*" (KomdtŞ)] is a commercial association created to run a commercial business under the trade name of the KomdtŞ. It has two types of partners: at least one of the partners is fully liable for all the debts and obligations of the KomdtŞ (unlimited or general partners—*Komplementare*), and the liability of one or more partners is limited to a fixed contribution (limited partner—*Kommanditisten*). The limited partners are not bound by the obligations of the KomdtŞ and cannot participate in the management of the KomdtŞ. Their liability is limited to their capital contributions. Only natural persons may be unlimited partners.

847. In many respects, the provisions and principles applicable to the K.Ş. apply to the KomdtŞ. The legal position of the general partner of a KomdtŞ is definitely the same as that of the partner of a K.Ş. The features which distinguish the KomdtŞ from the K.Ş. and the status of limited partners have been regulated in the TCC, in Articles 304–328.

§2. Formation

848. A KomdtŞ may only be created in accordance with the formalities prescribed by law, which are similar to those of the K.Ş. For the formation of the KomdtŞ a written partnership agreement must be prepared. Second, the KomdtŞ's Agreement must be signed by the founders, and their signatures must be notarized or affixed to the partnership agreement before the director or vice director of the relevant Trade Registry. Finally, the KomdtŞ's Agreement must be registered with the Trade Registry. Upon this registration, the KomdtŞ acquires legal personality (TCC 305, 212, 216). A KomdtŞ's Agreement, in order to be valid, must include those items which are required for the K.Ş. (TCC 213) and, in addition, the names of the limited partners, the amount and the kind of their capital contributions and management duties given to such limited partners which should not grant them any management authority should be included (TCC 305.2).

849. As per the provisions of TCC 306, it will be determined based on the provisions of the partnership agreement whether the partnership is in fact a "commandite" partnership. In other words, the title given to and type designation made for partnership by the partners shall not be conclusive for the determination of the type of the partnership. In case it may not be determined based on the partnership agreement that the company is in fact a "commandite" partnership, it shall be deemed as a "collective" partnership.

§3. RELATIONSHIP BETWEEN PARTNERS

850. The relationship between general and limited partners is regulated primarily by the KomdtŞ's Agreement. The provisions of the TCC (Articles 217–231) applicable to a K.Ş.'s internal relationship are also applicable to the relationship between partners in a KomdtŞ.

I. Management and Control

851. Each of the general and limited partners have only one vote and any provision in the partnership agreement to the contrary shall be null and void. The KomdtŞ is managed by the general partners (TCC 309). The limited partners are not authorized to conduct acts or transactions for the management of the partnership and they are not entitled to object to the management actions performed by the general partners. However, for extraordinary matters and transactions, structural changes such as amendment of the Articles of Association, conversion of the partnership, merger and spin-off and principal matters such as acceptance of a partner to the partnership or removal of one from the partnership and transfer of shares (collectively "*Material Resolutions*"); the limited partner shall also be entitled to a vote.

II. Resolutions

852. Material Resolutions require the unanimous vote of the partners. Others, unless provided to the contrary in the KomdtŞ's Agreement, may be taken by majority vote.

III. Capital Contributions of the Partners

853. The status of the general partners in relation to capital contribution is the same as that of the general partners in the K.Ş. In many respects, the principles applicable to general partners with regard to capital contributions also apply to general partners. They may contribute in cash or in kind, or provide services or their commercial reputation. Unlike general partners, a limited partner may not contribute a capital to his personal services and commercial reputation (TCC 307). This is the only feature which distinguishes limited partners from general partners with regard to capital contribution.

IV. Profits and Losses

854. The provisions governing profits and losses of a K.Ş. are also applicable to the general partners in a KomdtŞ.

855. As per TCC 312, the limited partner is entitled to profit distribution and interest payment that is determined in the partnership agreement. However, if the capital contribution made by the limited partner is lost due to any reason, he shall not be entitled to request payment of any profits or interest unless until the lost portion of capital is paid.

V. Inspection Rights

856. The status of the general partners in relation to inspection rights is equal to the status of the general partners in a K.Ş.

857. Limited partners have limited inspection rights. Inspection rights may be either (1) ordinary or (2) extraordinary. The *ordinary inspection rights* of a limited partner may be exercised exclusively at the end of the financial year during working hours. According to Article 310.1 of the TCC, he may examine the inventory and annual balance sheet of the partnership and check both for correctness. He may carry out this examination personally or through an expert. In the event of an objection pertaining to the expert, the court may appoint an expert upon the request of the limited partner. Such court decisions are final (TCC 310.2).

858. The limited partners enjoy extraordinary inspection rights in case of justified reasons. In case of existence of reason, the court may, upon the request of the limited partner, authorize, at any time, an inspection of the affairs and the assets of the partnership by the limited partner in person or through an expert (TCC 310.3).

859. Any clause of the KomdtŞ's Agreement which is contrary to the provisions of the TCC regarding the inspection rights of a limited partner(s), both ordinary and extraordinary, is invalid (TCC 310.4).

VI. Non-competition

860. The provisions of the TCC governing non-competition in a K.Ş. are applicable to the general partners in a KomdtŞ. The status of the limited partners differs from that of the general partners. Article 230 of the TCC, prohibiting partners of the collective partnership (and general partners in commandite partnerships) from dealing in the same field of activity as the partnership shall not apply to the limited partners of a KomdtŞ. However, if a limited partner competes with the partnership, he forfeits his inspection rights (TCC 311).

§4. Representation and Liability

861. In principle, the KomdtŞ is represented by the general partners and provisions pertaining to the representation of the collective partnership shall also apply to the representation of KomdtŞ. On the one hand, limited partners are not authorized to represent the partnership in their partner capacity. On the other hand, limited partners may be appointed as commercial representatives, commercial agents or traveling commercial officers (TCC 318.2).

862. The provisions concerning the liability of the partnership and the unlimited partners in a K.Ş. are also applied to the KomdtŞ and the general partners (TCC 246).

863. The status of the limited partners differs from the status of the general partners in a K.Ş.

864. The liability of the limited partners is limited to their capital contributions. The limited partner may not withdraw his capital contribution, directly or indirectly, as a compensation for his share of the profits or as interest. Furthermore, when his capital has diminished for any reason whatsoever, he is prohibited from receiving interest or his share of the profits until the lost portion of the capital is completed (TCC 323) otherwise, he will be liable to the creditors of the KomdtŞ up to the balance of capital contribution which he has agreed to contribute.

865. In the following cases, the limited partners lose their limited liability status and become liable without being subject to any limitation:

- the limited partner whose name is included in the title of the partnership shall be liable toward third parties as the general partner;
- the limited partner who conducts actions or enters into transactions in the name of the partnership without explicitly identifying his status as the commercial representative commercial agent or traveling commercial officer shall be liable toward third parties acting in good faith as the general partner with respect to such acts and actions (TCC 321.1); and
- if transactions have been made before the registry of the partnership with the Trade Registry, the limited partner shall be liable as the general partner toward third parties for such transactions unless he can prove that such third parties were in knowledge of his status as the limited partner (TCC 321.2);
- if a creditor proves that the value of the capital portion contributed by the limited partner is indicated in the partnership agreement at an amount above the actual value, the limited partner shall be liable for the difference.

866. If a creditor proves that the value of the capital portion contributed by the limited partner is indicated in the partnership agreement at an amount above the actual value, the limited partner shall be liable for the difference. The limited partner shall be liable for the debts of the partnership incurred before his entry into the partnership up to the capital amount he has contributed to the partnership.

867. The limited partner shall be liable towards creditors up to the capital contribution amount undertaken by the limited partner even if it is not fully paid. In the event that the limited partner pays to a creditor any unpaid portion of his capital contribution, he shall be relieved from liability to make such payment to the partnership.

868. The creditors shall not be entitled to pursue the limited partner unless the partnership is dissolved or the enforcement proceedings against the partnership do not yield any proceeds.

869. In the event of bankruptcy of the partnership, the rights of creditors enforceable against the limited partner shall pass to the bankruptcy administration.

870. If the limited partner has notified the creditors or announced that he shall be liable for an amount exceeding his capital contribution, he shall be liable toward third parties or the addressee of said notification for such exceeding amount.

§5. Changes among Partners and Termination

871. The provisions of the TCC concerning termination, dissolution of a K.Ş. and voluntary and forced exit of a partner of a K.Ş. shall also apply for KomdtŞ. However, death or placement under the guardianship of a limited partner does not result in the dissolution of the KomdtŞ (TCC 328). In the event that the limited partner is a legal entity, the dissolution of this partner is a ground for the dissolution of the KomdtŞ. In this case, however, any partner may demand the dissolution of the partnership.

§6. Liquidation

872. The provisions of the TCC concerning the dissolution and liquidation of a K.Ş. are also applied to the KomdtŞ.

Selected Bibliography

T. Ansay: *Anonim Şirketler Hukuku*, 6. Bası [the Law of Companies Limited by Shares, 6th Ed.], Ankara, 1982.

H. Arslanlı: *Kollektif ve Komandit Şirketler*, 2. Bası [General and Limited Partnerships, 2nd Ed.], İstanbul, 1960 [Partnerships].

H. Arslanlı: *Anonim Şirketler*, C. I (3. Bası); C. II ve III [Companies Limited by Shares] Vols. I (3rd Ed.) II and III, İstanbul, 1960.

H. Arslanlı: *Ticaret Kanunu Şerhi-Limited Şirketler*, C. I, İstanbul 1962, C II *İstanbul 1963* [Commentary on the Turkish Commercial Code-Partnerships with Limited Liability, Vol. I, *İstanbul 1962*, Vol. II], İstanbul 1963 [Commentary].

H. Arslanlı/H. Domaniç: *Limited ve Hisseli Komandit Şirketler, Türk Ticaret Kanunu Şerhi*, [Commentary on the Turkish Commercial Code-Partnerships with Limited Liability and Partnerships Limited by Shares], İstanbul, 1963.

T. Başbuğoglu: *Uygulamalı Türk Ticaret Kanunu, Açıklamalar, İçtihatlar*, 1. Cilt: Ticari İşletme, Ticaret Şirketleri, Kıymetli Evrak Hukuku, [The Application of the Turkish Commercial Code-Comments and Cases; Vol. 1: Commercial Enterprises, Commercial Enterprises, Negotiable Instruments] Ankara, 1983.

I. Doganay: *Türk Ticaret Kanunu Şerhi*, 2. Bası C. 1 ve 2 [Commentary on the Turkish Commercial Code, Vols. 1 and 2], Ankara, 1981.

H. Domaniç: *Adi, Kollektif ve Komandit Şirketler*, 4. Bası [Ordinary, General and Limited Partnerships, 4th Ed.], İstanbul, 1988.

H. Domaniç: *Anonim Şirketler*, [Companies Limited by Shares], İstanbul, 1978.

H. Domaniç: *Türk Ticaret Kanunu Şerhi*, C. I: *Adi, Kollektif ve Komandit Şirketler*, C. II: *Anonim Şirketler ve Uygulaması*, [Commentary on the Turkish Commercial Code; Vol. 1: Partnerships; Vol. II: Companies Limited by Shares] İstanbul, 1988.

G. Eriş: *Türk Ticaret Kanunu*, Birinci Cilt: Ticari İşletme ve Ticaret Şirketleri 1. Bası [1987], 2. Bası [1989] [Commentary on the Turkish Commercial Code; Vol. I: Commercial Enterprise and Commercial Enterprises, 1st Ed. (1987), 2nd Ed. (1989)], İstanbul.

Hirsch/Tekinalp: *Das türkische Aktien-und GmbH-Recht*, 2. Auflage, Baden-Baden 1993.

O. İmregün: *Anonim Ortaklıklar*, 4. Bası [Companies Limited by Shares, 4th Ed.], İstanbul, 1989.

Y. Karayalçın: *Ticaret Hukuku*, C. II: *Şirketler, Giriş, Adi Şirket, Şahıs Şirketleri Hukuku*, 2. Bası [Commercial Law; Vol. II: Introduction Partnerships, 2nd Ed.], Ankara, 1973.

Selected Bibliography

Poroy/Tekinalp/Çamoğlu: *Ortaklıklar Hukuku*, C. I, 2. Bası [1975], C. II, 2. Bası [1976] [The Law on Partnerships and Companies; Vol. I, 2nd Ed. (1975); Vol. II, 2nd Ed. (1976)], İstanbul.

Poroy/Tekinalp/Çamoğlu: *Ortaklıklar ve Kooperatif Hukuku*, Ders Kitabı, 5. Bası [The Law on Partnerships, Companies and Co-operatives; Textbook; 5th Ed.], İstanbul, 1993 [Textbook].

F. Tekil: *Şirketler Hukuku*, Cilt 1: *Adi Şirketler-Kollektif ve Komandit Şirketler*, 2. Bası (1976); C. 2: *Anonim Şirketler*, 2. Bası (1978); 3. Cilt: *Limited Şirketler ve Kooperatifler* (1978), [Partnership and Company Law; Vol. 1: Ordinary, General and Limited Partnerships; 2nd Ed. (1976); Vol. 2: Companies Limited by Shares, 2nd Ed. (1978); Vol. 3: Partnerships with Limited Liability (1978)] İstanbul.

Tekinalp/Çamoğlu: *Açıklamalı, Notlu ve Karşılaştırmalı Türk Ticaret Kanunu*, 8. Bası, [The Turkish Commercial Code with Commentary and Notes on Comparative Law, 8th Ed.], İstanbul, 1992.

Index

The numbers here refer to paragraphs

Index

www.ingramcontent.com/pod-product-compliance
Ingram Content Group UK Ltd.
Pitfield, Milton Keynes, MK11 3LW, UK
UKHW020141290926
15471UKWH00004B/629

9 789403 506968